Women and Our Panchayati Raj System

Women and Our Panchayati Raj System

M. S. Kulhari

Neha Publishers & Distributors
New Delhi - 110002 (INDIA)

Women and Our Panchayati Raj System

First Published in 2011

ISBN 978-93-80318-09-7

The responsibility for the facts or opinions expressed is entirely of the Author and not of the Publishers.

Published by : **Neha Publishers & Distributors**
4832/24, Prahlad Gali, S-204
Ansari Road, Daryaganj,
New Delhi - 110002
Tel. : 23278261, 43570976
E mail: gauravbookcentre@gmail.com
Website: www.gauravbookcentre.com

Laser Typesetting : Tamalika Computers, Delhi-110 009

Printed at : Balaji Offset, Delhi-32

PRINTED IN INDIA

Contents

Contents

Preface

The Panchayati Raj was in existence during the Vedic period in ancient India and worked well as the people carried out their personal and official duties based on Dharma. After independence, the Government of India, under the influence of Mahatma Gandhi, was committed to set up Panchayati Raj system to provide real Swaraj to the people of rural areas. The dream of decentralization of power in order to empower people at the grassroot level, particularly, to enable rural masses to join the mainstream and claim rightful participation in the process of their own development and governance attained its fulfilment on April 24, 1993. The people of India took over four decades to realize this dream of Mahatma Gandhi.

The Landmark 73rd Amendment to the Constitution of India has definitely empowered women in terms of numbers. From the miniscule figure of 2-4 per cent in most of the Indian states, the Amendment has for the first time brought 33-40 per cent rural women into the sphere of the decision-making process. But, being in large numbers is not enough as reservation provides only the possibility of a voice for women, it does not guarantee it. The awakening of women in India towards a society where justice and brotherhood prevail, can best be achieved by a women to women contact. Even though men have played a pioneering role in the case of women in India, their role has been effective bringing about constitution and legal changes in the status of women.

In this book, an attempt has been made to unveil the relationship between the political mobilisation of rural women and its impact on social justice with particular reference to their participation in Panchayati Raj institutions.

—Editor

1

Introduction to Panchayati Raj

The panchayat raj is a South Asian political system mainly in India, Pakistan, and Nepal. "Panchayat" literally means assembly (*yat*) of five (*panch*) wise and respected elders chosen and accepted by the village community. Traditionally, these assemblies settled disputes between individuals and villages. Modern Indian government has decentralized several administrative functions to the village level, empowering elected gram panchayats. Gram panchayats are not to be confused with the unelected khap panchayats (or caste panchayats) found in some parts of India.

PANCHAYATI RAJ

Panchayati Or Panchaayati Raj is a system of governance in which gram panchayats are the basic units of administration. It has 3 levels: village, block and district.

The term 'panchayat raj' is relatively new, having originated during the British administration. 'Raj' literally means governance or government. Mahatma Gandhi advocated *Panchayati Raj*, a decentralized form of Government where each village is responsible for its own affairs, as the foundation of India's political system. His term for such a vision was "Gram Swaraj" (Village Self-governance).

It was adopted by state governments during the 1950s and 60s as laws were passed to establish Panchayats in various states. It also found backing in the Indian Constitution, with the 73rd amendment in 1992 to accommodate the idea. The Amendment Act of 1992 contains provision for devolution of powers and responsibilities to the panchayats to both for preparation of plans for economic development and social justice and for implementation in relation to twenty-nine subjects listed in the eleventh schedule of the constitution.

The panchayats receive funds from three sources – (i) local body grants, as recommended by the Central Finance Commission, (ii) funds for implementation of centrally-sponsored schemes, and (iii) funds released by the state governments on the recommendations of the State Finance Commissions.

In the history of Panchayati Raj in India, on 24 April 1993, the Constitutional (73rd Amendment) Act, 1992 came into force to provide constitutional status to the Panchayati Raj institutions.

This Act was extended to Panchayats in the tribal areas of eight States, namely Andhra Pradesh, Bihar, Gujarat, Himachal Pradesh, Maharashtra, Madhya Pradesh, Orissa and Rajasthan from 24 December 1996. Now panchayati raj system exists in all the states except Nagaland, Meghalaya and Mizoram. Also all the UTs except Delhi.

The Act aims to provide 3-tier system of Panchayati Raj for all States having population of over 2 million, to hold Panchayat elections regularly every 5 years, to provide reservation of seats for Scheduled Castes, Scheduled Tribes and Women, to appoint State Finance Commission to make recommendations as regards the financial powers of the Panchayats and to constitute District Planning Committee to prepare draft development plan for the district. The 3-tier system of Panchayati Raj consists of a) village level panchayat b) block level panchayat c) district level panchayat.

Powers and responsibilities are delegated to Panchayats at the appropriate level :-

- Preparation of plan for economic development and social justice.
- Implementation of schemes for economic development and social justice in relation to 29 subjects given in Eleventh Schedule of the Constitution.
- To levy, collect and appropriate taxes, duties, tolls and fees.

Village level panchayat

It is called a Panchayat at the village level. It is a local body working for the good of the village. The number of members usually ranges from 7 to 31; occasionally, groups are larger, but they never have fewer than 7 members. The block-level institution is called the Panchayat Samiti. The district-level institution is called the Zilla Parishad.

Intermediate level panchayat

Panchayat samiti is a local government body at the tehsil or Taluka level in India. It works for the villages of the Tehsil or Taluka that together are called a Development Block. The Panchayat Samiti is the link between the Gram Panchayat and the district administration. There are a number of variations of this institution in various states. It is known as Mandal Praja Parishad in Andhra Pradesh, Taluka panchayat in Gujarat, Mandal Panchayat in Karnataka, etc. In general it's a kind of Panchayati raj at higher level.

Constitution

It is composed of ex-officio members (all sarpanchas of the panchayat samiti area, the MPs and MLAs of the area and the SDO of the subdivision), coopted members (representatives of SC/ST and women), associate members (a farmer of the area, a representative of the cooperative societies and one of the marketing services) and some elected members. The samiti is elected for 5 years and is headed by the chairman and the deputy chairman.

Departments

The common departments in the Samiti are as follows:

1. General administration
2. Finance
3. Public works
4. Agriculture
5. Health
6. Education
7. Social welfare
8. Information Technology and others.

There is an officer for every department. A government appointed block development officer is the executive officer to the samiti and the chief of its administration the department of:

Functions

1. Implement schemes for the development of agriculture.
2. Establishment of primary health centres and primary schools.
3. Supply of drinking water, drainage, construction/repair of roads.
4. Development of cottage and small-scale industries and opening of cooperative societies.
5. Establishment of youth organisations.

Sources of income

The main source of income of the panchayat samiti are grants-in-aid and loans from the State Government.

DISTRICT LEVEL PANCHAYAT

In the district level of the panchayati raj system you have the "zilla parishad". It looks after the administration of the rural area of the district and its office is located at the district headquarters. The Hindi word Parishad means Council and Zilla Parishad translates to District Council. It is headed by the "District Collector" or the "Distric Magistrate" or the "Deputy Comminissioner". It is the link between the state government and the panchayat samiti (local seld government at the block level)

Constitution

Members of the Zilla Parishad are elected from the district on the basis of adult franchise for a term of five years. Zilla Parishad has minimum of 50 and maximum of 75 members. There are seats reserved for Scheduled Castes, Scheduled Tribes, backward classes and women.

The Chairmen of all the Panchayat Samitis form the members of Zilla Parishad. The Parishad is headed by a President and a Vice-President.

Functions

1. Provide essential services and facilities to the rural population and the planning and execution of the development programmes for the district.
2. Supply improved seeds to farmers. Inform them of new techniques of training. Undertake construction of small-scale irrigation projects and percolation tanks. Maintain pastures and grazing lands.
3. Set up and run schools in villages. Execute programmes for adult literacy. Run libraries.
4. Start Primary Health Centres and hospitals in villages. Start mobile hospitals for hamlets, vaccination drives against epidemics and family welfare campaigns.
5. Construct bridges and roads.
6. Execute plans for the development of the scheduled castes and tribes. Run ashramshalas for adivasi children. Set up free hostels for scheduled caste students.
7. Encourage entrepreneurs to start small-scale industries like cottage industries, handicraft, agriculture produce processing mills, dairy farms, etc. implement rural employment schemes.
8. They construct roads, schools,& public properties. And they take care of the public properties.
9. They even supply work for the poor people.

FUNCTIONING OF TRADITIONAL PANCHAYAT

Lack of democracy in the functioning of traditional Panchayat is obvious. There are no women in Traditional Panchayat council. In many Panchayats the traditional Panchayats kept changing the leadership just to attract more money from the INGOs. Within a month after tsunami struck, the traditional Panchayat leaders came to know about INGOs and they started demanding more funds. There was no systematic interface between traditional panchayats and constitutional panchayats due to the domination of traditional panchayat leaders. NGOs directly dealt with the traditional Panchayats in spite of the lack of faith in equity and gender insensitivity. There was no proper sensitization among the officials, NGOs and INGOs on Panchayati Raj Institutions. Several Panchayat Presidents did not realize their role and responsibilities in disaster management. Sensitized Panchayat Presidents joined together with the traditional Panchayats and successfully carried out relief and rehabilitation activities.

They ensured the coordination among the government functionaries and departments, and sensitized the Village Panchayat Presidents and responded quickly by establishing contacts with the affected persons, and helped them to move to safe places. They made initial arrangements for the affected people food, drinking water, clothing and other basic needs. According to the president of Kameshwaram Panchayat, the Panchayat area is sandy so the sand suck the water quickly hence the village was affected by the flood miserably: the structure of the village is that it is surrounded by sand dunes and trees on both the sides. Only one side is low laying area, so the sand dunes and trees safeguarded the people from the sea water. Further, if at all the sea water entered the village, the water rushed out to the low lying area so the water did not stagnate in that village. The deaths occurred not only due to sea water, but also because of the trees that fell on the people.

During the cyclone and heavy rainy seasons –the thatched houses because of their light weight which did not fall down easily. So loss of life was meager; but, the tiles made up of mud got moistened and broke into pieces and fell. Each piece was like a stone and caused more injuries. To be safe from earthquake, some village people in Gujarat, preferred to have the traditional type of houses made up of light roof materials and thin round shape walls pasted with cow dung and camel dung. The study found that the training to the Gram Panchayat President is important, in relief and rehabilitation activities.

Relief activities started by the government only after three days of the occurrence. The food packets provided by the government were not eatable. Instead of providing food packets, government could have made arrangements to prepare food on the spot with the help of community and Panchayats. Linkages with block and district committees have not yet been initiated. The process of building up of disaster preparedness among the local body institutions has been initiated by the Government of Tamil Nadu and UNDP. Generally NGOs are not yet coming forward in building up disaster preparedness. They concentrated more on relief instead of involving community and empowering them. It has been noticed that there is no culture of working together and through a system. The role of women and Dalits in relief and rehabilitation activities did not get attention of the relief agencies. They were side lined and due representation was not given to them. The impact of tsunami on Dalit habitation and livelihood was not immediately realized. In respect of relief and rehabilitation activities there was no relief code and management policy from the perspective of grassroots institutions.

Traditional knowledge, wisdom and practices are not given recognition which resulted in wastages of resources, duplication and delay in the execution of relief and rehabilitation activities. All activities were supply-driven not on demand-driven. Even after the bitter experiences, lessons were not learnt from the past. In the 1977 Vedaranyam Flood, the Government forecast made the people stay inside the houses. This reduced human loss. Committees which were constituted did not work properly. No training was given to the committee members. Plans for preparedness have not yet been drafted in Tamil Nadu.

Panchayats in Disaster Management

The past experience shows that Government, INGOs and NGOs have taken number of measures for relief, rehabilitation and reconstruction activities regarding disaster. Based on experience an array of reports has been prepared for dissemination. Very useful recommendations have been made. But there is no proper initiative to make use of all those suggestions. Government structure in Orissa is very weak but bureaucrats in Tamil Nadu are efficient and they are delivering goods. When tsunami struck, decision making powers were decentralized and respective affected District Collectors were given powers to take decisions based on the ground realities. Apart from the District Collectors many officials efficiently worked. In that situation, the local body institutions were sidelined both by Government and NGOs. Not only in Tamil Nadu, had the same situation prevailed in Andhra Pradesh and Gujarat also. People and their assets were damaged due to flood, cyclone, tsunami and earthquake and they are still in the process of rehabilitation and reconstruction.

It is to be noted that assistance could be extended to the affected at any amount. And people must be made to work for their development. The external agencies can work with people in the system created for them. If any institution or organization or group works for them, community's pride and self respect will be eroded. People should have a feeling that they can manage on their own with support from others. Despite huge loss of lives and livelihoods in the recent disaster, generous support from the donor agencies and Government enabled the communities to overcome the shock and they started rebuilding. They spent huge amounts on relief, rehabilitation and reconstruction process. But this study found that it had not produced the results to the level of investment. The study found that the relief activities were not gender sensitive and equity oriented. It was supply driven and not demand driven. In this situation, the 73rd and 74th Constitutional Amendment envisages the panchayats should strive for the welfare, safety and the prosperity of the villages. According to the 74th Constitutional Amendment Act the panchayats should prepare the plan for the socio economic development of the people. While preparing the socio economic development plans the panchayats could include disaster management as one of its components. As there was no system, structure and procedures at the grassroots level, the resources dumped at that level had not met the felt needs of the community. In this situation, reconstruction could be done by preparing micro plan at the panchayat level. While preparing micro plan, panchayat could make reliable assessments on the nature and the extent of damages caused by the disaster. The environmental norms such as distance from the sea, identification of safe locations, designs, technologies and materials for construction of safe disaster resistance buildings should be considered. It could ensure that all the vulnerable are identified and included so that they get what is due to them from the reconstruction activities. Panchayats could make use of this opportunity to meet long felt needs.

For instance, they could develop new connecting roads that didn't exist earlier. With regard to damage assessment, the Panchayat could identify number of houses damaged and its magnitude. Public buildings (Anganwadi schools, health centres, community halls, Panchayat building, PDS shop, vocational training centres or any other government structures can be used very effectively). Basic services (including drinking water supply, access roads, sewage disposal, drainage, electricity and communication) apart from the physical damages Panchayats should be aware of the damages. Panchayats should take responsibility to assess the damages and accordingly the relief has to be given.

To ensure the rehabilitation for a long-term development the Panchayats must be made to concentrate on the following activities:

- Rebuilding livelihoods,
- Opportunity for adopting innovative approaches,
- Build their sustainable network of village-based economies,
- Use the opportunity to strengthen and improve the among the people of the village.

Through pro active and well-planned rehabilitation work, we can reduce gender based, caste-based, religion-based, class-based divisions in relief and rehabilitation activities. A few well trained, well oriented gram panchayat presidents took effects in relief rehabilitation and reconstruction activities. This yielded good results. Based on the field experience, this study suggested the following recommendations to strengthen the community and Panchayats. At every gram panchayat Disaster Management Committee headed by gram Panchayat presidents is to be formed. Government should form disaster management committees as statutory committees. In such disaster management committee SHGs, Youth and Elders should be integrated and they have to be oriented. At every ward, a sub committee at village level headed by ward member has to be constituted. Integrating Disaster Management Training with Panchayat Raj Capacity building exercise should be carried out regularly.

In every committee women and Dalit representatives should be incorporated. Allocation of separate Contingency fund for Disaster Management for every gram panchayat is an imperative. Government should allocate Rs.1 lakh as untied fund every year to each Gram Panchayat for disaster preparedness and management activities. There should be synergy between the constitutional panchayats and traditional panchayats. For all relief activities, the government departments have to rely on the committees constituted at the grassroots. A new culture has to be created at the ground to involve people. It requires a special training at all levels from Gram Sabha members to higher officials at district and state level. At every gram panchayat a contingency plan has to be developed. At every block and at every district, plan has to be prepared and implemented with the active participation of the stakeholders. Panchayats have to take responsibility from the stage of assessment of the loss to reconstruction.

Panchayats should have contingency fund. In the same way, every gram panchayat should have food stock through every ration shop. The entire physical infrastructure created through various government departments have to be handed over to the panchayats during the period of disaster. Every state should have a Disaster Management Act, policy and clear cut guidelines to carry out relief, rehabilitation and reconstruction works. Role clarity has to be ensured. Clear cut guidelines have to be prepared for disaster management at the gram panchayat level.

Since drought, flood and other disasters are now frequently occurring, each state should have a department meant for disaster relief with sufficient authority. In the regular development activities preparedness component has to be incorporated consciously. A well-maintained communication system has to be developed. With regard to data on the loss and compensation, the panchayat should be held responsible. Gram Panchayat should be made responsible for collecting vital statistics. It has to update the data regularly. This data should be validated by the Gram Sabha. The data have to be confirmed in the Gram Sabha meeting. All relief and rehabilitation activities will be carried out only based on the data already confirmed. Currently, we need people-centred approach. It should be community-based intervention. Involvement of Constitutional local bodies is more important. All reconstruction activities should be carried out with the support of Village micro plan. Building confidence among people to organize and respond to disaster is also essential.

Based on the 73rd Constitutional Amendment, Panchayats are established as institutionalized structure both in urban and rural areas. But, people are in the periphery. Empowering the people is the process if we include local bodies in the disaster management. This could be a much more profitable system. Usually context decides. As already seen in this study, the empowered and sensitized Panchayat leaders delivered services even during disasters. So Panchayats are the best deliverable institutions where they are not target oriented. They are working in a demand driven way. If we empower Panchayats and the reverse the supply driven process by way of demand driven process, the whole system and society will change for better. Institutionalized, efficient, well coordinated, participatory inclusive, gender sensitive, disaster management initiatives are the basic ingredients of good governance.

VILLAGE PANCHAYAT COUNCIL

One noteworthy point about the 17 target villages is their multi-cultural nature reflected through the presence of different castes. The council members are working in harmony and the relationship between the council members and the Presidents was understood to be cordial in all Panchayats except in a few. In the Chandrapadi village Panchayat, three ward members belonging to the fishermen community resigned due to difference of opinion in distributing relief materials to non-fishermen and in implementing rehabilitation activities in the non-fishermen habitation. With regards to the performance of women Presidents of our target villages, almost all of them have real interest and commitment in their activities. They are not completely independent but have facilitation and guidance from their male family members. There are exceptional women Presidents like the President of Kaveripoompattinam, Maruthampallam, Thennampattinam and Thirumullaivasal who are effectively involved in THP-GRI– Tsunami intervention project activities. Among the men Presidents of the target villages, almost all of them are seriously involved in the project activities. In some villages difference of opinion between the President and the representatives of fishermen community was evident that had resulted in cases of non-cooperation in the Gram Sabha meetings. Except on some issues, there exists a functional relationship between the President and the community. Irrespective of their party affiliation, almost all Panchayat Presidents were found to be having cordial relationship with their respective communities cutting across political party and caste differences. The periodical meetings of the Panchayat Council in all the 17 Panchayats are conducted properly. With regards to the Gram Sabha meetings, participation of women in Gram Sabha meeting is slowly increasing in number.

All the 17 Village Panchayats have very cordial relationship with the collaborative agencies like NGOs and other sectoral department of the Government of Tamil Nadu through which the welfare and development activities are implemented in their respective Panchayats. In some of the village Panchayats, difference of opinion between traditional Village Panchayat leaders and the elected Village Panchayat Presidents were found. All the Presidents spared their time in identifying the issues in Panchayati Raj and have dedicated their time/spirit to equip the village community.

Based on these issues, the plan documents of the Panchayats have included the following works to be attended to by the Gram Panchayats.

- Enrolling all the children who have completed five years of age in school.
- Ensuring that the enrolled children continue their studies without dropping out.
- Conducting school annual day celebration to enable the students to display their creative potential.
- Providing basic amenities like drinking water, toilet, playing ground and vegetable garden in the school.
- Creating a sanitation and toilet culture among the students.

- Establishing reading rooms to encourage the desire to learn among the villagers and putting to use the Ayyan Thiruvalluvar Library.
- Providing toilet facility and playthings for children in the anganwadi and trimming their nails to ensure hygiene.
- Enrolling all the children who have completed two and a half years of age in the anganwadi and helping them to learn the habit of attending to their personal cleanliness.
- Ensuring the age-specific weight and the general health of children by providing them with appropriate balanced nutritious meal and ensuring the proper conduct of activities such as providing nutritious flour and noon meal under the integrated child welfare scheme.
- Taking steps to ensure optimum utilization of the women's sanitary complexes.
- Ensuring that all the people get safe drinking water.
- Completely eradicating open air defecation.
- Arranging for common public toilets and their proper use.
- Showing the way for male as well as female self help groups to function robustly.
- Motivating and guiding self help groups participating fully in public welfare activities and in Gram Sabha meetings.
- Repairing and maintaining water sources such as ponds, tanks, ooranis and kanmois, collecting rainwater in them and using them properly.

Analysis of Micro-planning Process

During the course of the process, the facilitators made a few observations which have implications for furthering the planning from below both in the same areas and doing so in other areas. A consistent use of charity approach towards development has done more harm than good to the people. This was evident in the way people looked at the issues and problems concerning them and their villages. Having gotten used to being treated as mere recipients, they had started thinking of decisions about these to be taken by the government and others while it was their destiny to suffer from the wrong policies and benefit from the right ones. During the orientation at the beginning of the process, these were explained clearly through examples. Therefore, during the micro-planning process, people started looking at the issues as their own and this facilitated the process of articulation and integration of various spheres. The micro-planning process has not only been a discussion to come up with a document but one whereby a deliberate attempt was made to build the already existing capability among the participants.

The facilitators took it upon themselves to inform the people to be their own selves while sharing the problems and not to feel intimidated by the facilitators. These efforts at creating a feeling of ownership among the people went a long way to make people realize their strength individually, and most importantly, collectively. Prior to this exercise, the people themselves agreed of not having looked at the issue of disaster as something that can be managed.

A scientific and logical understanding of disaster in general and of tsunami in specific, with an analysis of the manner in which it makes people vulnerable to damages gradually made people to feel confident of managing natural disasters. It was during the discussion that people themselves shared the absence of disaster preparedness and lack of availability of infrastructures that can help them to overcome large-scale damages. Previously, people had looked at planning as a process that is necessarily directed from above. It was for the first time that they came to be part of a process meant for planning the development of the village. This entailed a process of collective envisioning that at one level brought the people together, and at another level, made them to look optimistically at the developmental issues.

Conclusion

Prior to the planning process, the facilitators had repeatedly debated about the manner in which sensitivity, people-centricity have to be maintained throughout the process. As has already been mentioned in the previous section, the idea behind facilitating this grassroots level planning was to take forward the process of decentralization started by the new Panchayati Raj Institutions system incorporated into the constitution through the 73rd amendment. This necessitated a methodology that would grant space to a pro-active participation of the community and to an inclusive process. In many senses, this could be termed as a novel method of planning for social development. The highlights of this method are:

- the participatory nature of the entire process ensured through a clear role for the facilitating agencies and the people. As has been repeatedly mentioned in the present document, people have been the chief planners in this project while GRI-SDC-THP along with the local NGO partners have been supporters of the process.
- the two-phased process based on public-private partnership that made the government to forge new partnerships with a facilitating group of the academic institution, NGOs and INGO chiefly for the development of the community. All the programmes undertaken in both the phases have been designed with people's participation and people's learning at the centre. The first phase focused on capacity building through orientation, focus on the Panchayats as the chief mediating agencies (for constituting planning group/ statutory committee, prioritizing of needs, identification of disparities, preparation of Panchayat Development Plan, approval of the plan and dissemination of the plan). The second phase concentrated on ensuring the continuing support of the government departments, strengthening the Panchayats through enhancing the pro-active participation by dalits/women in the meetings, resolving conflicts between the traditional and constitutional Panchayats, and partnership with agencies such as MSSRF.

It must be noted that special attention was given throughout the process to keep it as a people's plan where the agencies involved including the government played the role of guiding, supervising and facilitating the process. The process, however, has not been one without challenges and inconveniences. The challenges came in the shape of bringing the community together, facing the attitudes regarding caste and gender, and collection of data. While mobilising people for the planning process was not difficult given the repute of the institutes such as Gandhigram Rural Institute, the problem lay in keeping the people together. It took a great deal of energy to bring conflicting communities to one platform to discuss about the development of the village.

The facilitating agencies had to make use of techniques to resolve conflicts between the communities. Related to this has been discussing the issues of exclusion that are so much a part of the village society. Getting to talk about special needs of women is an issue that needs special mention. More difficult was integrating their needs into the planning process. Given the rigid patriarchal mindset that marks the village society, this task became even more difficult for the facilitators as it also involved creating space for the women to talk. Difficulties confronted while collecting data and later during the confirmation of data as a follow up was an extremely difficult task given the fact that most of the agencies, both governmental and non-governmental, focused on distribution of relief and efforts towards rehabilitation of tsunami-affected villages.

Political parties added to the chaos with lists based on biased collection of data. Therefore, the plan document based its analysis on the information available from the panchayats and from people through administering PRA exercises. The process of micro planning must be seen as one that not only led to a new process of planning from the below but has set a new trend by doing so. As a Panchayat president shared during the plan dissemination workshop: "the process was one of drawing a plan for the development of the people along side the village as also one whereby we all came to know what Panchayats stand for" (A. K. Ananthan, President of Pillaiperumalanullar on dt.13.6.2006 at the Collectorate, Nagapattinam). Indeed, the process has been one of understanding the real sense of planning from the grassroots.

2

History of Indian Panchayats

The district is the principal subdivision within the state (union territories are not subdivided). There are 476 districts in India; the districts vary in size and population. The average size of a district is approximately 4,300 square kilometres, and the average population numbered nearly 1.8 million in the early 1990s.

The district collector, a member of the Indian Administrative Service, is the preeminent official in the district. During the colonial period, the collector was responsible for collecting revenue and maintaining law and order. In the 1990s, the collector's role in most states is confined to heading the district revenue department and coordinating the efforts of the other departments, such as agriculture, irrigation, public works, forestry, and public health, that are responsible for promoting economic development and social welfare.

Definitions. In this Part, unless the context otherwise requires,-

(a) "district" means a district in a State;

(b) "Gram Sabha" means a body consisting of persons registered in the electoral rolls relating to a village comprised within the area of Panchayat at the village level;

(c) "intermediate level" means a level between the village and district levels specified by the Governor of a State by public notification to be the intermediate level for the purposes of this Part;

(d) "Panchayat" means an institution (by whatever name called) of self-government constituted under article 243B, for the rural areas;

(e) "Panchayat area" means the territorial area of a Panchayat;

(f) "Population" means the population as ascertained at the last preceding census of which the relevant figures have been published;

(g) "village" means a village specified by the Governor by public notification to be a village for the purposes of this Part and includes a group of villages so specified.

Gram Sabha. A Gram Sabha may exercise such powers and perform such functions at the village level as the Legislature of a State may, by law, provide.

Constitution of Panchayats.-

(1) There shall be constituted in every State, Panchayats at the village, intermediate and district levels in accordance with the provisions of this Part.

(2) Notwithstanding anything in clause (1), Panchayats at the intermediate level may not be constituted in a State having a population not exceeding twenty lakhs.

Composition of Panchayats.-

(1) Subject to the provisions of this Part, the Legislature of a State may, by law, make provisions with respect to the composition of Panchayats:

Provided that the ratio between the population of the territorial area of a Panchayat at any level and the number of seats in such Panchayat to be filled by election shall, so far as practicable, be the same throughout the State.

(2) All the seats in a Panchayat shall be filled by persons chosen by direct election from territorial constituencies in the Panchayat area and, for this purpose, each Panchayat area shall be divided into territorial constituencies in such manner that the ratio between the population of each constituency and the number of seats allotted to it shall, so far as practicable, be the same throughout the panchayat area.

(3) The Legislature of a State may, by law, provide for the representation-

(a) of the Chairpersons of the Panchayats at the village level, in the Panchayats at the intermediate level or, in the case of a State not having Panchayats at the intermediate level, in the Panchayats at the district level;

(b) of the Chairpersons of the Panchayats at the intermediate level, in the Panchayats at the district level;

(c) of the members of the House of the People and the members of the Legislative Assembly of the State representing constituencies which comprise wholly or partly a Panchayat area at a level other than the village level, in such Panchayat;

(d) of the members of the Council of States and the members of the Legislative Council of the State, where they are registered as electors within-

(i) a Panchayat area at the intermediate level, in Panchayat at the intermediate level;

(ii) a Panchayat area at the district level, in Panchayat at the district level.

(4) The Chairperson of a Panchayat and other members of a Panchayat whether or not chosen by direct election from territorial constituencies in the Panchayat area shall have the right to vote in the meetings of the Panchayats.

(5) The Chairperson of-

(a) a panchayat at the village level shall be elected in such manner as the Legislature of a State may, by law, provide; and

(b) a Panchayat at the intermediate level or district level shall be elected by, and from amongst, the elected members thereof.

Reservation of seats.-

(1) Seats shall be reserved for-

(a) the Scheduled Castes; and

(b) the Scheduled Tribes, in every Panchayat and the number of seats so reserved shall bear, as nearly as may be, the same proportion to the total number of seats to be filled by direct election in that Panchayat as the population of the Scheduled Castes in that Panchayat area or of the Scheduled Tribes in that Panchayat area bears to the total population of that area and such seats may be allotted by rotation to different constituencies in a Panchayat.

(2) Not less than one-third of the total number of seats reserved under clause (1) shall be reserved for women belonging to the Scheduled Castes or, as the case may be, the Scheduled Tribes.

(3) Not less than one-third (including the number of seats reserved for women belonging to the Scheduled Castes and the Scheduled Tribes) of the total number of seats to be filled by direct election in every Panchayat shall be reserved for women and such seats may be allotted by rotation to different constituencies in a Panchayat.

(4) The offices of the Chairpersons in the Panchayats at the village or any other level shall be reserved for the Scheduled Castes, the Scheduled Tribes and women in such manner as the Legislature of a State may, by law, provide:

Provided that the number of offices of Chairpersons reserved for the Scheduled Castes and the Scheduled Tribes in the Panchayats at each level in any State shall bear, as nearly as may be, the same proportion to the total number of such offices in the Panchayats at each level as the population of the Scheduled Castes in the State or of the Scheduled Tribes in the State bears to the total population of the State:

Provided further that not less than one-third of the total number of offices of Chairpersons in the Panchayats at each level shall be reserved for women:

Provided also that the number of offices reserved under this clause shall be allotted by rotation to different Panchayats at each level.

(5) The reservation of seats under clauses (1) and (2) and the reservation of offices of Chairpersons (other than the reservation for women) under clause (4) shall cease to have effect on the expiration of the period specified in article 334.

(6) Nothing in this Part shall prevent the Legislature of a State from making any provision for reservation of seats in any Panchayat or offices of Chairpersons in the Panchayats at any level in favour of backward class of citizens.

Duration of Panchayats, etc.-

(1) Every Panchayat, unless sooner dissolved under any law for the time being in force, shall continue for five years from the date appointed for its first meeting and no longer.

(2) No amendment of any law for the time being in force shall have the effect of causing dissolution of a Panchayat at any level, which is functioning immediately before such amendment, till the expiration of its duration specified in clause (1).

(3) An election to constitute a Panchayat shall be completed-

 (a) before the expiry of its duration specified in clause (1);

 (b) before the expiration of a period of six months from the date of its dissolution: Provided that where the remainder of the period for which the dissolved Panchayat would have continued is less than six months, it shall not be necessary to hold any election under this clause for constituting the Panchayat for such period.

(4) A Panchayat constituted upon the dissolution of a Panchayat before the expiration of its duration shall continue only for the remainder of the period for which the dissolved Panchayat would have continued under clause (1) had it not been so dissolved.

Disqualifications for membership.-

(1) A person shall be disqualified for being chosen as, and for being, a member of a Panchayat-

(a) if he is so disqualified by or under any law for the time being in force for the purposes of elections to the Legislature of the State concerned:

Provided that no person shall be disqualified on the ground that he is less than twenty-five years of age, if he has attained the age of twenty-one years;

(b) if he is so disqualified by or under any law made by the Legislature of the State.

(2) If any question arises as to whether a member of a Panchayat has become subject to any of the disqualifications mentioned in clause (1), the question shall be referred for the decision of such authority and in such manner as the Legislature of a State may, by law, provide.

Powers, authority and responsibilities of Panchayats.- Subject to the provisions of this Constitution, the Legislature of a State may, by law, endow the Panchayats with such powers and authority as may be necessary to enable them to function as institutions of self-government and such law may contain provisions for the devolution of powers and responsibilities upon Panchayats at the appropriate level, subject to such conditions as may be specified therein, with respect to-

(a) the preparation of plans for economic development and social justice;

(b) the implementation of schemes for economic development and social justice as may be entrusted to them including those in relation to the matters listed in the Eleventh Schedule.

Powers to impose taxes by, and Funds of, the Panchayats.-The Legislature of a State may, by law,-

(a) authorise a Panchayat to levy, collect and appropriate such taxes, duties, tolls and fees in accordance with such procedure and subject to such limits;

(b) assign to a Panchayat such taxes, duties, tolls and fees levied and collected by the State Government

for such purposes and subject to such conditions and limits;

(c) provide for making such grants-in-aid to the Panchayats from the Consolidated Fund of the State; and

(d) provide for constitution of such Funds for crediting all moneys received, respectively, by or on behalf of the Panchayats and also for the withdrawal of such moneys therefrom, as may be specified in the law.

Constitution of Finance Commission to review financial position.-

(1) The Governor of a State shall, as soon as may be within one year from the commencement of the Constitution (Seventy-third Amendment) Act, 1992, and thereafter at the expiration of every fifth year, constitute a Finance Commission to review the financial position of the Panchayats and to make recommendations to the Governor as to-

(a) the principles which should govern-

(i) the distribution between the State and the Panchayats of the net proceeds of the taxes, duties, tolls and fees leviable by the State, which may be divided between them under this Part and the allocation between the Panchayats at all levels of their respective shares of such proceeds;

(ii) the determination of the taxes, duties, tolls and fees which may be assigned to, or appropriated by, the Panchayats;

(iii) the grants-in-aid to the Panchayats from the Consolidated Fund of the State;

(b) the measures needed to improve the financial position of the Panchayats;

(c) any other matter referred to the Finance Commission by the Governor in the interests of sound finance of the Panchayats.

(2) The Legislature of a State may, by law, provide for the composition of the Commission, the qualifications which

shall be requisite for appointment as members thereof and the manner in which they shall be selected.

(3) The Commission shall determine their procedure and shall have such powers in the performance of their functions as the Legislature of the State may, by law, confer on them.

(4) The Governor shall cause every recommendation made by the Commission under this article together with an explanatory memorandum as to the action taken thereon to be laid before the Legislature of the State.

Audit of accounts of Panchayats. The Legislature of a State may, by law, make provisions with respect to the maintenance of accounts by the Panchayats and the auditing of such accounts.

Elections to the Panchayats.-

(1) The superintendence, direction and control of the preparation of electoral rolls for, and the conduct of, all elections to the Panchayats shall be vested in a State Election Commission consisting of a State Election Commissioner to be appointed by the Governor.

(2) Subject to the provisions of any law made by the Legislature of a State, the conditions of service and tenure of office of the State Election Commissioner shall be such as the Governor may by rule determine:

Provided that the State Election Commissioner shall not be removed from his office except in like manner and on the like grounds as a Judge of a High Court and the conditions of service of the State Election Commissioner shall not be varied to his disadvantage after his appointment.

(3) The Governor of a State shall, when so requested by the State Election Commission, make available to the State Election Commission such staff as may be necessary for the discharge of the functions conferred on the State Election Commission by clause (1).

(4) Subject to the provisions of this Constitution, the Legislature of a State may, by law, make provision with respect to all matters relating to, or in connection with, elections to the Panchayats.

Application to Union territories.-

The provisions of this Part shall apply to the Union territories and shall, in their application to a Union territory, have effect as if the references to the Governor of a State were references to the Administrator of the Union territory appointed under article 239 and references to the Legislature or the legislative Assembly of a State were references, in relation to a Union territory having a Legislative Assembly, to that Legislative Assembly:

Provided that the President may, by public notification, direct that the provisions of this Part shall apply to any Union territory or part thereof subject to such exceptions and modifications as he may specify in the notification.

Part not to apply to certain areas.-

(1) Nothing in this Part shall apply to the Scheduled Areas referred to in clause (1), and the tribal areas referred to in clause (2), of article 244.

(2) Nothing in this Part shall apply to-

(a) the States of Nagaland, Meghalaya and Mizoram;

(b) the hill areas in the State of Manipur for which District Councils exist under any law for the time being in force.

(3) Nothing in this Part-

(a) relating to Panchayats at the district level shall apply to the hill areas of the District of Darjeeling in the State of West Bengal for which Darjeeling Gorkha Hill Council exists under any law for the time being in force;

(b) shall be construed to affect the functions and powers of the Darjeeling Gorkha Hill Council constituted under such law.

(3A) Nothing in article 243D, relating to reservation of seats for the Scheduled Castes, shall apply to the State of Arunachal Pradesh.

(4) Notwithstanding anything in this Constitution,-

(a) the Legislature of a State referred to in sub-clause (a) of clause (2) may, by law, extend this part to that

State, except the areas, if any, referred to in clause (1), if the Legislative Assembly of that State passes a resolution to that effect by a majority of the total membership of that House and by a majority of not less than two-thirds of the members of that House present and voting;

(b) Parliament may, by law, extend the provisions of this Part to the Scheduled Areas and the tribal areas referred to in clause (1) subject to such exceptions and modifications as may be specified in such law, and no such law shall be deemed to be an amendment of this Constitution for the purposes of article 368.

Continuance of existing laws and Panchayats.-

Notwithstanding anything in this Part, any provision of any law relating to Panchayats in force in a State immediately before the commencement of the Constitution (Seventy-third Amendment) Act, 1992, which is inconsistent with the provisions of this Part, shall continue to be in force until amended or repealed by a competent Legislature or other competent authority or until the expiration of one year from such commencement, whichever is earlier:

Provided that all the Panchayats existing immediately before such commencement shall continue till the expiration of their duration, unless sooner dissolved by a resolution passed to that effect by the Legislative Assembly of that State or, in the case of a State having a Legislative Council, by each House of the Legislature of that State.

Bar to interference by courts in electoral matters.- Notwithstanding anything in this Constitution,-

(a) the validity of any law relating to the delimitation of constituencies or the allotment of seats to such constituencies, made or purporting to be made under article 243K, shall not be called in question in any court;

(b) no election to any Panchayat shall be called in question except by an election petition presented to such authority and in such manner as is provided for by or under any law made by the Legislature of a State.

PANCHAYATIRAJ SYSTEM

The System

Panchayati Raj Institutions – the grassroots units of self-government – have been proclaimed as the vehicles of socio-economic transformation in rural India. Effective and meaningful functioning of these bodies would depend on active involvement, contribution and participation of its citizens both male and female. Gandhiji's dream of every village being a republic and Panchayats having powers has been translated into reality with the introduction of the three-tier Panchayati Raj system to enlist people's participation in rural reconstruction. April 24, 1993 is a landmark day in the history of Panchayati Raj in India as on this day the Constitution (73rd Amendment) Act, 1992 came into force to provide constitutional status to the Panchayati Raj institutions.

Evolution of Panchayati Raj System in Assam

The Rural Panchayat Act 1948. Under this system there were two tiers of Panchayats – Primary Panchayats at village level and Rural Panchayats at Mouza level.

Assam Panchayati Raj Act 1959: Under this act a three-tier system was introduced they are Gaon Panchayat, Anchalik Panchayat and Mohokuma Parishad.

Assam Panchayati Raj Act 1972: Under this system again a two-tier system was introduced they are Gaon Panchayat and Mohokuma Parishad

Assam Panchayati Raj Act 1986: Under this act again a three-tier system is introduced – Gaon Panchayat, Anchalik Panchayat & Mohokuma Parishad.

Assam Panchayat Act 1994: A three-tier system with Zilla Parishad has been introduced – Gaon Panchayat, Anchalik Panchayat and Zilla Parishad.

73rd Amendment Act, 1992

The Salient Features of the Act are :

a. To provide 3-tier system of Panchayati Raj for all the States having population of over 20 Lakhs.
b. To hold Panchayat Elections regularly every 5 years.
c. To provide reservation of seats for Scheduled Castes, Scheduled Tribes and Women (not less than 33%)
d. To appoint State Finance Commission to make recommendations as regards the financial powers of the Panchayats.
e. To constitute District Planning Committee to prepare draft development plan for the district as a whole.

Powers and Responsibilities

According to the Constitution, Panchayats shall be given powers and authority to function as institutions of self-government. The following powers and responsibilities are to be delegated to Panchayats at the appropriate level :-

a. Preparation of Plan for economic development and social justice.
b. Implementation of schemes for economic development and social justice in relation to 29 subjects given in Eleventh Schedule of the Constitution.
c. To levy, collect and appropriate taxes, duties, tolls and fees.

Structure of the Panchayati Raj System in Assam

Gaon Panchayats:

a. President – directly elected by people.
b. One Vice President – to be elected from among the members of Gaon Panchayat.
c. Ten members – directly elected by people.

Zilla Parishad:

a. President – elected from among the directly elected members of Zilla Parishad.
b. Vice President-elected from among the directly elected members of Zilla Parishad.
c. Members –
   1. Members directly elected from the Zilla Parishad constituencies of the district.

2. Presidents of the Anchalik Panchayats.
3. Members of House of people & member of Legislative Assembly.

Anchalik Panchayats:

a. President – to be elected by the elected members of the Anchalik Panchayats.
b. Vice President-to be elected by the elected members of the Anchalik Panchayats.
c. Members –
    1. One member from each Gaon Panchayat area to be directly elected by people.
    2. President of the Gaon Panchayats falling within the jurisdiction of the Anchalik Panchayat.
    3. Members of Parliament and Legislative Assembly.

Functions of the Panchayati Raj Bodies:

Gaon Panchayat:

1. Preparation of Annual Plans for the development of the Gaon Panchayat area.
2. Preparation Annual Budget of Gaon Panchayat.
3. Mobilisation of reliefs in natural calamities.
4. Removal of encroachments on public properties.
5. Organising voluntary labours and contribution for community works.
6. Maintenance of essential statistics of villages.
7. Such other development works as may be entrusted.

Zilla Parishad:

It should be the function of a Zilla Parishad to prepare plans for economic development and social justice of the district and ensure the coordinated implementation of such plan.

Anchalik Panchayat:

a. Preparation of Annual Plan in respect of the schemes entrusted to it by virtue of the Act and those assigned to it by the Government or the Zilla Parishad and submission thereof to the Zilla Parishad within the prescribed time for integration with the District Plan;

b. Consideration and consolidation of the Annual Plans of all Gaon Panchayats under the Anchalik Panchayat and submission of consolidated plan to the Zilla Parishad;
c. Preparation of Annual Budget of the Anchalik Panchayat and submission to Zilla Parishad for approval within the prescribed time;
d. Performing such functions and executing such works as may be entrusted to it by government or the Zilla Parishad;
e. To assist the government in relief operation in natural calamities;
f. Such other development works as may be entrusted.

HISTORY OF PANCHAYATIRAJ IN INDIA

India has a chequered history of panchayati raj starting from a self-sufficient and self-governing village communities that survived the rise and fall of empires in the past to the modern legalized institutions of governance at the third tier provided with Constitutional support.

Early History

During the time of the Rig-Veda (1200 BC), evidences suggest that self-governing village bodies called 'sabhas' existed. With the passage of time, these bodies became panchayats (council of five persons). Panchayats were functional institutions of grassroots governance in almost every village. The Village Panchayat or elected council had large powers, both executive and judicial. Land was distributed by this panchayat which also collected taxes out of the produce and paid the government's share on behalf of the village. Above a number of these village councils there was a larger panchayat or council to supervise and interfere if necessary. Casteism and feudalistic system of governance under Mughal rule in the medieval period slowly eroded the self-government in villages. A new class of feudal chiefs and revenue collectors (zamindars) emerged between the ruler and the people. And, so began the stagnation and decline of self-government in villages. During the British rule, the autonomy of panchayats gradually declined with the establishment of local civil and criminal courts, revenue and police organisations, the increase in communications, the growth of individualism and the operation of the individual Ryotwari '(landholder-wise) system as against the Mahalwari or village tenure system.

During British Rule

The panchayat had never been the priority of the British rulers. The rulers were interested in the creation of 'controlled' local bodies, which could help them in their trading interests by collecting taxes for them. When the colonial administration came under severe financial pressure after the 1857 uprising, the remedy sought was decentralisation in terms of transferring responsibility for road and public works to local bodies. However, the thrust of this 'compelled' decentralisation was with respect to municipal administration.

From 1870 that Viceroy Lord Mayo's Resolution (for decentralisation of power to bring about administrative efficiency in meeting people's demand and to add to the finances of colonial regime) gave the needed impetus to the development of local institutions. It was a landmark in the evolution of colonial policy towards local government. The real benchmarking of the government policy on decentralisation can, however, be attributed to Lord Ripon who, in his famous resolution on local self-government on May 18, 1882, recognised the twin considerations of local government: (i) administrative efficiency and (ii) political education. The '"Ripon Resolution"', which focused on towns, provided for local bodies consisting of a large majority of elected non-official members and presided over by a non-official chairperson. This resolution met with resistance from colonial administrators. The progress of local self-government was tardy with only half-hearted steps taken in setting up municipal bodies. Rural decentralisation remained a neglected area of administrative reform.

The Royal Commission on Decentralisation (1907) under the chairmanship of C.E.H. Hobhouse recognised the importance of panchayats at the village level. The commission recommended that "it is most desirable, alike in the interests of decentralisation and in order to associate the people with the local tasks of administration, that an attempt should be made to constitute and develop village panchayats for the administration of local village affairs".

But, the Montague-Chemsford reforms (1919) brought local self-government as a provincial transferred subject, under the domain of Indian ministers in the provinces. Due to organisational and fiscal constraints, the reform was unable to make panchayat institutions truly democratic and vibrant. However, the most significant development of this period was the 'establishment of village panchayats in a number of provinces, that were no longer mere ad hoc judicial tribunal, but representative institutions symbolising the corporate character of the village and having a wide jurisdiction in respect of civic matters'. By 1925, eight provinces had passed panchayat acts and by 1926, six native states had also passed panchayat laws.

The provincial autonomy under the Government of India Act, 1935, marked the evolution of panchayats in India. Popularly elected governments in provinces enacted legislations to further democratise institutions of local self-government. But the system of responsible government at the grassroots level was least responsible. D.P. Mishra, the then minister for local self-government under the Government of India Act of 1935 in Central Provinces was of the view that 'the working of our local bodies... in our province and perhaps in the whole country presents a tragic picture... 'Inefficiency' and 'local body' have become synonymous terms....'.

In spite of various committees such as the Royal Commission on Decentralization (1907), the report of Montague and Chemsford on constitutional reform (1919), the Government of India Resolution (1918), etc., a hierarchical administrative structure based on supervision and control evolved. The administrator became the focal point of rural governance. The British were not concerned with decentralised democracy but were aiming for colonial objectives.

The Indian National Congress from the 1920s to 1947, emphasized the issue of all-India Swaraj, and organized movements for Independence under the leadership of Mahatma Gandhi. The task of preparing any sort of blueprint for the local level was neglected as a result. There was no consensus among the top leaders regarding the status and role to be assigned to the institution of rural local self-government; rather there were divergent views on the subject. On the one end Gandhi favoured Village Swaraj and strengthening the village panchayat to the fullest extent and on the other end, Dr. B.R. Ambedkar opposed this idea. He believed that the village represented regressive India, a source of oppression. The model state hence had to build safeguards against such social oppression and the only way it could be done was through the adoption of the parliamentary model of politics During the drafting of the Constitution of India, Panchayati Raj Institutions were placed in the non-justiciable part of the Constitution, the Directive Principles of State Policy, as Article 40.

The Article read 'the State shall take steps to organise village panchayats and endow them with such powers and authority as may be necessary to enable them to function as units of self-government'. However, no worthwhile legislation was enacted either at the national or state level to implement it. In the four decades since the adoption of the Constitution, panchayat raj institutions have travelled from the non-justiciable part of the Constitution to one where, through a separate amendment, a whole new status has been added to their history

Post-independence Period

Panchayat raj had to go through various stages. The First Five Year Plan failed to bring about active participation and involvement of the people in the Plan processes, which included Plan formulation implementation and monitoring. The Second Five Year Plan attempted to cover the entire countryside with National Extensive Service Blocks through the institutions of Block Development Officers, Assistant Development Officers, Village Level Workers, in addition to nominated representatives of village panchayats of that area and some other popular organisations like cooperative societies. But the plan failed to satisfactorily accomplish decentralisation. Hence, committees were constituted by various authorities to advise the Centre on different aspects of decentralisation.

The Balwantrai Mehta Committee (1957)

In 1957, Balwantrai Mehta Committee studied the Community Development Projects and the National Extension Service and assessed the extent to which the movement had succeeded in utilising local initiatives and in creating institutions to ensure continuity in the process of improving economic and social conditions in rural areas. The Committee held that community development would only be deep and enduring when the community was involved in the planning, decision-making and implementation process. The suggestions were for as follows :-

- an early establishment of elected local bodies and devolution to them of necessary resources, power and authority,
- that the basic unit of democratic decentralisation was at the block/samiti level since the area of jurisdiction of the local body should neither be too large nor too small. The block was large enough for efficiency and economy of administration, and small enough for sustaining a sense of involvement in the citizens,
- such body must not be constrained by too much control by the government or government agencies,
- the body must be constituted for five years by indirect elections from the village panchayats,
- its functions should cover the development of agriculture in all its aspects, the promotion of local industries and others
- services such as drinking water, road building, etc., and
- the higher level body, Zilla Parishad, would play an advisory role.

The PRI structure did not develop the requisite democratic momentum and failed to cater to the needs of rural development. There are various reasons for such an outcome which include political and bureaucratic resistance at the state level to share power and resources with local level institutions, domination of local elites over the major share of the benefits of welfare schemes, lack of capability at the local level and lack of political will.

K. Santhanam Committee (1963)

One of the prime areas of concern in this long debate on panchayati raj institutions was fiscal decentralisation. The K. Santhanam Committee was appointed to look solely at the issue of PRI finance, in 1963. The fiscal capacity of PRIs tends to be limited, as rich resources of revenue are pre-empted by higher levels of government, and issue is still debated today. The Committee was asked to determine issues related to sanctioning of grants to PRIs by the state government, evolving mutual financial relations between the three tiers of PRIs, gifts and donation, handing over revenue in full or part to PRIs. The Committee recommended the following :

- panchayats should have special powers to levy special tax on land revenues and home taxes, etc.,
- people should not be burdened with too many demands (taxes),
- all grants and subventions at the state level should be mobilised and sent in a consolidated form to various PRIs,
- a Panchayat Raj Finance Corporation should be set up to look into the financial resource of PRIs at all levels, provide loans and financial assistance to these grassroots level governments and also provide non-financial requirements of villages.

These issues have been debated over the last three decades and have been taken up by the State Finance Commissions which are required to select taxes for assignment and sharing, identifying the principles for such sharing and assignment, determine the level of grants and recommend the final distribution of state's transfers to local authorities.

Ashok Mehta Committee (1978)

With the coming of the Janata Party into power at the Centre in 1977, a serious view was taken of the weaknesses in the functioning of Panchayati Raj. It was decided to appoint a high-level committee under the chairmanship of Ashok Mehta to examine and suggest measures to strengthen PRIs. The Committee had to evolve an effective decentralised system of development for PRIs. They made the following recommendations :-

- the district is a viable administrative unit for which planning, coordination and resource allocation are feasible and technical expertise available,
- PRIs as a two-tier system, with Mandal Panchayat at the base and Zilla Parishad at the top,
- the PRIs are capable of planning for themselves with the resources available to them,
- district planning should take care of the urban-rural continuum,
- representation of SCs and STs in the election to PRIs on the basis of their population,
- four-year term of PRIs,
- participation of political parties in elections,
- any financial devolution should be committed to accepting that much of the developmental functions at the district level would be played by the panchayats.

The states of Karnataka, Andhra Pradesh and West Bengal passed new legislation based on this report. However, the flux in politics at the state level did not allow these institutions to develop their own political dynamics.

V.K. Rao Committee (1985)

The G.V.K. Rao Committee was appointed to once again look at various aspects of PRIs.

The Committee was of the opinion that a total view of rural development must be taken in which PRIs must play a central role in handling people's problems. It recommended the following :-

- PRIs have to be activated and provided with all the required support to become effective organisations,
- PRIs at the district level and below should be assigned the work of planning, implementation and monitoring of rural development programmes, and
- the block development office should be the spinal cord of the rural development process.

L.M., Singhvi Committee (1986)

L.M. Singhvi Committee studied panchayatiraj. The Gram Sabha was considered as the base of a decentralised democracy, and PRIs viewed as institutions of self-governance which would actually facilitate the participation of the people in the process of planning and development. It recommended :

- local self-government should be constitutionally recognised, protected and preserved by the inclusion of new chapter in the Constitution,
- non-involvement of political parties in Panchayat elections.

The suggestion of giving panchayats constitutional status was opposed by the Sarkaria Commission, but the idea, however, gained momentum in the late 1980s especially because of the endorsement by the late Prime Minister Rajiv Gandhi, who introduced the 64th Constitutional Amendment Bill in 1989. The 64th Amendment Bill was prepared and introduced in the lower house of Parliament. But it got defeated in the Rajya Sabha as non-convincing. He lost the general elections too. In 1989, the National Front introduced the 74th Constitutional Amendment Bill, which could not become an Act because of the dissolution of the Ninth Lok Sabha. All these various suggestions and recommendations and means of strengthening PRIs were considered while formulating the new Constitutional Amendment Act.

The 73rd Constitutional Amendment Act

The idea that produced the 73rd Amendment was not a response to pressure from the grassroots, but to an increasing recognition that the institutional initiatives of the preceding decade had not delivered, that the extent of rural poverty was still much too large and thus the existing structure of government needed to be reformed. It is interesting to note that this idea evolved from the Centre and the state governments. It was a political drive to see PRIs as a solution to the governmental crises that India was experiencing. The Constitutional (73rd Amendment) Act, passed in 1992 by the Narasimha Rao government, came into force on April 24, 1993. It was meant to provide constitutional sanction to establish "democracy at the grassroots level as it is at the state level or national level". Its main features are as follows :

- The Gram Sabha or village assembly as a deliberative body to decentralised governance has been envisaged as the foundation of the Panchayati Raj System.
- A uniform three-tier structure of panchayats at village (Gram Panchayat — GP), intermediate (Panchayat Samiti — PS) and district (Zilla Parishad — ZP) levels.
- All the seats in a panchayat at every level are to be filled by elections from respective territorial constituencies.
- Not less than one-third of the total seats for membership as well as office of chairpersons of each tier have to be reserved for women.
- Reservation for weaker castes and tribes (SCs and STs) have to be provided at all levels in proportion to their population in the panchayats.
- To supervise, direct and control the regular and smooth elections to panchayats, a State Election Commission has to be constituted in every State and UT.
- The Act has ensured constitution of a State Finance Commission in every State/UT, for every five years, to suggest measures to strengthen finances of PRIs.
- To promote bottom-up-planning, the District Planning Committee (DPC) in every district has been accorded constitutional status.
- An indicative list of 29 items has been given in Eleventh Schedule of the Constitution. Panchayats are expected to play an effective role in planning and implementation of works related to these 29 items.

THE PANCHAYATI RAJ CAMPAIGN

Communication Strategies

The holds that effective bottom-up strategies for ending hunger and poverty combine 3 factors: mobilising people at the grassroots level to build self-reliance, empowering women as key change agents, and forging effective partnerships with local government and non-governmental organisations (NGOs).

Through partnerships with 55 local NGOs across 14 states, THP state and national staff trained more than 800 staff trainers of these organisations to lead workshops and provide ongoing empowerment to women leaders. These organisations make up a national alliance that advocates for change at the state and national levels. Drawing on this multi-pronged approach, THP's Panchayati Raj Campaign implements specific interventions in each year of a woman leader's term in an effort to empower her to succeed.

In the first year after election, women participate in a 3-day Women's Leadership Workshop (WLW) that alerts women to their human rights, educates them about their powers and responsibilities as panchayat leaders, builds their capacity to create a vision and plan actions to achieve it, and links them with government and other resource people in their area. This is reinforced 3 months later in a follow-up workshop and through needs-based workshops that women request to strengthen their skills in communication, finances, and knowledge of laws and government programmes. Women leaders are trained to organise the women of their villages into self-help groups (SHGs) for mutual support and economic activity. SHGs become a constituency to stand with the elected leader for women's priorities. The SHGs are mobilised to attend mandatory open meetings known as gram sabhas, where they can hold panchayats to account. They are empowered to meet beforehand to prepare a clear list of priorities. In Year 2, THP works with panchayats to create bottom-up plans ("microplans") for villages to meet basic needs. These plans involve assessing available resources and creating strategies for actions that people can take themselves. When governmental resources are required, planning includes establishing good partnerships with local officials.

During Year 2, there are additional capacity-building workshops for elected women leaders, and THP takes additional action to mobilise women to participate in the gram sabhas. The focus in Year 3 is on creating federations of elected women representatives. THP has observed that, as villages take action, they inevitably run up against bureaucratic obstacles. To overcome these obstacles-and to sustain villages' process of empowerment on their own-federations are formed at the block (100+ villages), district, and state levels. Block-level federations provide regular monthly forums for mutual support, and state federations rally elected women to demand change at the policy level. In Year 4, THP ensures that panchayats have successfully implemented their plans and that lives have truly improved on a sustainable basis.

In addition, where leaders have run up against major legal obstacles, the women demand policy changes and engage in public-interest litigation. For example, in Bihar in 2004, THP mobilised 2,000 women to protest the failure of the state government to implement key provisions of the 73rd amendment, and then followed up with litigation for change.

In the run-up to elections, THP carries out campaigns to encourage the participation of women-both as independently minded voters and as candidates. As the reserved seats rotate to different areas each term, new women are encouraged to step forward to run for those seats. In addition, women who have already served are encouraged to stand for re-election against men in unreserved seats.

Hunger Project in India

The Hunger Project in India is committing itself to ignite and sustain a coordinated, strategic campaign of action for women's leadership and the success of panchayati raj. The Hunger Project is beginning this initiative in four states where there has been strong official support for panchayati raj: Gujarat, Karnataka, Madhya Pradesh and Rajasthan. It intends to expand the campaign to all 11 states where The Hunger Project works.

Four-pronged Strategy: The Hunger Project's Panchayati Raj Campaign initially has four major components: alliance-building, leadership training, increasing media coverage and generating international support. The Hunger Project will identify additional high-leverage pathways for action as the campaign unfolds.

1. *Building Alliances for Advocacy and Action*: Women's leadership and panchayati raj are opportunities of such

scale and importance that such a campaign can only be carried out by an alliance of organisations in each state committed to this issue. The Hunger Project is working strategically to build strong and active alliances among government agencies, NGOs, self-help groups, academics and media in support of women's leadership in panchayati raj.

2. *Leadership Skills Training*: India is blessed with many organisations providing training to equip women panchayat leaders with key factual information, such as the roles and responsibilities of panchayats, and details of government programmes. What appears to be missing-and what The Hunger Project is in a unique position to provide-is training for these women in fundamental leadership skills.

   Elected women representatives have grown up in an environment that tells them, day after day, that they-as women-are powerless. They have had precious few opportunities to develop their leadership skills. The Hunger Project has created a new Women's Leadership Workshop to enable women to have a breakthrough in their leadership skills, and to empower their leadership over time.

   Vision, Commitment and Action: In the workshop, women discover that they possess the power to actually change conditions they have considered both intolerable and hopeless. They generate their own vision for what they want to achieve, and learn how to inspire others to stand with them to achieve it. After a lifetime of doing only what they have been told, women discover their ability to create their own strategies and action plans. In the months following the training, participants come back together to support each other in achieving their goals.

3. *Increasing and Improving Media Coverage*: The Hunger Project has held workshops and press conferences to educate reporters about the untold success stories of women in panchayati raj. To enhance and expand this effort, The Hunger Project is launching the Sarojini

Naidu Prize for Best Reporting on Women in Panchayati Raj.

4. *International Support*: India's pioneering work in panchayati raj sets an important example for countries around the world. People in both developed and developing countries need to know about and maintain support for these efforts. Through strategic communications and site visits, The Hunger Project is mobilising its global constituency to put and keep the international spotlight on this historic phenomenon.

JUDICIAL FUNCTIONS OF GRAM PANCHAYATS

Powers and jurisdiction of Gram Panchayat over criminal offences. (1) Gram Panchayat shall exercise powers and shall have jurisdiction over matters laid down in Schedule II. (2) For the purpose of deciding whether an offence falls within the jurisdiction of a Gram Panchayat, the provisions of sections 178 to 181 of the Code of Criminal Procedure, 1973 shall apply. (3) A Gram Panchayat shall be deemed to be criminal court when trying criminal cases.

Transfer of proceedings. Any Magistrate before whom a complaint or report by the Police of any offence triable by a Gram Panchayat Is brought or who takes cognizance of any such offence upon his own knowledge or suspicion shall transfer the proceedings to a Gram Panchayat of competent jurisdiction:

Provided that a Chief Judicial Magistrate may for reasons to be recorded in writing, transfer any criminal case from Gram Panchayat to another Gram Panchayat of competent jurisdiction or to another court subordinate to him.

Exclusion of certain case. (1) Subject to the provisions of sub-section (3), no Gram Panchayat shall take cognizance of any offence under the Indian Penal Code, 18960, in which either complainant or the accused is a public servant. (2) When information relating to the commission of a cognizable offence triable by a Gram Panchayat has been given to an officer incharge of a police station, he shall forthwith send a copy of the First Information Report, to the Gram Panchayat competent to try such an offence and such Gram Panchayat shall not proceed to try any complaint relating to the same facts nor shall it issue any summons in the matter, until the officer has intimated in writing that the investigation has been concluded; Provided that such an officer shall send the information to the Gram Panchayat after the conclusion of the investigation. (3) No criminal cases shall be heard, by any Gram panchayat when criminal case on substantially the same facts against the same facts against the same person has been heard and finally decided by the competent court or Gram Panchayat or is pending therein, or before it.

Cognizance of criminal cases. (1) A criminal case before a Gram panchayat shall be instituted on a complaint in writing and on payment of fee prescribed in Schedule III by presenting it in person to the Sarpanch, and in his absence, to any Panch or by sending it by registered post Gram Panchayat : Provided that If the court fee stamp is not available at the place where the Gram Panchayat ordinarily sits or at the place from where the complaint is sent an equivalent amount may be paid in cash sent to the Gram Panchayat by money order. (2) The particulars of the complaint shall be recorded by the Secretary the Gram Panchayat in the register prescribed for the purpose. (3) Notwithstanding anything contained in sub-section (1). a Gram Panchayat shall be competent to take cognizance *suo moto* of cases falling under sections 160, 228, 264, 277, 289, 290, 294, 510 of the Indian Penal Code, 1860 and under sections 3 and 4 of the Punjab Juvenile Smoking Act, 1918.

Action on complaint. (1) The Gram Panchayat may, after examining the complainant and the witnesses, if any, and after such further enquiry, as it may deem necessary, either dismiss the complaint or summons accused. (2) The Gram Panchayat may dismiss the case if the complainant is absent on any day fixed for hearing of the case or for want of prosecution and such order shall, subject to the provisions of sub-section (3), operate as an acquittal. (3) If the complainant satisfies the Gram Panchayat that his absence for want of prosecution of the case on his part was due to a sufficient cause, the Gram Panchayat may set aside the order of dismissal and revive the proceedings:

Provided that no order of dismissal shall be set aside unless:

(i) an application for the purpose is made by the

complainant within thirty days of the passing of such order; and

(ii) a notice of the application has been served upon the accused if the dismissal was made after appearance of the accused before the Gram Panchayat.

Power of Gram Panchayat to refuse to entertain criminal case. (1) If at any time it appears to the Gram Panchayat that the offence is one for which the sentence which the Grain Panchayat is competent to pass would be Inadequate, It shall send the record of the case by order in writing to the Chief Judicial Magistrate.

Proceeding on failure of the accused to appear. (1) If the accused fails to appear or cannot be found, the Gram Panchayat shall report the facts to the Magistrate having jurisdiction over the area. (2) The Magistrate shall Issue the summons or warrant for the arrest of he accused and in case of a warrant, shall direct by endorsement on the warrant that if such person executes a bond in certain amount with or without sureties for his attendance before himself in the manner provided in section 71 of the Code of Criminal Procedure, 1973, he shall be released from custody. (3) When the accused appears before the Magistrate he may direct him to execute a bond with or without sureties in the amount to be named to appear before the Gram Panchayat at its next meetings and it shall be the duty of such accused to enquire the date and time of the next meeting of the Gram Panchayat. (4) On his failure to execute such a bond if required to do so under sub-section (3) of the Magistrate shall order that the accused may be produced in custody before the Gram Panchayat at its next meeting. (5) If the accused fails to appear before the Gram Panchayat after executing a bond under sub-section (3) the Gram Panchayat shall report the fact m the bond was executed and such Magistrate before whom the bond was executed and such Magistrate shall proceed under sub-section (2) to compel the attendance of the accused amount of bond under Chapter XXXIII of the Code of Criminal Procedure, 1973.

Prompt disposal of criminal cases. (1) The Gram Panchayat shall, if possible, try a criminal case and pass orders on the day on which the accused appears and. If that is not possible may, if he is not already on ball, require him to execute a bond with or without sureties for a sum not exceeding five hundred rupees to appear before the Gram Panchayat on any subsequent day or days to which the trial may be adjourned. (2) The amount of bond to be executed under sub-section (1) if, forfeited shall be recoverable by the Gram Panchayat as if were a fine imposed by it. (3) If the accused fails to execute the bond required by sub-section (1) the Gram Panchayat shall inform the Magistrate of the fact and the date fixed, for the next hearing and the Magistrate shall proceed as provided under sub-sections (4) and (5) of section 50.

Punishment. A Gram Panchayat may on conviction –

(a) sentence the accused to a fine not exceeding two hundred rupees or double the value of the damage or loss caused by this Act, whichever is greater : Provided that no fine shall exceed the maximum fine prescribed by the law for that offence:

(b) discharge him after due admonition.

(c) require him to execute within such time as the Gram Panchayat may fix, a bond with or without sureties of an amount not exceeding one hundred rupees, binding himself that he will not be again guilty of an offence triable by the Gram Panchayat for any period not exceeding twelve months, or

(d) where in the opinion of Gram Panchayat he is under eighteen years of age, require his father or his guardian to execute within such time as the Gram Panchayat may fix, a bond with or without sureties of an amount not exceeding one hundred rupees, binding himself to prevent such offender from committing any offence triable by the Gram Panchayat for any period not exceeding twelve months.

(2) The amount of any bond taken under clauses (c) and (d) of the foregoing sub-section if forfeited, shall be recoverable by the Gram Panchayat as if it were a fine imposed by itself and if the accused or his father or his guardian as the case may be, fails to execute such a bond within the time fixed the accused shall be punishable with fine which may extend to one hundred rupees. (3) Where a Gram Panchayat imposes a fine

under the provisions of this section and such fine is not paid as required it shall record an order declaring the amount of fine imposed and that it has not been paid, and shall forward the same to the nearest Judicial Magistrate who shall proceed to execute it as if were an order passed by himself, and such Judicial Magistrate may also sentence the accused to imprisonment in default of payment.

Compensation. (1) If a fine is imposed under this Act, the Gram Panchayat may order the whole or any part of the fine recovered to be applied

(a) in defraying expenses properly incurred in the case by the complainant; and

(b) in compensation for any material damage or loss caused by the offence committed.

(2) If the Gram Panchayat considers that a case is flaw or frivolous or vexatious it may call upon the complainant to show cause why he should not pay compensation to the accused. (3) The Gram Panchayat shall record and consider any cause which the complainant may show under sub-section (2) and if it is as satisfied that the case was false, frivolous or vexatious, may for reason, to be recorded direct that compensation not exceeding rupees fifty shall be paid by the complainant to the accused.

Conviction by Gram Panchayat not Previous Conviction. No conviction under this Act shall be deemed to be previous conviction for the purpose of section 75 of the Indian Penal Code, 1860 or section 356 or section 360 of the Code of Criminal Procedure, 1973.

Supervision of Criminal proceedings by Chief Judicial Magistrate. (1) The Chief Judicial Magistrate, if satisfied that a failure of justice has occurred, may, of his own motion or on an application of the party aggrieved by order in writing after notice to the accused, or the complainant, as the case may be, cancel or modify any order in a judicial proceeding made by a Gram Panchayat or direct the retrial of any criminal case by the same or any other Gram Panchayat of competent jurisdiction subordinate to him. (2) A fee of one rupee shall be paid on every application, to be filed under sub-section (1).

Civil, revenue and judicial powers. (1) Notwithstanding anything contained in any other law for the time being In force and subject to the other provisions of this Act, the jurisdiction to try any of the suits mentioned hereunder shall vest In a Gram Panchayat,-

(a) suits for the recovery of movable property or the value of such property:

(b) suits for money or goods due on contracts or price thereof,

(c) suits for compensation for wrongfully taking or injuring movable property; and

(d) suits mentioned In clauses U), (k), (1) and (n) of sub-section (3) of section 77 of the Punjab Tenancy Act, 1887, or any other law for the time being in force.

(2) The pecuniary limits of jurisdiction of a Gram Panchayat shall be five hundred rupees in respect of all suits falling under sub-section (1). Gram Panchayat to he deemed to be civil or revenue court. The Gram Panchayat When trying suits referred to in section 56 shall be deemed to be a civil court or revenue courts, as the case may be, unless relinquished in part, the suits shall include the whole of the claim and no subsequent suits shall lie before the Gram Panchayat or any other court for any claim or a part thereof relinquished or omitted.

Limits to jurisdiction. No suit shall lie before a Gram Panchayat unless the defendant or one of the defendants sought to be made liable for the claim where there are more than one at the time of the institution of the suit resides or carries on business or personally works for gain, or has within one year of the institution of the suit resided or carried on business or personally worked for gain, within the limits of its jurisdiction or the cause of action has arisen wholly or in part within these limits.

Transfer of suits. (1) Any other court before whom a suit triable by a Gram Panchayat is filed shall transfer the suit to the Gram Panchayat of competent jurisdiction. (2) The District Judge or Collector may, for reasons to be recorded in writing, transfer any civil or revenue suit respectively from the Gram Panchayat to another Gram Panchayat of a competent jurisdiction or to another court subordinate to him.

Exclusion of Gram Panchayat jurisdiction. No suit shall lie in a Gram Panchayat –

(a) on a balance of a partnership account;

(b) for a share or a part of share under an intestacy or for a legacy of part of legacy under a Will;

(c) by or against the Central Government or a State Government or local authority or a public servant or a Gram Panchayat or Market Committee constituted under the Punjab Agricultural Produce Markets Act, 1961 or any other law for the time being in force, or when any such party is, in the opinion of the Gram Panchayat necessary party;

(d) by or against a minor or a person of unsound mind or when any such person is in the opinion of the Gram Panchayat a necessary party;

(e) against an insolvent for a claim pertaining to the time prior to the admission of his insolvency petition;

(f) on account of any dispute or matter regarding which any suit or application may be made in a revenue court as defined in the Punjab Tenancy Act, 1887 except as provided by clause (d) of sub-section (1) of section 56;

(g) in which the matter directly and substantially in issue is pending for decision or has been heard and finally decided by a Court of competent jurisdiction in a former suit between the same parties or those

Limitation. (1) The provisions of any law fixing a period of limitation for civil or revenue proceedings shall be deemed to be amended to the extent that the period of limitation of any suit triable by a Gram Panchayat shall not exceed three years. (2) Any time spent on proceedings before a Gram Panchayat to which the Provisions of this section are applicable shall be excluded from any period of limitation of any prescribed by law for suits in other courts.

Institution of suits. (1) Any person, who wishes to institute a suit before a Gram Panchayat, shall present a petition in writing to the Sarpanch, or, in his absence, to any Panch and shall at the time pay the fees prescribed in Schedule III: Provided that if the court fee stamp is not available at the place where the Gram Panchayat ordinarily sits, an equivalent amount in cash shall be paid. (2) Any petition presented under sub-section (1) shall be entered in a register of suits, to be maintained in such form and by such person as the State Government may prescribe, Wrong institution of suits. If at any time, it appears to the Grain jurisdiction to try a suit it shall direct the petitioner, by order in writing, to file his suit in the proper court.

Summary dismissal. If upon the face of the petition, or on examining he petitioner, a Gram Panchayat is of opinion that the petition is vexatious or frivolous or barred by limitation or discloses no cause of action, it shall dismiss the petition by order in writing.

Necessary Parties in suits. (1) Subject to the provisions of clauses (c) and (d) of section 56 of the Gram Panchayat shall add as parties to suit person whose presence as parties it considers necessary for a proper decision thereof and shall enter the names of such parties in the register of suit and suit shall be tried as between the parties whose names are entered in the said register: Provided that when any party is added notice shall be given to him and he shall be given an opportunity of appearing before the trial of the suit is proceeded with. (2) In all cases where new party appears under the proviso to sub-section (1) during the trial of a civil suit, he may require that the trial shall beg, *de novo*. (3) If the plaintiff or dependant in any suit dies before a case has beer finally decided and the right to sue still survives the suit shall subject to the provision of clause (d) of section 56 be proceeded with at the instance of, or against the legal representatives of the deceased plaintiff or the deceased defendant, as the case may be: Provided that application in this behalf it has been presented to the Gram Panchayat within thirty days of the death or within such fur titter period as the Gram Panchayat may, for sufficient cause allow.

Summons. If suit is not dismissed under section 64 the Gram Panchayat shall by summons require the defendant to appear before It and answer the petition.

Dismissal in default and restoration. (1) If the petitioner fails to appear on the date fixed for hearing or If In the opinion of the Gram Panchayat he shows negligence In prosecuting his suit, the Gram Panchayat may dismiss the suit unless the defendant admits all or any part of the claim, when it shall be decreed accordingly. (2) A Gram Panchayat shall restore a suit dismissed for failure to appear if, within fifteen days from the date of such dismissal, or such further period which for sufficient cause the Gram Panchayat may allow, the plain tiff satisfies the Gram Panchayat that he was prevented by any sufficient cause from appearing; but no order of dismissal shall be set aside without notice to the defendant. If it has been passed after his appearance before the Gram Panchayat. (3) A fee of one rupee shall be paid on every application for restoration, under sub-section (2).

Ex pane decision. (1) If the defendant fails to appear and the Gram Panchayat is satisfied that he has received notice of the date fixed for the hearing or that he is intentionally evading service, the Gram Panchayat may proceed ex parte. (2) Any defendant against whom a suit has been decided ex parte, may within thirty days from the date of executing any process for enforcement of the decision or within such further period as the Gram Panchayat may for sufficient cause allow, apply orally or in writing to the Gram Panchayat, to set aside the order; and the Gram Panchayat, if satisfied that the defendant did not receive due notice of the hearing or was prevented from appearing by any sufficient cause or was not intentionally evading service of summons, shall act aside the decision and shall appoint a day for proceeding with the suit, but no such order shall be passed without notice to the opposite party. (3) A fee of one rupee shall be paid on every application under sub-section (2) for setting aside an ex parte decision.

Final decision. (1) At the conclusion of the trial, the Gram Panchayat shall pass a decree in writing with or without costs of the suits in such forms as the State Government may by rules prescribe and shall enter particulars of the decision in register of suits. (2) If any money is paid over or if any property is transferred in the presence of Gram Panchayat in satisfaction of a decree it shall enter the Payment or the transfer in the register of suits. (3) A decree passed by a Gram Panchayat shall be executed by It In sue Manner as may be prescribed and If the Gram Panchayat finds any difficulty in executing a decree, it may forward the decree to the civil or revenue court having jurisdiction and such court shall thereupon proceed to execute the decree as if it were a decree passed by itself.

Supervision. The District Judge in respect of civil suits or the Collector in respect of revenue suits may of his own motion or on an application of the party aggrieved set aside or modify any decree or order made by a Gram Panchayat in civil or revenue suit or direct the retrial of the suit by the same or any other Gram Panchayat of competent jurisdiction or by any other court subordinate to him if he is satisfied that there has been a failure of justice whether on a point of fact or point of law.

Supervisions of the Code of Criminal Procedure, 1973, and the Code of Civil Procedure, 1908 to apply only where provided. (1) The Provisions of the Code of Criminal Procedure, 1973, the Code of Civil Procedure, 1908, and of the Indian Evidence Act, 1972, shall not apply to proceedings before Gram Panchayats save to the extent mentioned in this Act, but the Gram Panchayat may ascertain the facts of any criminal case or civil or revenue suit by all legitimate means in its power and thereafter ass such order, sentence or decree as may be in accordance with justice, equity and good conscience. (2) Every Gram Panchayat shall maintain a brief memorandum of Proceedings of each case tried by it. (3) All orders, sentences and decrees shall be passed in accordance with the decision of the majority of the members present and voting: Provided that in the case of equality of votes, person, presiding at such meeting shall in addition to his own vote as a member, have a second or casting vote. (4) All orders, sentences and decrees passed under sub-section (1) shall be announced In an open meeting of the Gram Panchayat by the person presiding at such meeting and decision shall be recorded and it shall be duly signed by an the members of the Gram Panchayat attending the meeting: Provided that any member not concurring in the decision may record the dissenting note which will form part of the decision.

Bar to Personal interests. (1) No Sarpanch or Panch of a Gram Panchayat shall take part in any case, suit or proceeding to which he or his employer, employee or partner in business or near relative is a party or in which any of them may be personally interested. (2) If by reason of the number of Panches disqualified under sub-section (1) there remains no quorum the Gram Panchayat shall send the case or he suit to the Chief Judicial Magistrate or the District Judge or the Collector having jurisdiction, as the case may be, for disposal in accordance with law.

Compromise and decision on oath. (1) Notwithstanding anything contained in this Act or any other law for the time being in force, it shall be lawful for the Gram Panchayat to allow any criminal case to be compounded or to decide any suit within its jurisdiction in accordance with any lawful and valid compromise agreed upon between the parties. 2) The provisions of the Oaths Act, 1969 shall apply to judicial proceedings before a Gram Panchayat.

Bar to legal practitioners. Notwithstanding anything contained in the Legal Practitioners Act, 1879, no legal practitioner shall be permitted to appear, plead or act before a Gram Panchayat for any party in any judicial proceedings under this Act.

Appearance of agents. (1) A woman or any other person specially permitted by a Gram Panchayat, being a party to any judicial proceedings before it may appear through an agent authorized in this behalf. (2) For the purposes of this section 'agent' shall not include any legal practitioner or any person employed as a clerk to any legal practitioner or any petition writer or tout declared as such under section 36 of the Legal Practitioners Act, 1879.

Difficulties in respect of having no jurisdiction. If at any time, it appears to a Gram Panchayat. –

(a) that it has no jurisdiction to try a case or a suit;

(b) that a case or a suit Is of such a nature or of such difficulties that it should be tried by another court.

it shall, by order in writing, stating, therein, the dates of presentation and return of the petition, direct the complainant or the petitioner, as the case may be, to present the complaint or petition to the proper court.

Attendance witnesses. (1) A Gram Panchayat may by summons send for any person to appear and give evidence or cause the production of any document. –

(a) no person who is exempt from personal appearance in court under sub-section (1) of section 133 of the Code of Civil Procedure. 1908 shall be required to appear in person before a Gram Panchayat in a civil suit.,

(b) a Gram Panchayat may refuse to summon a witness or to enforce a summons already issued against a witness, when in its opinion the attendance of the witnesses cannot be procured without an amount of delay, expense or inconvenience which in the circumstances would be unreasonable;

(c) a Gram Panchayat shall not require any person living beyond its jurisdiction to give evidence or to produce a document unless such a sum of money be paid to him as appears to the Gram Panchayat to be sufficient to defray his reasonable expenses;

(d) no woman shall be compelled to appear as a witness in person before a Gram Panchayat, she may, however, be examined on commission in the manner prescribed; and

(e) if a document is produced in obedience to a summons issued under this section, the Gram Panchayat shall cause the document to be copied, mark the copy after comparing with the original to be a true copy and return the original to the person producing the same.

(2) If any person, whom the Gram Panchayat summons by written order to appear or give evidence or to produce any document before it, wilfully fails to obey such summons, the Gram Panchayat may take cognizance of such disobedience and after giving such person, an opportunity to explain may, on conviction sentence him to a fine not exceeding twenty-five rupees.

Processes. (1) Every summons issued by a Gram Panchayat shall be drawn up in such form and shall be signed or sealed in such manner as may be prescribed. (2) When the person on whom the summons is to be served resides within its jurisdiction such summons shall ordinarily be served by one of the

Chaukidars of the local area but the Gram Panchayat may in its discretion have it served by any other person willing to do so. (3) If the accused or the defendant resides at the time of the issue of the summons outside the local area of its jurisdiction the Gram panchayat may forward the summons to the Gram panchayat within the local area of whose jurisdiction the accused or the defendant resides and such Gram Panchayat shall cause it to be served as if it were a summons issued by itself. (4) If the accused or the defendant resides at the time of the issue of the summons outside the jurisdiction of a Gram Panchayat, the Gram Panchayat may, where it is not possible to serve the summons, through another Gram Panchayat forward the summons to the nearest Judicial Magistrate who shall cause it to he served as if it were a summons issued by himself.

Transfer application. (1) If in any criminal case or civil or revenue, suit before a Gram Panchayat any party intimates at any stage before the announcement of the final order or decree that he intends to make an applications under this section to the Chief Judicial Magistrate or the District Judge or the Collector, as the case may be, for the transfer of the case or suit, the Gram Panchayat, shall upon his executing, if so required, a bond without sureties of an amount not exceeding ten rupees that he will make such application within a reasonable time to he fixed by the Gram Panchayat which shall not be less than fifteen days, adjourn the case or suit for such a period as will afford sufficient time for the application to be made and an order to be obtained thereon : Provided that nothing herein contained shall require the Gram Panchayat to adjourn the case or suit upon a second or subsequent intimation form the same party. (2) If the application be not made within the time allowed, the amount of such bond shall be forfeited and may be recoverable by the Gram Panchayat as if it were a fine imposed by itself.

Stay of proceedings. The Chief Judicial Magistrate or the District Judge or the Collector, as the case may be, on an application for transfer, order a Gram Panchayat to stay the proceedings pending before it and on receipt of such order the Gram Panchayat shall stay the proceedings.

Payment by installments. A Gram Panchayat may, when imposing a fine or ordering the payment of a sum of money or the delivery of any movable property direct that the money be paid or the movable property by delivered by installments

Finality of decisions. (1) A Gram Panchayat shall not be competent to cancel, revise or alter any sentence, decree or final orders passed by it in any judicial proceedings, except *ex parts* decree or orders; and subject to the provisions of sections 59 and 74 no sentence, decree or other order passed by Gram Panchayat in judicial proceedings shall be subject to appeal, or revision by any other court or authority.

Resjudicata. (2) The provisions of sections 10 and 11 of the Code of Civil Procedure, 1908 and section 300 of the Code of Criminal Procedure, 1973, shall apply to all civil, revenue and criminal proceedings before a Gram Panchayat.

Custody of money. Any sum realised by a Gram Panchayat by way of judicial fees or of judicial fines shall be credited to the Consolidated Fund of the State in the manner prescribed.

Contempt of Court-(1) The provisions of sections 345 and 346 of the Code of Criminal Procedure, 1973, shall apply to judicial proceedings under this Act; Provided that the fine imposed for contempt of court shall not exceed one hundred rupees. (2) The provisions of sections 299, 452 and 456 of the Code of Criminal Procedure, 1973, shall apply to criminal proceedings before a Gram Panchayat and if any order made by a Gram Panchayat in relation to section 452 and section 456 of said Code is not complied with, the Gram Panchayat shall forward the same to the nearest Judicial Magistrate who shall proceed to execute it as it were an order passed by himself.

3

Civil Society and Women in Panchayat

Debates on reservation of seats for women in parliament and state legislatures still continues, a decade after the enactment of the 73rd and 74th Amendments. Women in the remotest corners are now empowered to participate in the decision-making process not only as ordinary members of the three-tier Panchayati Raj Institution (PRI), but also as chairpersons and deputy chairpersons. Except Bihar, where the panchayat elections were held only in 2001, most of the states have passed legislation to give effect to the 73rd Amendment within two to three years of its enactment. West Bengal and Karnataka, two states, one under the Left rule and the other under the Janata Dal, had set up the present system of party-based PRI in 1978. The Amendment, however, makes the three-tier Panchayati Raj mandatory for the state governments with 33% reservation of seats for women in all the three tiers and proportional reservation of scheduled caste and scheduled tribe. It is expected that devolution of power to local bodies along with reservation for those sections so far excluded from the political arena will necessarily be followed by certain major changes in traditional caste-class domain. The amendment envisages decentralization not only region-wise but also along the social hierarchy to tilt it towards the marginal group.

This new enactment is recognition of the pious wishes of the makers of the constitution. They paid homage to the father of the nation by making an appeal to the state governments in Part IV, Directive Principles of State Policy for giving shape to the panchayats in a suitable time and in a befitting manner. It took nearly four and a half decades to make provision for a mandatory three-tier system. We will not focus on the factors responsible for this unusual delay in recognizing the right for self-governance here. How does the civil society react to this belated but telling and far-reaching political decision will be the focus of this book.

The legacy of women's participation in the political movements in India can be traced from the Gandhian clarion call for the non-cooperation movement. Women came out en masse for the first time from the confines of their four walls to raise their voice in protest against the Salt Law. In 1920, Smt. Sarojini Naidu led 25,000 people in the salt satyagraha. Women were seen picketing in front of wine shops and shops dealing in foreign clothes and goods during the non-cooperation movement. The demand for franchise for Indian Women was first raised in 1917 when an Indian Delegation of 14 women went before the British Parliament led by Sarojini Naidu. In 1921 these women whose husbands were educated and owned some property were considered eligible to vote. The revolutionary movement in the early years of the twentieth century also involved a few women revolutionaries.

The sacrifices of Bina Das, Kalpana Dutt and Pritilata Wadder gave a new dimension to the armed resistance to British rule. Communist ideology attracted a significant number of women who actively took part in the historical movements of Tebhaga, Telengana and food movement in post-independence period. The historical anecdotes of these movements reveal, when the movement transformed from a peaceful agitation to violent upsurges the women came forward even with their kitchen implements to fight the class enemies. During the Tebhaga movement, it is said that a woman gave shelter to one of the leaders. When the police knocked at her door, she sent her son who was immediately arrested! Her firm commitment to the movement's cause inspired her to provide protection to the leader. She felt the need to prevent the arrest of the leader for the success and continuation of the movement allowing her son to be arrested instead. The dream of the struggling women of undivided Bengal was cracked down with the bloody event of partition.

The women's organizations and the left activists involved themselves in repatriation and rescue operations. The legal battle for women's right launched and monitored by the women's organizations became abundant with the adoption of the Indian Constitution. Women were the worst sufferers of partition. The rootless, shelter less women had to shoulder the responsibility of uprooted families and a large number of them joined the work force immediately after independence. The gender equity has always been considered as the domain of women activists and social action groups. Section 326 of the constitution of India expands the voting right to all irrespective of sex, caste or religion. The political parties do not take much trouble to nominate the women candidates. The politics has been considered as the domain of the male only. The 73rd and 74th Amendments have changed this scenario. The political parties have to nominate women candidates to honour the constitutional provisions of 33% reservation of seats for women in local bodies.

Literacy becomes a major determining factor in implementing this newly amended provision. The women representatives in Kerala with cent percent literacy rate are considered to be more effective in the decision making process than the semi and illiterate representatives in Madhya Pradesh. In a comparative study on women's participation in local governance in Bangladesh and India, I.Shamin and R.Kumari pointed out that the percentage of illiterate women representatives in India is much higher than in that of Bangladesh.

This, they have explained in terms of activist groups' involvement in adult education programmes in Bangladesh. Besides poor literacy rate, the caste hierarchy is the other major stumbling block in empowerment of women. This has mediated a new phase of Panchayati Raj run by *Sarpanchpati*. Here comes the role of civil society. The reaction of the civil society, to this state sponsored effort for women empowerment becomes to some extent decisive. Our focus in this book is not to evaluate the performances of the women representatives but to know the responsiveness of civil society to this very question of women reservation in panchayats. This is urgent in view of the pending reservation bill for the representation of women in state and national legislatures. The law can only be given shape effectively when the community and the enforcement authorities would have decided to act in unison. The repressive laws can be executed without the co-operation of the community. The progressive laws, for its proper execution needs the approval of the majority otherwise the laws may not serve those for whom they have actually been enacted. Some sort of maneuvering by the traditional groups will stand in way.

"In South Asia affirmative action to bring more women into local government structures are mapped onto existing and deeply ingrained structures of inequality based on gender, caste, class, religion and other hierarchies. It is no wonder then that families, political parties and other agencies that have power over women work the quotas as best they know how to gain leverage and often to the disadvantage of women. This has led several researchers to conclude that affirmative action is necessary but not a sufficient condition to overcome the rigid social and cultural barriers that women face and which disallows their participation in the public sphere"

The women's forums and organizations of different political parties are now extremely vocal to extend the right of reservation of women in state and national legislatures. Unlike their western counterparts the women organizations in India did not lead any independent movement for women suffrage. Neither did they ever move for women reservation in local bodies. The question remains why was the provision for the reservation of seats for women in local bodies been incorporated in the 73rd and 74th Amendments when the women's organizations remained silent on this specific demand. Hence, this also raises a related question how the civil society accepts this proposal for reservation. Is it ready to accord such position to women in matters of state running? Technically, Mahi Pal has explained the necessity for women's reservation in local units in terms of partial fulfillment of the women specific programmes by government agencies and panchayats. Targets under the programme of Development of Women and Children in Rural

Area (DWCRA) were not achieved either in the sixth plan or in the seventh plan. The District Rural Development Authority gave a low priority to DWCRA. Integration of various women's development programmes being implemented by different departments at different levels has been urgently felt.

WOMEN AND PANCHAYAT

The Central Council of Local Government first dealt the issue of reservation of seats for women in panchayats in the year 1957. The Balvantray Mehta study team recommended (as suggested by the Central Council of Local Government) cooption of two women to the local bodies who are interested in work among women and children. The council however, categorically noted in 1958 in its fourth session that ideal position would be to keep half of the total seats reserved for women. The world conference of women in Nairobi in 1985, declared "for true equality to become a reality for women, the sharing of power on equal terms with men must be a major strategy". This declaration perhaps led some of the South Asian countries to introduce new policies of reservation of seats for women in local governments. The Parity movement in France in 1992 raised a similar demand with the slogan 'all local and national elected assemblies will be made up of as many women as men'. In 1992, only 4.3% women were elected to public office in France. Sweden topped the European Union with 40.4% women in its parliament. Holland had one-third followed by Germany and Austria with one-fourth women members.

In 1974, the Committee on the Status of women in India proposed formation of statutory women's panchayat as part of the panchayat structure. The objective is to ensure greater political participation by rural women. In Maharashtra, Shetkari Sanghatana Mahila Aghadi proposed to prepare a panel to all the women panchayats in the late 80's. This experiment in Maharashtra though it initially suffered from many obstacles, social and legal, the determination and sincerity of the women members made a good imprint on decentralization process where women in some areas are readily invited to shoulder the responsibility in local decision-making. They overcame the barrier of illiteracy and successfully gave a blow to the asymmetrical social relation.

"They show that while it helps to have at least one educated woman in the 'team', illiterate women can take leading role and that they provide the main collective strength of the campaign. .... Women once elected, take up need-oriented development programmes. The village has reported providing water taps, biogas plants, toilets especially in the Dalit areas, playgrounds for the village schools" The panches in Vinter, Maharashtra complained that initially they were not allowed by the former male sarpanch to work for four months. "He also gave us a pot of dung and asked us to use it, saying that is what we were meant for." Sharad Joshi, the 'mangdarshak' (guide) and 'guru' of the Maharashtra farmers' movement in the 80's raised the slogan of India vs. Bharat. He asked the Shetkari Sanghataks to make their wives financially independent without which political participation would remain a myth. This movement in Vinter empowered the women to assert their own voice and enjoy equal rights in major decision-making at home and in the panchayats. "Sharad Joshi had urged husbands to transfer some of the money from their land to women in their family. Instead, the men of Vinter actually gave portions of the land itself to their wives.". While the women-elect in All Women Panchayats in Maharashtra were fighting against upper caste encroachment, the upper caste domination in urban Maharashtra took a very ugly shape in the mid 80s. The women from upper caste and middle class background participated in an anti-reservation agitation in which over 200 people died and more than 2000 were injured, about 200 huts and tenements were burnt. This sharpens Joshi's theory of distinction between India and Bharat.

Women in West Bengal are said to be comparatively more aware and more politicized than their counterparts in the neighboring states. They have realized that the exercise of electoral rights can improve their economic status. The movement for recovery of surplus land initiated during the late 60s and restructured in a new form of operation barga and distribution of land among the landless, by the left front government during the 80s has significantly changed the class structure. Almost eighty to eighty-five percent of cultivable land is now in the possession of the marginal peasants. The family members of the landless peasants and the bargadars have a first hand experience of a pro-poor government. This made them more and more pro-active in political programmes organized by the mass organizations of the left parties. The tenth five year plan noted that West Bengal registered a sharp decline in both rural and urban poverty (from 63% in 1973 to 27.02%). It further states that, "the policy of increasing the access of the rural poor to assets, i.e. agricultural land, through a programme of asset redistribution (land reforms) may have helped spread income earning opportunities more evenly and contributed to a major decline in rural poverty during this period." This upward trend in West Bengal economy has further been reinforced by the finding of the National Sample Survey. It has been reported that nearly Rs.13,000/-crore was spent by the common people in rural areas on industrial goods every year. The purchasing power of the people in rural areas has been increasing at the rate of nearly 10% every year. All this leads to empowerment of women which a single piece of legislation cannot do.

The women's organizations have spread their network to the farthest corners and motivated the village women to take the help of the Panchayati Raj to meet their everyday necessaries as well as reconstructing the infrastructure facilities. However, does this participation of women in Panchayati Raj have any direct impact on multifarious social barriers from which they suffered? Does empowerment in a sense getting chance for electing and to be elected really address women-specific problems? The political organs of the ruling parties by and large particularly the frontal organizations keep themselves engaged in routine work like collection of subscription, fulfilling the membership quota and participate in those movements, launched by the national and state level party units.

In West Bengal, the Kultikri Panchayat, the pioneer women panchayat was elected consecutively for three terms. In the 2003 elections ten other panchayats were turned into all women panchayats. The politics for these villages is no more the exclusive domain of the male voters. The Kultikri experiment proves beyond doubt that the voters irrespective of their sex bias have faith in the capabilities of the women panchayat members without which the panchayat could not have worked as a woman panchayat for three consecutive elections. The women candidates nominated by the left front have to fight the elections against the male candidates nominated by the opposition parties.

The National Perspective Plan for women in 1988 (NPP) focused on under representation of women at all levels. It recommended 30% reservation for women in local bodies. With the announcement of emergency in 1975, moves for decentralisation by all political parties were shelved. Instead, all democratic bodies and political parties, except the ruling one, jumped into the fray for the restoration of democracy. The Janta Dal and its alliance which came to power in 1977 pledged for devolution of power to the local bodies and to build up Panchayati Raj in its true sprit. Ashok Mehta Committee, appointed to review the PRI submitted its report in 1978. It proposed co-option of two women members at district and block level if they remain un-represented. Karnataka government made a provision for the reservation of 25% seats for women at district and block levels. This attempt of Karnataka government perhaps induced the union government to place 64th Constitutional Amendment bill with 30% reservation of seats for women in the year 1989. The example set by the W.B. in implementing land ceiling law, and poverty eradication programme through panchayat inspired states like Andhra Pradesh, Maharashtra and Orissa to undergo second generation Panchayati Raj. V.P.Singh in 1990 reintroduced the 64th Amendment which had been later passed as 73rd Amendment by the Congress government in 1991.

With the enactment of the 73rd Amendment Bill the third generation of PRI with a mandate for elected panchayat as the third tier of government has started functioning. Unlike the previous panchayats the third generation panchayats have not only been vested with the power of implementation of schemes but also entrusted with the task of planning for ensuring equitable justice. Art 243 (D) maintains reservation of not less than 1/3rd of the total number of seats for women. Such seats are to be allotted by rotation to different constituencies in a panchayat. The reserved quotas for the SC/St communities will be in proportion to the total population. The offices of the chairperson at the village or any other level shall be reserved for the SC/St and women.

Panchayati Raj in West Bengal started its journey with a single mission of implementation of the developmental policies with active participation of the village people. With the massive programme of distribution of land to the landless and operation barga along with the successful implementation of food-for-work programme the poor and marginal people have already become aware of their democratic rights and began to consider Panchayat as their own institution. A study conducted in 1993 by Girish Kumar and B.Ghosh in four districts of West Bengal reveals that the panchayat system has taken 'deep roots in the socio-political life of the villagers'. Most importantly, an overwhelming proportion of people (about ninety percent) feel that the panchayat as an institution is useful and the people would suffer if the institution was to be abolished.. Nearly, four decades of experience has changed the world's view of the villagers.

In 1978, just one year after the left front government came to power the newly elected Panchayat came closer to the people who were severely affected by a devastating flood. The people depended upon democratic machinery for relief and shelter came to realise that a local self government with its limited power could reconstruct the flood affected villages much more efficiently. The approachability of the panchayat functionaries made them more and more assertive. With the help of JRY, IRDP they successfully maintained a safe distance from the jotedars and the mahajans. The kitchen manager of the half starved families, the mothers and the housewives felt assured of getting their *chulas* burnt everyday. They came to respond to the panchayat leaders' call for different programmes. The overwhelming presence of women in literacy campaign during the late 80s prepared them for working outside the four walls. Emancipation of women will be easier once the old guards have been driven out G.K.Lieten and Ravi Srivastava while conducting a survey in UP in 1994 found that the higher the caste status, the more rigid the purdah regulations. They (higher caste) supported the idea of education for women but they should not be given equal rights. The women should remain under the control of men otherwise they would become dangerous for society. In anticipation to the enactment of the 73rd Amendment the West Bengal government gave effect to the proposed reservation policy in 1993 for the fourth Panchayat election. The policy of reservation of seats for chairpersons at three levels was not given effect to in 1993. This was made effective in 1998 election.

Women in West Bengal are enjoying their rights and get themselves involved in decision making on local issues at village level. The panchayat bodies played a crucial role in generating political awareness among different target groups

Prior to reservation the percentage of elected women members in panchayat was 9.84%. This does not necessarily mean that women remained passive spectators. One chairperson Aparna Gupta of North 24 parganas ZP spoke of an old woman who as early as in 1980 stopped a group of young men who were looking for a suitable site for the installation of a tube well saying, "It is none of your business. This is our prerogative as the young girls of my locality will have to go to the tube well ten times more than you. So who are you to take a decision"?

Since the early 90s with the acceptance of the New Economic policy the panchayat has become instrumental in promoting self-employment through implementation of self employment schemes and setting up self-help groups. Without some sort of economic independence it becomes pretty difficult for the women to enjoy their political rights. The western feminism, of late is arguing for expansion of micro-credit to the developing countries. In 1997, in a micro-credit summit held in Washington the organisers fixed a target of reaching 100 million poor with micro-credit within ten years. In West Bengal the new strategy of the formation of self help groups mostly by those people below the poverty line has been officially adopted. The journey adopted by Md.Yunus in Bangaladesh has taken a definite shape with the acceptance of this policy by quite a small number of developing countries. It has been reported in the budget statement of the year 2002-03 that as against the target of setting up of thirty thousand new self help groups, the number has exceeded the target and reached the figure of thirty-five thousand with membership strength of over 3.5 lakhs, of which nearly 90% are women. By the end of 2004 the number of SHG groups has been raised to more than seventy-three thousand. The District of North 24pgs.organized a massive rally with 18,000 representatives from nine thousand self help groups. It was reported that the attendance to gram sansad meetings has been enhanced in a remarkable manner. The women members of the SHGs have raised issues like the trafficking of women and children, better health amenities, misanagement in mid-day meals. The women who are usually kept behind the curtain and expected to do all the domestic and household chores without any wages, now get themselves involved to get rid of their everyday scarcity. They usually spend their income for the upkeep of their family members especially for the health and education of their children. Their membership to SHGs gives them the voice to raise their demands and a determination not to recede. Mukhopadhyay and Meer in their book "Creating Voice and Carving Space" (2004) narrated a story.

The provision for reservation of women and SC/ST population in local governments has been aimed to provide a space for the disadvantaged people to place their demands and make the local units serve their purpose. The decentralisation of power in its true spirit signifies devolution of power from the 'old guards'. Chattopadhyay and Dufflo in a comparative study on PRI made out that the women participation in gram sansad meetings is not gender-neutral. "In West Bengal the percentage of women among participants in the gram sansad is significantly higher when the pradhan is a woman (increasing from 6.9% to 9.9%). This is consistent with the idea that political communication is influenced by the fact that citizens and leaders are of the same sex. The study further reveals that women feel more comfortable to approach a woman pradhan. "Women in villages with reserved pradhans are twice as likely to have addressed a request or a complaint to the G.P. pradhan in the previous six months, and this difference is significant".

SOCIO-ECONOMIC PROFILE OF WOMEN PANCHAYAT MEMBERS

The mandatory pancahayat system with its reservation provision has made a structural change of the elected bodies in the villages. "Earlier studies of women representatives in panchayats before the 73rd Amendment noted the major presence of women from the dominant sections, e.g. from Marathas and families owning more than 20 acres of land in Maharashtra and Lingayats and Vokkalingas in Karnataka. But the profile of the new women in post 73rd Amendment panchayats showed that the majority were illiterate and a large percentage were from families in the lower socio-economic strata".

The reaction to this amendment varies from state to state. The initial inhibition to women's participation in public affairs is gradually waning. "The husband who opposed her ended with bringing lunch for her". When asked whether everybody attended the gram sansad meetings the members of All Women Pancahayats in Maharashtra gave an affirmative answer. To them everybody means the men voters. The surrogate representation has been epitomised in a father-in law's clear confession, 'My bahu stood for election as I ordered her to do so'.

The ex-members and their relatives are found controlling the panchayat affairs. The male dominated bureaucracy and the vested interest usually make use of illiteracy and political inexperience of the women members and continue their uninterrupted rule. Patriarchy can be effectively challenged only when women establish themselves at their workplace and in the world beyond their four walls. In Haryana, Janwadi Mahila Samity organised a rally in Hissar to raise their voice in protest against violence against women. An activist was beaten up by her husband for participating in that rally. The next time when she was going to attend a rally against Gujrat violence her husband threatened her.

The NGO activities to train and make the women aware to identify their rights and fight for the same have been multiplied after the enactment of the 73rd Amendment Act. A nation wide protest against the violence committed against Draupadi Bai, a woman panchayat member in Raigarh District in 1995 gradually sensitised the issue of reservation and demanded more safety value for the women members. The women representatives are approaching more and more towards the centre stage. Ganga Devi Rawat in UP refused to sign on a set of suspect accounts – 'this hand and this signature are no longer my own'.

In West Bengal, Pancahayat is a shelter for the marginal and low income group. 88% of the respondents in a study conducted by Girish Kumar and Buddhadeb Ghosh stated that the greatest achievement of the Panchayati Raj is that it has made the rural people free from the grip of *mahajan* and landlords. For the well-to-do people panchayat is a service centre for the poor, distributing government relief. Majority of the panchayat members also belong to the poorer section of the community. Their representation has further been increased after the implementation of the 73rd Amendment Act. From Dilip Ghosh's account of socio-economic profile of panchayat members of four districts we have compared Hoogly and Bankura. It appears that in both the districts the highest per cent of the respondents came from the agricultural labourer family. In Hoogly it stands for 21% and in Bankura for 31%. While in Hoogly 52% belong to lowest income group (i.e. below Rs.1000/-annual income) in Bankura it is 41%.

The educational status of the district level leaders is much higher than those of the two other tiers. They are nominated as members of different Sthayee Samities and have to co-ordinate with the Chairpersons of the Z.P., P.S. as well as with different ministers. They are the chief spokespersons of their area and they have to attend the meetings of the samities regularly, to chalk out plans for the future and assessment of the jobs done. From Chairperson to opposition leaders as well as the common people cutting across the party lines are reported to be satisfied with the sincerity and efficiency of the works done by the women members. Attendance of the members of the Sthayee Samities in North 24 pgs. will endorse this. The register shows at least 65% of the meetings of the Sthayee Samities have been attended by the women members. Four of them (incidentally all are Muslim) have attended 88% to 99% of the meetings.

However, poor level of education status of the GP members and to some extent of the panchayat samity members make them handicapped. They have to take the help of the extension officers to write even a note or for that matter any confidential letter to the respective authority. They are not conversant with the intricacies of rules and regularities of the panchayat law. Decentralisation of training programme and new curriculum for educating these women members are urgently needed when almost 19,000 women have occupied the seats of Panchayat. Empowerment of women and quickening the pace of development are to be achieved simultaneously.

ATTITUDE OF THE COMMUNITY TOWARDS THE RESERVATION OF SEATS FOR WOMEN

A field study has been conducted in Gaighata block in North 24 pgs. to assess what sort of approval the community bears for the new policy of reservation in Panachayats. Geographically the block is in the south west part of Bengal with Nadia in the west and Habra in the south. The block is demarcated by the international border with Bangladesh in the east. There are thirteen gram panchayats encompassing 94 square miles of which we have chosen Jahswar II and Ichapur I gram panchayats. Four booths from each of the gram panchayats were selected by simple random sampling without replacement. From these eight booths we have selected 323 voters again with the help of randomized number.

Method

The study involves a survey method along with focus group discussions and interviews of elected members at different tiers of the panchayat. A survey team was sent to the areas under study in the month of October/November 2003. The questionnaire has been framed to conduct a major study involving four districts covering five blocks. The objective is to identify and prioritize the factors determining the electoral behaviour during panchayat elections.

The present study focuses on the attitude of the civil society towards the policy of reservation for women in local self government. Dilly dallying of the political leaders with the proposal for reservation of seats in parliament and state legislatures has made the issue even more pertinent. The study will bring home the changing perspective of the civil society after the policy of reservation has already been implemented in panchayat raj institution.

About 69% of the entire population gives their verdict in favour of women reservation. Only 16% are not satisfied while 14% are not aware of such reservation. When interviewed an aged Muslim woman panchayat member working in a paddy field sarcastically commented, "You the urban educated youth have come here to take interviews of people like me. Is this not enough to prove our elevated status? This is for reservation." Initial inhibition of the men folk to approach the women members is now waning.

The study conducted by G.Kumar and B.Ghosh during and after 1993 Panchayat election revealed that almost 50% of the total sample population were positive about the need for fair representation being given to women. This percentage has been increased by 19 after a decade.

The elected male panchayat members who have to swallow the pill unwillingly have a mixed reaction to the performance of the women members. A political activist who has been elected for all the five consecutive panchayat elections since 1978 stated that many of the newly elected women members whom they were compelled to nominate knowing well of their incompetence, however, after assuming power they very quickly got themselves accustomed to their new role.

In areas with strong left base the acting members of the frontal women's organizations are generally nominated. The policy of rotation of reserved seats makes the task of finding out suitable candidates furthermore difficult. Very often willingly or un-willingly the wife or sisters of the elected members are nominated.

The most difficult part of the game is to trace women to be nominated from scheduled caste and scheduled tribe community. Once elected the women members are generally found to be more honest and sincere than the male members; but are less competent in decision-making. It is usually their husbands or the local party leaders who make the decisions. The village people complain that it becomes pretty difficult for a woman panchayat pradhan to attend '*Salishi*' (arbitration) meetings which are most often conducted at night and at places may be far away from the pradhan's residence. The women members of ZP who generally come from educated semi-urban families can overcome these difficulties with less effort.

Of the sample population 54% are male while 46% are women. The reveals, nearly 72% of those dis-satisfied with the policy are male voters. Only 28% who oppose the reservation policy are women. Nearly 46% of the total female population appreciate the new policy of reservation for women in local bodies. As high as 68.0% in comparison to 32% of the male respondents fail to make up their mind. This indecisiveness suggests some sort of incapacity in decision making on the part of the women.

To our specific question whether women's reservation hinder panchayat work, almost majority of the population disagree to the query. The disapproval to the question on Women's reservation hindering panchayat work is not that alarming in our study. Only 23.2% bear a negative attitude to women's participation in the panchayat.

However, the percentage of respondents appreciating women's representation in the panchayat is not very high (50.8%), while 26.0% of the population refusing to give a specific answer either due to ignorance or avoidance signifying the hesitation still persisting on women's reservation issue. This is quite unexpected in a block like Gaighata where competitive politics marks the panchayat and state elections since the beginning of the left rule.

During the survey the Panchayat Samiti was run by an anti-left alliance. The people here usually have exposure to the programmes of both the ruling and the opposition parties. Hence, it is expected that they will be able to make their decisions with far more conviction. To trace the root of opposition to women's reservation the population has been divided into sex, occupation, land ownership and caste.

The males (68.0%) are more averse to women's reservation than the females (32.0%). Similarly, the percentage of women (48.8%) stating that women's reservation does not hinder panchayat work is less than the male representation of (51.5%). Women in our sample area do not support women's representation in panchayat en masse. They themselves have much reservation in sending women to the panchayat. Further research is required to see whether this ambivalence on women's reservation issue is caused by poor performance of the women members of the panchayat or due to lack of awareness.

The situation becomes more precarious with 46.4% of the male respondents belonging to the Don't Know column. This is slightly less than the female respondents (53.6%). Such insignificant difference between male and female respondents belonging to the Don't Know group raises the question whether the respondents belonging to this group are unaware of the recent reservation or intentionally avoid to give specific answers.

A three fold classification of the sample population has been made in terms of occupation: I) agricultural workers ii) non-agricultural workers and iii) Non-workers.

Opposition to the reservation issue is found to be minimum (10.9%) among the non-workers and strongest (24.5%) among the agricultural workers. The corresponding figure for non-agricultural workers is 15.8%. Attachment to traditional occupation perhaps made the agricultural population more conservative.

Till now, production in agriculture requires the service of the female members of the households for the completion of the entire process. The apathy to reservation among the agriculturalists has been positively related to the ownership of land. In Gaighata block, a *ryot* dominated area, big landowners even within permissible limit of land ceiling is conspicuously absent. A three fold classification of landholding has been made; land owning i) below two bighas including landless, ii) two to five bighas iii) five bighas and above.

CONCLUSION

The study reveals a mixed reaction to women's reservation policy In a state with twenty-eight years of left rule the patriarchy has been challenged and women feel more comfortable in exercising their political rights. Women's disapproval to this policy indicates their inability to change their mindset and to accept politics as a domain of both men and women. Their personal apathy to joining politics perhaps has been superimposed on their reaction to issues on women's reservation in elected bodies. The women specific issues like dowry, multiple marriages, drinking and wife beating to name a few are not dealt with seriously by the panchayats in our state.

The ideology behind this is, the upliftment of the economic status will gradually do away with all other vices in the society. A woman pradhan narrated her bitter experience to make the panchayat members fight against dowry and increasing incidents of dowry death in her locality. A second thought perhaps is needed to get rid of this unbearable custom in Indian society. A girl child can never be treated equally unless this evil practice of dowry is rooted out. Dowry prohibition Act is the most glaring example to show how vested interest can bypass a progressive law and continue its operation. Though joint *patta* was first introduced in this state, a study reveals, the marginal peasants most of who own distributed surplus land had to sell their land to meet the dowry hungry bridegroom and his family.

The study attempts to decipher the population sharing a critical view on the issue of women's reservation and locates the root of dissention convincingly in sex, class and caste divisions. Relatively free from caste and class oppression, the women in West Bengal are expected to be more active and more communicative in comparison to their sisters in caste-dominant states. The elected women representatives in those states have to proceed with more antagonistic civil society.

Even the state machinery also passes discriminatory orders like two children norm (U.P.), class ten certificate (Rajasthan, Haryana) as eligibility conditions. The bureaucrats with 4.9 percent women officials also rarely help the women in their official work.

In West Bengal, the women representatives have to put up with by the policies and programmes of the political parties which nominate them to fight the election. The NGOs, unlike in other states are not much active in W.B in organizing training programmes or similar other awareness building activities. The dependence of the women representatives on family members and caste leaders in panchayat functioning has been transformed to dependence on party leaders in West Bengal.

The programme of Total Literacy Campaign fails to rule out illiteracy. The aversion of the civil society to the women's reservation issue may be explained with reference to the existing 40% illiteracy among women.

This coupled with women's apathy to join active politics makes the civil society a little bit lukewarm on reservation issue. Civil society must come forward to make a law effective. Protest and participation are the two catchwords of the new legislation. However, the ultimate fate of this legislation depends upon how the civil society accepts the newly empowered role of women as decision makers.

4

Women's Participation in Urban Local Governance

Women's Participation in Local Government

Limits and Constraints that Prevent Women from Participating Equally with Men Inormal and Informal Forums.

Involvement of women in the political arena and in decision-making roles is an important tool for empowerment as well as monitoring standards of political performance at local level. However, in the present political process of entry into decision making political institutions, there is growing influence of money and muscle power, backroom dealings, communalisation and criminalisation.

In many respects women and men elected representatives face similar problems on election to office. Above all there is a need to understand just how to be a good local politician. The role of political representatives at local level is demanding and all new 'recruits' need time to gain experience and to understand the rules, regulations and procedures governing the administrative bureaucracy with which they now have to work – often quite closely in the urban service delivery system. Some of the major constraints that prevent women from effective participation at local level are as follows:

1. Lack of orientation/training in urban development issues and municipal administration.
2. No proper knowledge/orientation about municipal acts and rules and regulations.

3. No prior experience about dealing with multidimensional urban development issues/civic issues and its complexities.
4. Lack of knowledge about technical in-puts related to urban service delivery system.
5. Lack of support from senior male/female colleagues in the party/municipal body.
6. Less co-operation from municipal officials understanding about various facets of the budget, such as allocation of budget at ward level (at central/ward level).
7. Lack of party support and poor organisational structure.
8. Lack of money and resources to sustain the electoral campaigns (inspite of code of conduct by election commission).
9. Discrimination in decision making at party level.
10. Specific notions towards politics and political atmosphere.
11. Fear and insecurity.
12. Lack of confidence in public speaking.
13. Criminalisation of politics and use of money power.
14. Family responsibilities.

Laws / legislation Promoting the Participation of Women in Local Government

The 74th Amendment to the Indian Constitution, 1992 has served as a major breakthrough towards ensuring women's equal access and increased participation in local government. The Constitution (74th Amendment) Act, 1992 aims at Constitutional guarantees to safeguard the interests of urban local self government to enable them to function as effective democratic and self governing institutions at the grass root level. This Amendment provides for reservation of 33 1/3 percent of elected seats for women at local government level in urban and rural areas.

There is also a one-third reservation for women of posts of chairpersons of these local bodies. A very active role for women in local governance is envisaged as compared to governance at the state and national levels in India. These provisions have provided great opportunities and challenges to women in India, particularly in the local government field. This is of great significance, since this grass-root level participation has considerably broadened the base of women's participation in politics at city level.

Civil Society initiatives aimed at increasing women's participation in local government

Political system in India works through political parties who contend for power by invoking popular support. Therefore it is necessary that if women want to share power they have to make a place for themselves within the political parties through which the Indian democratic system operates. The experience of the last 52 years show an inability to create 'this space' and recent studies show that there has been no significant change in either the nature of women's functioning or in the political parties' approach to women and women's issues.

If we examine women's participation (prior to 1993) it is seen that the political parties have given less importance to women's issues in terms of ideology, either in priority in their party manifesto or in terms of the number and importance of the position that women occupied in individual political parties. Women are not seen as a vote bank to be approached, and once the men are mobilised, women will merely endorse their choice of party and candidate.

Male candidates rarely have access to the female electorate and there are not enough women involved in political campaigns to be able to reach out to a large section of women even in big cities. As a result, the exposure of women to political debates and issues has always remained indirect. According to women from all parties the political environment was not conducive to women's participation in politics.

The analysis made by Kumari and Kidwai (1996) stated that political parties have dominated the conservative 'cultural' perspective and no conscious attempt has been made to increase active participation of women. Women in India today are agitating at the doors of Parliament, demanding reservation for 33 per cent of the seats. The issue at stake here is more complex than it may seem.

It is not only a question of a few more or a few less women in the corridors of Parliament and legislatures but also a response to the fact that a large section of society has historically been denied its legitimate share in the exercise of political power, power that ultimately determines its destiny. In this demand for reservation, women are also raising their voice against a system, which has consistently denied them space by harnessing the forces of tradition in order to marginalise and trivialize their role. Reservation of seats for women in Panchayats/Municipal bodies have shown that it has tremendous implications, not merely in terms of the number of women entering the public arena and holding public office, but also in terms of the social, economic and political impact that these reservations have had for the total system.

It is for these reasons that women are increasingly demanding political roles for themselves. They recognise that constitutional guarantees do not ensure effective participation and that these cannot ensure political equality. Hence the need to gain entry into political institutions and in the functioning of the state, and to share control over the power the state exercises. This alone would lead to a situation where women are able to reverse the existing situation, which has consistently been against their interests, and bring about the necessary changes in policy and the social structure so as to ensure a more equitable and humane order. The role of women's participation in elected bodies should not be undervalued.

Elections are after all a forum for self government and democracy, they are significant in drawing the attention of the nation to the problems and needs of disadvantaged sections; the manifestos, campaigns, promises made by individual candidates, track record and future course of action of political parties are indicative of national concerns as well as mandates for action. Proper selection of candidates in an election is vital if this representative democracy is to function in the interests of a majority of the population that is depressed and disadvantaged. Hence, opportunities for participation at this level are significant for the adoption of politics and measures for women's development. Strong and dynamic women who would not dream of appropriating privilege are today talking of reservation because they have come to recognize that they will not give "easy entry" in the corridors of power without reservation.

This hierarchy is so rigid that the natural processes of democracy and constitutional guarantees have not been able to make a dent in these fortresses of power. The demand for reservation should not therefore be seen as either a gift or a privilege that women are seeking. For most women it is the last straw and a desperate measure to ensure their coming into the political mainstream.

Their participation becomes vital in the context of the adoption of development strategies that are negative and harmful to women. Today most of the political parties in India have initiated some initiatives to activate political participation of women and develop their capacities. However, most of the political parties have not yet developed any special programmes to meet the special requirements of women in urban or rural areas, despite the fact that most of the women activists felt that if planned efforts were made, they could be easily mobilised. Different debates concerning struggles of women as well as various actions by women's groups and NGOs on local as well as national problems have forced the mainstream political parties to accept women's concerns in their political programmes.

The political parties started changing their attitude towards women which is reflected in their election manifestos, their attitudes towards women candidates, speeches and slogans. Statistics on women's participation in the electoral process are not very encouraging. It is important not only to pressurise the political parties but also to make the leaders understand the significance of organising systematic training of women possessing leadership qualities, of carefully selecting women candidates and ensuring financial, technical and human resources for affirmative action (Patel, Vibhuti, 1992). The need to strengthen womens' participation and leadership is constantly emphasised by various institutions viz, All India Institute of Local Self Government, NIUA, HSMI, Rambhau Mhalaji Prabhodini, etc and several NGOs and Women's groups like SEWA, Working Womens' Forum, YUVA, Disha, Prayas, Astha, Winavani, SNDT University, Aalochana, Agni, FASDSP

(Forum Against Sex determination and Sex Preselection), Stree Mukti Sanghathana, etc.

Many NGOs/CBOs, Womens' groups have provided some training, however systematic training of women possessing leadership qualities is not enough and more concentrated efforts are required to facilitate the process of women's ascent to key positions in political field. It is essential that the women's groups and movement recognise the importance of women as a constitutency and ensure their participation and representation in policy formulation. The movement must provide a support system for women who enter political processes to win elections. As stated by Nath Kamale (1997) 'The women's movement has been a powerful agent of empowerment and has provided an alternative perspective for fundamental structural changes. The movement has created organisational strength of women, has focused on women's issues and mobilised them around these issues. The women in the movement, however, have shied away from active participation in politics. The women's groups and women activists thus aim to bring about a change in the women's perceptions, but not necessarily in the structures which subordinate women. If we want to bring about change in the lives of women and transform mainstream politics, there is no other way than to get involved in politics and transform it.

The women's movement and groups have to recognise the importance of women as a constituency and ensure their participation and representation in policy formulation. This can be achieved through reorienting existing structures for entry into decision-making including the political party system and introduce quotas or reservation as a temporary means of women's representation. The movement should also provide a support system (women's groups) for women who enter political processes to win elections.

The women's groups working at the grassroots level are small and scattered and have diverse ways of empowering women. There are no infrastructural facilities of networking available that could bring them together and strengthen them while allowing autonomy in their functioning. It is important to create unity in diversity between women's groups, organisations and individuals involved with women's empowerment. They need to adopt a common strategy, informed by a common vision, to be able to bring about changes in the policies and structures that perpetuate their subordinate status.

Local government initiatives to encourage women to participate in local governance

Reservation for women in local government is not just a question of getting a certain number 'in'; it also develops their capacities to play their rightful roles in the development process and makes an important difference as the local governments deals mostly with the quality of life for citizens. Municipal responsibilities relate both to women's practical needs and their strategic needs. The better we meet women's strategic needs, the better they are able to contribute to good city governance. Good Local Governance, in turn, enables a better response to women's practical needs. Most local governments have initiated orientation/training programmes to encourage women to participate in local governance by organising city-specific induction or theme-based training programmes, wherein intensive training is given in various subject areas, such as, municipal acts and its implementation, laws of meetings, municipal budgeting, budgeting at ward level, municipal taxation, mobilisation of resources, urban service delivery systems (solid waste management, water supply, sewerage, health care services, traffic and transportation), poverty alleviation schemes, community management, environment management, shelter programmes, new reforms in municipal administration, functioning of ward committees, motivation techniques, communication skills, women and development, handling the media etc.

The Ministry of Urban Development, Government of India and Urban Development Department of State Governments organise a number of training programmes, workshops, seminars for women elected representatives at local level through various training institutions.

Many municipal bodies have initiated a series of in-house training in municipal administration and urban development, in collaboration with premier training institutions in India.

State governments through their State Training Centres organise capacity building programmes for women elected members from municipal bodies in their States. Special training/ orientation programmes are organised by Ministry of Urban Development and Poverty Alleviation, Government of India under the UNICEF assistance and government's funds in the area of poverty alleviation schemes and its implementation in urban areas (e.g. SJSRY, NSDP, etc.)

Gender Sensitizing of local Government

Using sex-disaggregated data for policy and programme formulation

Local governments are using sex-desegregated data for policy and programme formulation. It is an obligatory duty of municipal governments in India to collect, compile and maintain vital statistics in their city limits. Sex-disaggregated data is in use in many cities of the States in India for policy programme formulation and implementation of some special programmes and projects at local city level.

The Government of India regularly collects, analyses and disseminates quantitative and qualitative data on the number of women and men employed at various levels in government on an annual basis and many mechanisms have been set up within governmental structures for monitoring progress in this field. The Department of Women and Child Development, Government of India is collecting and using gender-disaggregated data to evaluate development from a gender perspective.

The Department is also developing a Gender Development Index (GDI) for the construction of EDI and Gender Empowerment Measure (GEM). Bringing women to positions of political power in local government is just the first step in social transformation. Gender sensitization of those in power, be they men or women, is of critical importance. Influencing the choices of those at decision– making levels and bringing gender issues to the political agenda are important factors. Over the years, this perspective has gained acceptance within organisations, action groups and political parties. Government departments, other institutions, non-governmental organisations, and women's organisations have undertaken several programmes to sensitise local governments about the issues and needs of women in their cities. It is recognised that law enforcement is a critical factor for bringing about enduring changes in gender perceptions.

Several initiatives have been taken by the Government of India and the voluntary sector to sensitise law enforcement personnel and policy makers. Gender sensitisation of police personnel and urban administrators in the National and State level training centres is now a regular programme. A National Centre for Gender Training and Research has set up in the National Academy of Administration in Mussourie with the objective of sensitising young administrators and policy makers on gender issues. The Election Commission of India maintains updated information on women representatives in each Parliament, including categorised information on the number of scheduled castes women representatives. With the recent revolution in information technology, the entire information is available not only in print but also on the Internet in the Parliament and Election Commission websites.

This increases outreach and access of this information to the general public. The Ministry of Rural Development, Government of India maintains updated information on the representation of women in local self-government or Panchayati Raj. The Department of Women and Child Development, Government of India also has come out with publications like 'Women in India – A Statistical Profile' in 1997, which compiled information on all aspects related to women in India.

The Planning Commission, which is mooting the process of collection of gender desegregated data by all concerned departments in various Ministers, has included information on women's representation in power and decision-making in its Ninth Five Year Plan Document.

Besides these, several independent organisations are carrying out their own research and surveys that provide updated information on the same. These are also widely used and are quoted in different public documents. Sensitising the leadership of people's movements in the country to gender issues need to be prioritised.

WOMEN AND LOCAL SELF GOVERNANCE

The ideology of division of labor forces women to be confined to the private sphere of life & restricts women's existence within domestic roles as wives & mothers. The male hegemony prevails in the decision-making processes both in private as well as public domains. Politics should be a democratic, participatory, accountable & transparent means to bring about a just, humane & equitable society. Political system should incorporate the interests of & be accessible to all sections of society, of which women constitute half of the population. High cost of electioneering, improper & illegal practices, violence & corruption are some reasons that prevent women from participating in politics. It is high time to seek & work towards transformation of politics that would establish a decisive role for women at all levels of governance & politics.

The 73rd Constitutional Amendment has constitutionalized the elected grassroots level local governing bodies i.e. Panchayats & Municipal Corporation as the third strata of the Government structure. These are self-governing institutions that stand for a decentralized, participatory, accountable, transparent, relevant polity administration. The Constitutional Acts have also set into motion a process that has made women's representation in local level decision-making a reality.

WOMEN IN LOCAL GOVERNANCE: A HISTORICAL BACKGROUND

The Panchayat Raj, a system of self-governance, was introduced in 1959, following the submission of Balwant Rai Mehta Committee Report of 1957. The Balwant Rai Mehta Committee had recommended that besides 20 members of the Panchayat Samiti (block level body), there should be two women as co-opted members. This may be said to be the first official declaration for women to enter active politics at the grassroots. Following this, the Maharashtra Zilla Parishad (district body) & Panchayat Act of 1961, provided for nomination of one or two women to each of the three bodies, in case no women were elected. As it happened, out of a total of 320 women representatives of Panchayat Samities & Zilha Parishads in Maharashtra 1978, only 6 were elected members. In many parts of India, women were recruited to the Panchayat Raj by co-option rather than through election. The 64th Constitutional Amendment Bill was introduced in Parliament in 1989, which provided for 30% reservation for women. But it could not be passed. The Bill was defeated by a narrow margin in the Upper House. The Bill was reintroduced in September 1991, as the 72nd & 73rd Constitutional Amendment Bills with an additional provision such as one-third representation for women in chairperson positions. The Bills were finally passed on December 1992. Ratified by half the states by April 1993, they came into operation as 73rd & 74th amendments to the Constitution of India on 24th April 1993.

The provisions of the 73rd & 74th Amendment had far reaching consequences. It provided for direct elections to all the seats for the Panchayat – from the village level to the intermediary block committee (Panchayat Samiti) to the district level (Zilha Parishad) for a period of five years. The act is most significant for the reservation for women & Scheduled Caste (lower caste) & Scheduled Tribes. There are certain general features, which could be taken advantage of by women. Such as direct elections for membership & Sarpanch (village head or chairperson) post, at the local as well as the block level. If the states so desired, they could make provisions for reservation to the membership for chairpersons to citizens of backward classes.

This amendment can be considered as a landmark in the empowerment of women, as shortly after the 1992 election in Maharashtra, a total of 28,000 Panchayat Raj yielded positions of power to 93,333 women in various Panchayats as members & as chairpersons.

EXPERIENCE OF THE PANCHAYAT RAJ

The situation created by the Act was so drastic that it brought out women straight from the kitchen into the fray of politics & administration with no training or experience whatsoever in public life. Women have been given power but they are not seen as political entities. They are seen as a source of status enhancement. Thus these elected women were mere fronts for their father or husbands or father-in-law or sons &

very often did not attend the Gram Panchayat (village governing body) out of fear or ignorance. As a result, they are considered as proxy members or absentee members. New appellations such as "Sarpanch Pati" are used to describe husband chairpersons & members of Gram Panchayats, implying that they performed the Panchayat's work on behalf of their wives. Elected women Sarpanch in many villages could not answer questions posed to them since their husbands would answer on their behalf.

Further, although the reservation of 33% of seats under the Panchayat Raj system has been a morale booster for women in rural India, their husbands & other men in the village were yet to reconcile themselves with the women's new status. Women Sarpanchs who go out with men for work related to the Gram Panchayat or Zilha Parishad, are castigated as 'bad women' & they becomes victims of character assassination. For e.g. 1) Ratnamala Vaidya faced the bad tactics of opposition party during the district level election. Since 1994 she is wining the elections of Gram Panchayat. She has done very good village development work.

People appreciate her a lot. And this created problems for her. Last year at the time of Zilha Parishad (district level) election, opposition party started spreading rumours like her character is bad, she has two husbands etc. They also published a pamphlet, which amounted to character assassination in the worst form. As a result she was defeated in the election. 2) Maya (a member of Vadval Gram Panchayat), along with a colleague from the village had gone to Latur to attend a program of women's organization. The program was to be held in the hall of a hotel that had lodging-boarding facilities. The schoolteacher saw the women entering this lodge & that was it! He spread around vulgar rumours about the two women. "These women go to hotel rooms!" he publicized. All men of the village looked at the two with doubting & accusing eyes, the other women stopped talking to them. Organization's work came to a stand still. However, women who have been active in the people's struggles are able to work independently. A case in point was that of Kamalkar Hilam, a 25-year-old married tribal women who catered to the need of seven villages &

thirteen tribal colonies in an effort to implement water supply & road construction schemes.

Women in both states complained of the lack of information & experience, which made them diffident of their ability to handle the job, or working in the system. They had no idea as to what constituted a meeting, what was an agenda, how meetings were to be conducted & what was expected of them as elected representatives. Women Sarpanchs are often marginalized. Men, who still turn to the previous male Panchayat members for guidance & advice, do not take their leadership in the village seriously. Added to this was the age-old tradition of deferring to the males for decision making & seeking their advice. Men expectedly, in many cases, were antagonistic to the women.

In Kotgal Gram Panchayat of Gadchiroli district in Maharashtra, for the first time 11 candidates from lower caste won the elections in 2002. This year the post of Sarpanch is reserved for the women. Here Jyoti Meshram won the Sarpanch election. She is from the Schedule Caste (low caste). People from the upper caste were shocked by the fact that though they have the majority, a candidate from a SC community won the Sarpanch elections. They tried to create obstacles in the working of Panchayat. In the first Gram Sabha held in December 2002, they protested against the one topic in the agenda of the meeting relating to "The right of the Sarpanch & Secretary over authority in financial transactions". Forcefully, they made a resolution that the Sarpanch & the Secretary would have no authority in financial transactions. Her basic right, by the virtue of being the Sarpanch, was denied. Women soon acquired confidence & started taking independent action. Retribution, however, was immediate, which ranged from intimidation to physical violence.

Another example that one can sight is that of Ms. Sunita Agham. After being elected as the Sarpanch of Shirsgaon Pandhari village in Maharashtra she took charge of her office. On the day of first Gramsabha (public meeting in village which should be conducted once in month), Gram Panchayat Secretary was reading the information about the administrative procedures of the Panchayat. At this instance, the Ex-Sarpanch & his supporters got up & created a ruckus. They denied the appointments of Sarpanch & deputy Sarpanch & demanded to stop Gramsabha. Then after a big drama was created by Ex-Sarpanch & his men. They threw the chilly powder in Sarpanch's eye, on the Secretary, deputy Sarpanch & the members of Gram Panchayat. Soon they started beating them & abusing Sarpanch as she came from a low caste. The elected women members often faced the un-cooperative, manipulative staff & officialdom.

The other example of harassment is a Women Sarpanch in Nagpur district of Maharashtra, who was being sexually harassed by Gram Panchayat Secretary. He used to write vulgar letters to her. One day after receiving the same type of letter she committed suicide.

On the other hand, participation in the political process has also helped women to break out of the traditional moulds. It was stated that the adoption of the Panchayat Raj Act by all the states would ensure the presence of approximately 7.95 millions women in the Panchayat Raj system at the village block & district level. There would be at least 15 to 20 million women contesting in the polls. A third of chairperson at three levels of Panchayat administration about 76,200 – would be women.

Across the country today, there is a marked presence of women in the Panchayats. There are estimated more than 10 millions women in all three tiers of Panchayat Raj Institutions (PRI). Thus, the positive discrimination of PRI has initiated a momentum of change. Women's entry into local Government in such large numbers has shattered the myth that women are not interested in Politics & have no time to go to meetings or to undertake all the other work that is required in political party processes. The analysis of emerging patterns of women leadership at Panchayats has revealed that elected women Sarpanch were less than 50 years of age. They mostly belonged to the age group between 25 & 45 years. Almost all of them were married. This dispels the myth that rural power is the monopoly of the aged. The younger generation of women opting for political representation is a sign of change. A substantial number of women members, particularly at Gram Panchayat level, were illiterate or partially illiterate. But now many well-educated women are taking part in politics. Initially there was a preponderance of women representatives from well to do dominant caste groups. Now women from backward classes & low caste are effectively mobilized to participate. Almost half of the women representatives are from lower caste & tribal, 30% are from families below the poverty line, 14% are from landless families & 22% are working as hired labor. Reservation of Seats has enabled not only the poor & marginalized women but also the women from conservative minority sections. In West Bengal State a large number of Muslims have been elected in the Panchayats. In Kanpur, where Muslim women had to defy fatwas (an order by religion) to fight elections, 14 Muslim women won from 30 women reserved seats in the corporation elections. Reservation of seats has given these women an opportunity to demonstrate their deep political consciousness & interest in obtaining power. For them, politics & elections are very practical routes out of poverty & are instruments of social change. The findings also dispel the myth that only Hindu well to do & upper class women benefit from the reservations.

IMPACT OF WOMEN RESERVATION

Reservation policies clearly have a strong impact on women's representation. Women participate more in the political process in Gram Panchayat in which seats are reserved for women. In that Gram Panchayat, there are significantly more investments in drinking water, road construction, health, public toilets etc. Women representatives devote more energy to women-specific issues than men do, and to are more successful in passing legislation on women's issues when they propose them.

Women's experience of being involved with the PRI has transformed many of them. They have gained a sense of empowerment by asserting control over resources, officials & most of all, by challenging men. They have become articulate & conscious of their power. Despite their low-literacy level, they have been able to tackle the political & bureaucratic system successfully. They have reported regular attendance at Panchayats meetings. They have used their elected authority to address, critical issues such as education, drinking water facilities, family planning facilities, hygiene & health, quality of healthcare & village development. They have also brought alcohol abuse & domestic violence onto the agendas of political campaigns. In these & other ways, the issues that women have chosen differ from conventional political platforms, which are usually caste/ethnic/religion based.

For decades, the Panchayats in Metikheda village in Yavatmal district of Maharashtra had done no work at all, till in 1998 the women took over & brought about a total transformation in the village. The women's Panchayat initiated & implemented water supply schemes, additional school rooms, provided fuel & sanitation facilities which reduced the burden of rural women drastically. All women Panchayat in Kultikri in West Bengal took up several income augmenting schemes such as waste land development, leasing of small ponds for aqua culture, organization of loan repayment, fairs, distribution of pattas, construction of roads & tube wells as utilized under the Employment Guarantee scheme. The most important achievement of the Panchayat has been the fulfillment of 100% literacy in its area. Forty teams of women in Sonabhadra (Uttar Pradesh) area carried out systematic campaigns covering ten villages each, to explain the salient features of the 73rd Amendment & the place given in to women. Women, who took part in these campaigns, were very clear about their cattle & for their families. They were equally determined to prevent the inflow of liquor into their area.

Women & men have different policy priorities. In developed countries, women are more likely to support liberal policies, a difference known as the "gender gap". The primary responsibilities of women in rural areas in India, besides working on the fields, are to fetch water, fuel & to take care of children. Child health has been shown to be more responsive to women's income than to men's income.

ROLE OF MAHILA RAJSATTA ANDOLAN (MRA)

The Constitutional Amendment Acts have entitled over a million of women to become members & heads of political institutions. They need a supportive infrastructure that gives them political education & training. Mahila Rajsatta Andolan (Campaign for Women in Governance) works in this direction in state of Maharashtra. We are making elected women representatives conversant with the Panchayat laws, procedures, their rights, powers & functioning of the administrative mechanism through training programs & the use of posters, songs, street-theatres, stories, banners & other media. Mahila Rajsatta Andolan (MRA) is movement that has been working all over Maharashtra at both policy & program level with a firm stand of women's active participation in the process of village development. MRA is a campaign for Women in Governance initiated by Resource & Support Centre for Development (RSCD), Mumbai in collaboration with its regional networks in Maharashtra in the year 2000, with specific strategies & campaigns:

'The magnitude of the problem like lack of people's governance is a multi political matrix. Only specific campaign with clearly defined focus, can create the sense of urgency, mobilize popular support, & marshal all possible resources to sustain mass action, continuity & follow-up of such issues.' To achieve these objectives, focus on 3 major campaigns related to the Panchayati System to bring about a social change:

- Empowerment of Gramsabha (village public meeting) & women's Gramsabha where women can actively participate in decisions concerning the village.
- Economic changes where community resources are available to all & its control by Gramsabha, & decentralization of finance from the State to the Panchayati bodies.
- Political decentralization from Panchayati to sub-committees whereby the political power is shared with a larger body of developmental actors.

Major Concepts Of Campaign

- Let village learn village governance
- Let's activate the village committees & their members.
- Let the villagers plan their budget

Campaign Strategies

- Information generation on various policies & resolutions through reliable sources.

- Dissemination of useful information through district centres.
- Field & policy analysis.
- Policy actions.

Achievements At The Field Level

- Publication of Diwali (Indian Festival) Magazine as a medium to initiate dialogue between intellectuals & grassroots of the society. In this magazine activist from village level & village level leaders share their field experiences. This is a platform for them.
- Pre-session workshops to address local issues. In these workshops we discuss the current major policy gaps & strategize how these issues should be presented, both inside & outside the legislative assembly during the session.
- Struggle documentation process to re-visit the vision of MRA. This is an effort to document the struggle of Elected Women Representatives of the Gram Panchayat. We try to highlight their issues and represent them at the policy-making levels.
- Gramsabha (Village Public Meeting) Gaurav Abhiyan. Gramsabha is the platform provided by the Government to the people to keep a check on the village administration. But unfortunately people are unaware of their own rights. In order to create awareness among the mass this campaign was initiated.
- Show us Accounts Campaign – this campaign was initiated to make people – both the elected representatives and common people aware of their rights to know about the village budgets, expenditures and related documents and hold the village administration responsible for the same.
- Campaign on 10% reserved budget for women. There is provision of 10% women & child welfare fund in the budgets of all the three levels of local self-governing bodies. But very few Gram Panchayats keep the fund for the women related issues. Many a times this fund is utilized for other work. Women are unaware about

this provision, therefore our aim is to make them aware and demand for 10 % budget!

- Series of women leadership workshops. In these workshops we give training related to women empowerment, Panchayat Raj System, Rights & duties of elected representatives, legal advice etc.
- Pre-election Campaign. By this campaign we guide people about their political rights, duties of citizens, qualities of right candidate etc.
- Gram Panchayat Darshan (visit) campaign by women leaders. Women often feel embarrassed or fearful to enter the Village Administration Office (Gram Panchayat). Gram Panchayat Darshan Campaign is an effort to rid women of this fear. Women get a chance to visit the office & gain information about the proceedings of the Gram Panchayat.
- Felicitation of Husbands & Families of women leaders, for supporting women to participate in village administration.
- Joint Ownership of Houses through Women Gramsabha. There is law made by Government about the joint ownership of houses. This states that a house should be in the name of both husband & wife i.e. joint ownership. But this is not implemented properly. So through Women Gramsabhas we try to inculcate this thought and encourage implementation of this law.
- Grassroot Scholarship to identify grassroot issues. MRA has undertaken reality studies in several villages to asses whether all the laws are being implemented well. In the process, we were also able to analyze the problems and obstacles that the Elected Women Representatives face.
- Media Advocacy through print media, Radio, T.V. & even folk media like street play & songs on legal provisions.
- Daughters of Savitri – a series for neo-representatives. A documentation of the life struggles of women who have entered politics at local levels.

- Inter State Workshop for national policy initiatives.
- Dialogue with Maharashtra State Assembly Speaker & policy makers.
- MAVIM (State Government's Board for women's economic development) – MRA collaboration for economic & political governance.
- Huldi Kumkum – cultural campaign to share ideas on governance with women.
- Lobbying with political parties, on specific issues.
- Lokarpan Campaign to initiate people's leadership in Organization at grassroot.
- Novel on MRA process, written by NGO leader.
- Emerging front of forty women leaders.
- Creative participation in an election. Many MRA Activists across the State contested elections. MRA extended full support to such potential women leaders.

Achievement At The Policy-Advocacy Level

- Demand for the allocation of effective powers to the Gramsabha accepted by the State Government & a law came into effect on December 2002.
- State Government has agreed to start District level Consultation Centres for Women in Panchayat Raj.
- Women Gramsabha now made mandatory before the general Gramsabha.
- State Government has accepted to make suitable amendments to resolve the issue of suspended Gramsabha.
- Block Development Officers are advised to give adequate publicity to Block meetings to ensure women's participation.
- Three-fourth majority is made Mandatory to unseat women Sarpanch through No-Confidence motion, thus putting a check on improper & gender biased use of statutory provisions.
- State Government has agreed to employ Women Village Secretaries on an experimental basis.
- 10% Budget for women will be implemented rigorously.

- Priority to be given to Women Groups for allocation of land by the Government.
- Presently financial powers enjoyed by Water supply & Irrigation sub-committees is to be extended to other committees as well.
- As a result of MRA lobbying, State Government has issued a resolution stating that women should be entitled to Flag hosting where she is heading the bodies such as Gram Panchayats, Taluka Panchayat & Zilha Parishad.

Concerns And Challenges:

- NGO in village politics has emerged as a new trend. Villagers do not readily accept their increasing interference.
- Exclusion of Elected Women Representative (EWR's) from selection process of the Sarpanch by strategic actions like collective "Visit To Temples" Programs.
- Physical attack on EWR's, their families & supporters creates lot of insecurity among newly elected women members & their families. Participation of EWR's in Gramsabha, Women Gramsabha, Gram Panchayat meetings is decided by Male members of the family.
- Problems arising due to Alcoholism hinder women's participation in governance.
- Character Assassination of active women member is an often-used weapon by opponents.
- EWR's are in dual mind – family role Vs governance role.
- Passive EWR's are Tolerable; Active EWR's are eligible only for no confidence motion.
- Women have 33% reservations in the Panchayat Raj Institutions, but societal expectations are far beyond reality. EWR's are expected to become "development magician".
- Women are expected to execute 100% value based politics within the existing self-centred, party focused and value-less context of governance.

Draft Resolution for Public Debate:

- Raise reservation for women in Panchayats to 50% & provide at least 33% reservation for women in Parliament & State Legislatures.
- Introduce regular gender sensitive reorientation campaigns for MPs, MLAs & bureaucrats about the funds, functions & functionaries of the Panchayats.
- Ensure that due consideration is given by authorities at all levels to the proposals of the Gramsabha, particularly those relating to issues of women & children.
- Facilitate formation of women's associations at different levels of governance to act as pressure groups.
- Ensure that every state Government opens a toll-free help line for Panchayat women at the state & district levels to attend to emergent needs (adverse or otherwise) of elected women functionaries of PRIs in terms of police assistance, information dissemination, legal assistance, counseling etc. With a view to strengthen women's participation in local governance. Set up a national centre in Delhi to co-ordinate all the state-level help lines & act as a resource centre.
- Implementation of the Women Component of the Five-Year Plan through Panchayats.
- Provide for stringent laws to deal with those committing violence against women candidates during & after elections.
- Scrap the two-child norm as applicable at present in respect of the representatives of Panchayats.
- Strict implementation of laws regarding employment guarantee and equal wages for women, through gramsabha.
- Provide literacy training under special crash programs for illiterate women Panchayat members.
- Facilitate exchange programs for Panchayat women representatives inside & outside the country.
- Give awards for outstanding performance by women representatives at all levels of the Panchayat in the country.

- Ensure that the Government provides funds for celebrating women's governance day at the national, state & district levels.
- The no confidence motion should not be tabled within two years of functioning of PRIs. 3/4th majority should pass the motion. When tabled & passed a person from the same reserved category to be reelected to the same post.
- Setting up a mechanism to monitor the implementation of the POLICIES related to women in governance in all spheres of life, at least at the national and global levels.

Women's Issues are Human Issues & Women's Rights are Human Rights

A few micro realities and Mayatai's insights on Governance for Human Rights. In a democratic country, everybody has a 'Right to Express' his/her opinion. If we want to ensure success of democracy and well being of a just society, we have to encourage and elicit everybody's participation. Every person has unique skills. We should give each individual the scope to realize her/his potentials and utilize them for the betterment of our society. Especially women, she is mother of creation. She is capable of ensuring a healthy society. It is believed that if a woman is educated, the entire family reaps the benefit. Therefore participation of this indispensable component of our society in political & decision-making process is must.

Due to lack of sensitivity, we are unaware of others' plight. We always tend to engage in self-pity. We feel that we are the most deprived individuals on this earth and that everybody else is better off. It is therefore essential to communicate with others. This is the only way to discover people who are facing extreme challenges and hardships in life...but are still at peace and enjoy every second of their existence. We should try to use our governing skills to ensure better conditions for such people.

Fight the Menace of Caste & Race

Several strong laws have been enforced till date to tackle the menace of caste, untouchability and race. However, we need purposeful and organized efforts to strike at their roots and uproot them. Women are still engulfed in the web of these inhuman practices. Often one's surname provides the key to one's caste status. Women should make conscious efforts to get rid of such biased notions and strike towards equality.

Always Remain Down to Earth

Whenever we get power, we should utilize it for the creation of a just society. We should ensure the use of power for the betterment of the larger masses. While working for a good cause, one should forgo her/his vested interests.

Need of Formal and Informal Political Education

In India, even today political illiteracy is extremely low. As a result, politicians and bureaucrats often exploit such citizens. Literate people too face such problems, as they are ill equipped to deal with such complex socio-political issues and exercise their rights. Therefore there is need of both formal and informal political education. Organizing mass training programs to enlighten people about the system and their fundamental rights-is the need of the hour.

50% Reservation for Women

In India, the 73rd and 74th Constitutional Amendment provides 33% reservation for women in the rural and urban Local Self Governing Bodies. However some practical difficulties have been experienced at the filed level. For e.g. a particular Grampanchayat has 9-member body. According to 33% reservation for women, there will be 6 men and 3 women in this body. Therefore while taking decisions or passing a resolution, the men have the majority. This amounts to disregard and rejection of most of the resolutions tabled by the women members. If women try opposing such tactics of the male members, they are pressurized to keep their mouth shut. Women are forced to maintain silence since the men have numerical majority in most of the Grampanchayats. Gradually women start withdrawing from the Grampanchayat proceedings. Same is the scenario at different levels in the government, where women officials are less in numbers. Dominating attitude of the male officials often obstruct the smooth functioning of the women officials.

Men's Participation in Savitri's Nation

In India, Savitribai Phule & her husband Jyotiba Phule are considered as the pioneers of "Women's Education". In 18th century, Jyotiba first educated his wife. Then Savitribai decided to use her knowledge for the others. She started teaching 7-8 girls in her village. Men from the high caste communities tried to obstruct her in several ways. Savitribai and Jyotiba were ostracized by their own family and were forced to leave their house. However, Savitribai did not step back and Jyotiba supported and encouraged her in all possible ways. Today we are in dire need of many such "Jyotibas" who will support their wives. With such backing, women and the nation are bound to progress at a greater pace.

Importance of Organization and Unity

We need to bring to the notice of women the importance of mass organization in resolving issues. E.g.: to ensure smooth and regular supply of food grains in the Rationing Shops (Government Fair Price shops) United, women can fight against the corruption of the shop owners and demand their rightful. Through united and organized efforts, women can demand the Grampanchayat to provide water hand pumps. Proper and timely justice is being given to Dowry cases because of organization's interventions. Women have succeeded in many cases because of the power of unity. Therefore we all should fight against injustice unitedly, at the micro and macro levels.

Sustaining in Building the Process

Several activists are working relentlessly for a just and humane society. However, when it comes to Process Building they lag behind due to the lack of necessary knowledge and skills. Developing new relations is possible is only through meeting and interacting with different people. There is a need for process building; so that people of similar philosophies can come closer. Such associations will build and strengthen the process. As a result, our struggle gains the power to fight against any injustice.

Government & Administration

People cannot identify with the Government's laws &

administration. so it is our duty to create awareness, orient people towards government laws, GRs, schemes and make them realize that these laws are for their betterment. we need to bridge the gap between the people and the administration.

Understand Internal Relations and Contradictions Within the Society

While working in the field we come across different kinds of people. At times, due to personal disputes some people may try disrupt our work or even usurp resources for their vested self-interests. We need to assess the backing and support that we have. Our leadership is determined by the kind of people's support we have. We should try to transform our opponents into our supporters in peaceful and diplomatic manner.

Priority Needs to be Given to People's Interest, Rather than Self-interest

One needs to realize that being the Village Head does not entitle one to usurp the benefits of all the schemes and fulfil vested interest. Such adverse mentality among leadership will prove to be disastrous. One should always think about the people first. Only then will our leadership get optimum acceptance from the larger society.

Self Confidence & Positive Attitude

Always keep positive attitude. Don't be frightened to confront problems. Don't harness thoughts that you will be unable to do certain things. Nothing is impossible in this world. Sometimes women feel that they are incapable of handling financial matters. However, this is just a misconception. A positive attitude contributes to our confidence and helps in enhancing our personality.

RAISE THE VOICE FOR A GLOBAL PLATFORM FOR WOMEN IN GOVERNANCE

We should unite women from all over the world. For this we can use women's groups, Elected Women Representatives and SHGs (Self-Help Groups). We can organize common programs for these groups to strengthen women financially, socially and politically. We should form strong networks of such groups. We should encourage them to unite and emerge as a global pressure group. We should ensure the availability of all types of legal aid, training and support to these women. In such training, laws related to women in governance, women's fundamental rights, etc should be highlighted.

We will have to facilitate the development of healthy and fearless communications between women and men. We should also try to defeat women's patriarchal mindsets. Every woman should feel proud to be "a woman "-the creator of human beings on this EARTH. This platform will be instrumental in maintaining and enhancing equality in this world, by creating a just space for all the women in the Local and Global Self Governance.

5

Women Empowerment Through Self Help Groups

INTRODUCTION

Poverty and unemployment are the major problems of any under developed countries, to which India is no exception. In India, at the end of ninth five year pan 26.1% of the population was living below poverty line. In the rural area 27.1% of the population was living under poverty. The overall unemployment rate is estimated to 7.32%. The female unemployment rate is 8.5%. The rate of growth of women unemployment in the rural area is 9.8%. This is because of the low growth rate of new and productive employment. In the end of IX plan the rate of growth of implemented various schemes to reduce poverty and to promote the gainful employment. But the more attractive scheme with less effort (finance) is "Self Help Group". It is a too to remove poverty and improve the rural development (Sabyasachi Das. 2003).

ORIGIN AND CONCEPT OF SHGS

The origin of SHGs is from the brainchild of Grameen Bank of Bangladesh, which was founded by Mohammed Yunus. SHGs were started and formed in 1975. In India NABARD is initiated in 1986-87. But the real effort was taken after 1991-92 from the linkage of SHGs with the banks. A SHG is a small economically homogeneous affinity group of the rural poor voluntarily coming together to save small amount regularly, which are deposited in a common fund to meet members emergency needs and to provide collateral free loans decided by the group. They have been recognized as useful tool to help the poor and as an alternative mechanism to meet the urgent credit needs of poor through thrift SHG is a media for the development of saving habit among the women. SHGs enhance the equality of status of women as participants, decision-makers and beneficiaries in the democratic, economic, social and cultural spheres of life.

The basic principles of the SHGs are group approach, mutual trust, organization of small and manageable groups, group cohesiveness, sprit of thrift, demand based lending, collateral free, women friendly loan, peer group pressure in repayment, skill training capacity building and empowerment. In Tamil Nadu the SHGs were started in 1989 at Dharmapuri District. At present 1.40 lakh groups are function with 23.83 lakh members. At present, many men also eager to form a SHGs.

WORKING OF SHGS

SHGs are working in democratic manner. The upper limit of members in a group is restricted to 20. Among them a member is selected as an 'animator' and two members are selected as the representatives. The animator is selected for the period of two years. The group members meet every week. They discuss about the group savings, rotation of sangha funds, bank loan, repayment of loan, social and community action programmes.

FUNCTIONS OF SHGS

- Create a common fund by the members through their regular savings.
- Flexible working system and pool the resources in a democratic way.
- Periodical meeting. The decision making through group meeting.
- The loan amount is small and reasonable. So that easy to repay in time.
- The rate of interest is affordable, varying group to group and loan to loan. However it is little higher than the banks but lower than the money lenders.

From the previous studies related to SHGs, it is clearly understood that the SHGs are tool to promote rural savings and gainful employment. Through this the rural poverty is reduced considerably. Therefore women members are economically independent and their contribution to household income is also increased. The present study is also focusing the economic improvement of women after they joining SHGs.

Objectives

The overall objective of the present study is to analysis the economic empowerment of women through SHGs in the north districts of Tamil Nadu. However more specifically:

1. To study the income, expenditure and savings of the members after joining SHGs.
2. To know the role of SHGs in providing rural credit.

Methodology

The present study has covered the three villages from north districts of Tamil Nadu Viz., Ponneri Village of Vellore District, Koodamalai Village of Thiruvannamalai District, and Paparpatti Village of Dharmapuri District. These three villages were selected for this study, because of the SHGs in these villages are functioning very successful manner. The ponneri village of Vellore district is pioneer in starting make SHGs. Therefore these villages were selected for the present study.

This study is compiled with the help of the primary data covered only one year period (2004-05). The primary data were collected with the help of specially prepared interview schedule.

The schedule included the questions related to the general information about the SHGs members, income, expenditure, savings and loan schemes available to SHGs' members. Totally 134 respondents were selected from 20 SHGs (398 total members) of three districts simple random sapling method. The sample size was 1/3 of the total members in the SHGs. This is purely a descriptive study. Therefore no complicated models and tools were used, only percentage and average were used for the analysis.

ANALYSIS AND INTERPRETATION

The present study is related to the economic empowerment of women in the north Tamil Nadu. For this study three villages were selected from three districts.

This section deals the economic improvement of women through SHGs. In the study area totally twenty SHGs are functioning with 398 members. From the 398 members 134 respondents were selected for the study.

Age Group of Members of SHGs

Age and socio-economic activities are inter-related. The young and middle age group people can actively participate in the socio-economic activities, which is true in the activities of SHGs in the study area. In the three south district of Tamil Nadu, 20-30 and 30-40 age groups are actively participated in the SHGs activities. The aged people (40-50) are also in the SHGs, their role is also important for SHGs. They can only control and solve the problems arise in the groups.

Reasons for Joining SHGs

The major aim of the SHGs is to promote savings and to credit for the productive and consumption purposes. This is true because many people in the study area joins the SHGs for getting loan and promote their personal savings, in addition to get social status. In the study area many people (43.28%) joins the SHGs for getting financial assistance, 32.84% of the respondents joins the SHGs for the social status, because SHGs give the identify to the members. 14.92% of the respondents join for improving their savings. For social, cultural and political improvement (other reasons 8.96%) some members join in the SHGs.

Income Level of the Members

Income is the major determinant of the standard of living of the people. The SHGs member income has been increased after joining the SHGs. Hence women members of the groups are independent to meet their personal expenditure, and they contribute more to their household income. Many housewives (22.39%) did not earn anything before joining SHGs, but after a member of the SHGs, they are also earning reasonably. This increases the willingness to participate in the SHGs' activities. Many women members independently involve in the economic activities individually and with other group members after joining SHGs. Therefore they are now economically independent and contribute to increase their household income.

EXPENDITURE OF THE SHG MEMBERS FAMILY

The family expenditure has been increased due to positive change in the SHGs members' income. The incremental income not only enhance the expenditure of the family but also promote the savings of the family after they join in the SHGs. Here the objective of the SHGs is fulfilled. This is a achievement of the women SHGs in the study area. Usually working women are being respected by the household members and the society. Nowadays the women in the SHGs are also respected by the others, because they are independent in earning the income and they are contributing to household income, expenditure and savings. Therefore the above discussion clearly states that after joining in the SHGs, the members' well-being has been increased.

RURAL CREDIT AND SHGS

One of the reasons for joining SHGs is to avails credit, which is true in the present study area. The second objective of the present is to know the rural credit by SHGs. This part is discussed the rural credit and SHGs in study area. The credit organizations like nationalized banks, Co-operative Societies and so on, follow many formalities to provide credit to the rural people. At the sometime village money lenders change very high rate of interest. In this situation SHGs are the boon to the rural people, because instead of approaching banks individual, SHGs can easily approach the banks and other institutions to get loan. The SHGs get loan from credit institutions then, they refinance (share) to the members in the SHGs. The SHGs charge reasonable interest. In the study are the prevailing interest rate is 1% to 4%. All the members are responsible to repay the loan to the banks. Therefore members are repaid the loan in time. Moreover banks instruct the members to save minimum Rs. 200 per month. So re-payment is very easy to SHGs. The loans can be used by individual group members for their personal needs, sometime the group may invest on any economic activities. Nowadays many SHGs are starting small business, cottage industries, food processing units etc. The SHGs in the study area grant the loan to their member for various purposes. The maximum loan amount per members is decided by the general body meeting. Almost all the members in the study area are availing the loan facilities in their SHGs.

The study was undertaken the women empowerment through SHGs in the north Tamil Nadu. It is found that the income of the women has been increased after joining the SHGs. So that the monthly household expenditure also has been raised considerable level. But the savings is increasing at slow rate, because the incremental expenditure is higher. Mostly they are spending for present consumption. The members should change it. The good practice of the women SHGs in the study area is repayment of the loan in time. Nearly 64% of the debtor paid their monthly due with in the time, even some members 19% paid their due in advance. A few members do not pay in time but this is not affecting the further credit of SHGs. Since the repayment of loan is regular and within the time, we may conclude that the economic activities of SHGs are quite success. In this way SHGs in north Tamil Nadu are very successful to develop women empowerment and rural areas.

PROBLEMS OF WORKING WOMEN

It is an open truth that working women have to face problems just by virtue of their being women. Working women here are referred to those who are in paid employment. Social attitude to the role of women lags much behind the law. This attitude which considers women fit for certain jobs and not others colours those who recruit employees. Thus women find employment easily as nurses, doctors, teachers the caring and nurturing sectors, secretaries or in assembling jobs-the routine submissive sectors. But even if well qualified women engineers or managers or geologists are available, preference will be given to a male of equal qualification. A gender bias creates an obstacle at the recruitment stage itself. When it comes to remuneration the law proclaims equality but it is seldom put into practice. The inbuilt conviction that women are capable of less work than men or less efficient than men governs this injustice of unequal salaries and wages for the same job. The age old belief of male superiority over women creates several hurdles for women at their place of work. Women on the way up the corporate ladder discover that they must be much better than their male colleagues to reach the top. Once at the top male colleagues and subordinates often expect much greater expertise and efficiency from a woman boss than from a male boss. Conditioned by social and psychological tradition women colleagues too don't lend support to their own sex. Working in such conditions inevitably put much greater strain on women than what men experience. These problems tend to make women less eager to progress in their careers. Indeed many of them choose less demanding jobs for which they may even be over-qualified. A woman's work is not merely confined to paid employment.

She has to almost always shoulder the burden of household chores as well. A woman could still bear up with these problems if she had control over the money she earns. But in most families even now her salary is handed over to father, husband or in-laws. So the basic motive for seeking employment of getting independence is nullified in many women's case. Problems of gender bias beset women in the industrial sector.

Technological advancement results in retrenchment of women employees. No one thinks of upgrading their skills. Maternity leave is seldom given. It is much easier to terminate the woman's employment and hire someone else. Trade Unions do little to ameliorate the lot of women workers. Women's issues do not occur on the priority list of most of the trade unions. Women going to work are often subject to sexual harassment. Public transport system is over crowded and men take advantage of the circumstances to physically harass women. Colleagues offer unwanted attention which can still be shaken off but a woman is placed in a difficult situation if the higher officer demands sexual favours. If refused the boss can easily take it out on the woman in other ways to make life miserable for her. There have been several cases of sexual harassment recently involving even the senior women officials. On the other hand if a woman is praised for her work or promoted on merit, her colleagues do not hesitate to attribute it to sexual favours. The psychological pressure of all this can easily lead to a woman quitting her job. Most of the problems that beset working women are in reality rooted in the social perspective of the position of women. Traditionally men are seen as the bread winner and women as the house-keepers, child bearers and rearers. This typecast role model continues to put obstacles before the working women. A fundamental change is required in the attitudes of the employers, policy makers, family members and other relatives and the public at large.

GIRLS, WOMEN AND POVERTY

Systematic discrimination against girls and women in the world's poorest countries will prevent the United Nations from meeting its goals to reduce poverty. Girls and women were more likely to be poor, hungry, illiterate or sick than boys and men. According to Action Aid which produced the report in South Asia women are getting a shrinking share of income as the economy grows. Amid growing concern that the millennium development goals set by UN for 2015 will not be met, Action Aid said a focus on women was vital to put the international community back on track. Ten million more girls than boys miss out on primary school while African women accounted for 75% of all young people living with the human immunodeficiency virus/AIDS. The aim of universal primary education was being hampered in Africa by the 40 billion hours spent each year by women and children collecting water-equivalent to a year's labor for the entire workforce of France.

A special session of the UN will be held in September to discuss ways of making speedier progress with discussions centrad on four areas: health and education; climate change and the environment; the role of business and trade and growth.

The disproportionate impact of poverty on girls is not an accident but the result of systematic discrimination. On current trends the goal of halving hunger would not be until 2035, 40 countries would have equal enrolments for boys and girls until after 2025 and current progress in cutting maternal mortality rates was less than 1/5th of what was needed to meet the goal.

The total number of HIV/AIDS infections in 2007 was 33 million-the highest ever. According to Action Aid discussions at the UN and this year's meeting of the G-8 industrial nations in Japan would only succeed if they started with the recognition that the development emergency is first and foremost an emergency for women and girls. The lack of progress on maternal health shows people's lives are at stake.

REPRODUCTIVE HEALTH STATUS OF WOMEN IN INDIA

India's maternal mortality ratio (MMR) is highest in South Asia: 540 deaths per 100,000 live births or one woman dying roughly every five minutes. An estimated 1, 36,000 women die in India every year due to pregnancy related setbacks. The number of maternity-related deaths which occur in a week in India is equivalent to what occurs in a whole year in Europe. However government has not taken any effective measures till date.

Despite the fact that an high fatalities occur among women in a year due to poor reproductive health practices no one is exercised enough to create a movement for improving women's health. One of the reasons why women succumb to reproduction related complications is lack of timely transportation to the nearest hospital. Experts estimate that 70% of the maternal-related deaths are preventable. Tetanus and anemia claim a large number of women because mothers get very little or no care in the post natal period. Anaemia can be overcome with proper nutrition and supplements.

In US MMR has dropped by 99% in recent years largely because of improvements in sanitation and post natal care rather than new medication. Good sanitation and nutrition and avoiding overwork and stress will improve the health of the women here.

The need is to shift focus from the medical to the social, beginning with healthy antenatal care. But cultural, social and economic barriers delay or prevent women from seeking reproductive health care at any stage-antenatal, delivery or post natal. Safe maternity is a vital social indicator which requires immediate attention.

DEVELOPMENTS IN WOMEN EMPOWERMENT

Despite many international agreements affirming their human rights, women are still much more likely than men to be poor and illiterate. They usually have less access than men to medical care, property ownership, credit, training and employment. They are far less likely than men to be politically active and far more likely to be victims of domestic violence.

The ability of women to control their own fertility is absolutely fundamental to women's empowerment and equality. When a woman can plan her family, she can plan the rest of her life. When she is healthy, she can be more productive. And when her reproductive rights—including the right to decide the number, timing and spacing of her children, and to make decisions regarding reproduction free of discrimination, coercion and violence—are promoted and protected, she has freedom to participate more fully and equally in society.

UNDERSTANDING GENDER EQUALITY AND WOMEN'S EMPOWERMENT

Gender equality implies a society in which women and men enjoy the same opportunities, outcomes, rights and obligations in all spheres of life. Equality between men and women exists when both sexes are able to share equally in the distribution of power and influence; have equal opportunities for financial independence through work or through setting up businesses; enjoy equal access to education and the opportunity to develop personal ambitions. A critical aspect of promoting gender equality is the empowerment of women, with a focus on identifying and redressing power imbalances and giving women more autonomy to manage their own lives. Women's empowerment is vital to sustainable development and the realization of human rights for all.

Where women's status is low, family size tends to be large, which makes it more difficult for families to thrive. Population and development and reproductive health programmes are more effective when they address the educational opportunities, status and empowerment of women. When women are empowered, whole families benefit, and these benefits often have ripple effects to future generations. The roles that men and women play in society are not biologically determined — they are socially determined, changing and changeable. Although they may be justified as being required by culture or religion, these roles vary widely by locality and change over time. UNFPA has found that applying culturally sensitive approaches can be key to advancing women's rights while respecting different forms of social organization. Addressing women's issues also requires recognizing that women are a diverse group, in the roles they play as well as in characteristics such as age, social status, urban or rural orientation and educational attainment. Although women may have many interests in common, the fabric of their lives and the choices available to them may vary widely. UNFPA seeks to identify groups of women who are most marginalized and vulnerable (women refugees, for example, or those who are heads of households or living in extreme poverty), so that interventions address their specific needs and concerns. This task is related to the critical need for sex-dis-aggregated data, and UNFPA helps countries build capacity in this area.

Key Issues and Linkages

Reproductive health: Women, for both physiological and social reasons, are more vulnerable than men to reproductive health problems. Reproductive health problems, including maternal mortality and morbidity, represent a major – but preventable — cause of death and disability for women in developing countries. Failure to provide information, services and conditions to help women protect their reproduction health therefore constitutes gender-based discrimination and a violation of women's rights to health and life.

Stewardship of natural resources: Women in developing nations are usually in charge of securing water, food and fuel and of overseeing family health and diet. Therefore, they tend to put into immediate practice whatever they learn about nutrition and preserving the environment and natural resources.

Economic empowerment: More women than men live in poverty. Economic disparities persist partly because much of the unpaid work within families and communities falls on the shoulders of women and because they face discrimination in the economic sphere.

Educational empowerment: About two thirds of the illiterate adults in the world are female. Higher levels of women's education are strongly associated with both lower infant mortality and lower fertility, as well as with higher levels of education and economic opportunity for their children.

Political empowerment: Social and legal institutions still do not guarantee women equality in basic legal and human rights, in access to or control of land or other resources, in employment and earning, and social and political participation. Laws against domestic violence are often not enforced on behalf of women.

Empowerment throughout the life cycle: Reproductive health is a lifetime concern for both women and men, from infancy to old age. UNFPA supports programming tailored to the different challenges they face at different times in life.

Experience has shown that addressing gender equality and women's empowerment requires strategic interventions at all levels of programming and policy-making.

WOMEN'S WORK AND ECONOMIC EMPOWERMENT

In nearly every country, women work longer hours than men, but are usually paid less and are more likely to live in poverty. In subsistence economies, women spend much of the day performing tasks to maintain the household, such as carrying water and collecting fuel wood. In many countries women are also responsible for agricultural production and selling. Often they take on paid work or entrepreneurial enterprises as well.

Unpaid domestic work – from food preparation to caregiving – directly affects the health and overall well being and quality of life of children and other household members. The need for women's unpaid labour often increases with economic shocks, such as those associated with the AIDS pandemic or economic restructuring. Yet women's voices and lived experiences – whether as workers (paid and unpaid), citizens, or consumers – are still largely missing from debates on finance and development. Poor women do more unpaid work, work longer hours and may accept degrading working conditions during times of crisis, just to ensure that their families survive.

Intergenerational Gender Gaps

The differences in the work patterns of men and women, and the 'invisibility' of work that is not included in national accounts, lead to lower entitlements to women than to men. Women's lower access to resources and the lack of attention to gender in macroeconomic policy adds to the inequity, which, in turn, perpetuates gender gaps. For example, when girls reach adolescence they are typically expected to spend more time in household activities, while boys spend more time on farming or wage work. By the time girls and boys become adults, females generally work longer hours than males, have less experience in the labour force, earn less income and have less leisure, recreation or rest time. This has implications for investments in the next generation. If parents view daughters as less likely to take paid work or earn market wages, they may be less inclined to invest in their education, women's fastest route out of poverty.

UNFPA in Action

UNFPA is committed to actions to attack poverty and powerlessness, especially among women. About half of the UNFPA programme countries have developed strategies to provide women with economic opportunities. The Fund has supported economic empowerment and micro-credit initiatives in Bangladesh, Chad, Kenya, Morocco, Palestinian women's centres, Tajikistan and elsewhere. As part of its Campaign to End Fistula, UNFPA also supports skills training for who have been marginalized by this debilitating injury of childbirth. UNFPA strongly supports addressing the feminization of poverty through the integration of gender concerns in macro economic policy and in poverty reduction strategies.

In Chad, a two-pronged programme unites microcredit and reproductive health education: while young women receive support that can lead to economic independence, they also learn to protect themselves against HIV and other reproductive health problems. In the Lao People's Democratic Republic, a seed fund is helping women gain respect – as economic partners, as well as mothers and wives. Women are learning about reproductive health issues through the programme as well.

In Bangladesh, a UNFPA-supported microcredit project provides skills training and small business loans to women, and also supports reproductive health and family planning services. In Viet Nam, UNFPA and partners support national efforts that link economic empowerment, environmental management and reproductive health services. Participation involves 500 Women's Savings Groups in nine provinces with a membership of over 12,000 women.

Empowering Women through Education

> *"Education is one of the most important means of empowering women with the knowledge, skills and self-confidence necessary to participate fully in the development process." —ICPD Programme of Action, paragraph 4.2*

Education is important for everyone, but it is especially significant for girls and women. This is true not only because education is an entry point to other opportunities, but also because the educational achievements of women can have ripple effects within the family and across generations. Investing in girls' education is one of the most effective ways to reduce poverty. Investments in secondary school education for girls yields especially high dividends.

Girls who have been educated are likely to marry later and to have smaller and healthier families. Educated women can recognize the importance of health care and know how to seek it for themselves and their children. Education helps girls and women to know their rights and to gain confidence to claim them. However, women's literacy rates are significantly lower than men's in most developing countries.

Education has Far-reaching Effects

The education of parents is linked to their children's educational attainment, and the mother's education is usually more influential than the father's. An educated mother's greater influence in household negotiations may allow her to secure more resources for her children. Educated mothers are more likely to be in the labour force, allowing them to pay some of the costs of schooling, and may be more aware of returns to schooling. And educated mothers, averaging fewer children, can concentrate more attention on each child. Besides having fewer children, mothers with schooling are less likely to have mistimed or unintended births. This has implications for schooling, because poor parents often must choose which of their children to educate. Closing the gender gap in education is a development priority. The 1994 Cairo Consensus recognized education, especially for women, as a force for social and economic development. Universal completion of primary education was set as a 20-year goal, as was wider access to secondary and higher education among girls and women. Closing the gender gap in education by 2015 is also one of the benchmarks for the Millennium Development Goals.

What UNFPA is Doing

UNFPA advocates widely for universal education and has been instrumental in advancing legislation in many countries to reduce gender disparities in schooling. The 2003 UNFPA global survey on ICPD+10 showed that most programme countries formally recognize the important of reducing the gender gap in education between boys and girls. UNFPA supports a variety of educational programmes, from literacy projects to curricula development with a focus on reproductive and sexual health. Because of the sensitivity of these issues, the focus and names of the educational programmes have gone through a number of changes over the past decades.

Gender issues now receive more attention than they did in past programmes, and instruction methods have changed, from a didactic approach to one emphasizing student participation and communications skills. In Jamaica, through an alliance with the Women's Centre of Jamaica Foundation and funding from the European Union, UNFPA supported a programme that enabled thousands of girls to return to school following pregnancies and to acquire technical skills.

In a UNFPA-supported project in Bolivia, women are learning to read in their indigenous language while learning about reproductive health, safe motherhood and health insurance. In Mali, a literacy project reaches adolescents both in and out of school, with a focus on migrant girls, domestic workers, victims of violence and abuse, and those living on the margins of society. In Mauritania, UNFPA is collaborating on an educational initiative in four of the poorest regions of the country. The initiative aims to reduce the dropout rate by half and equip at least 5,000 girls with a range skills, from home economics and information technology to environmental preservation.

POLITICAL EMPOWERMENT

Throughout much of the world, women's equality is undermined by historical imbalances in decision-making power and access to resources, rights, and entitlements for women. Either by law or by custom, women in many countries still lack rights to:

- Own land and to inherit property
- Obtain access to credit
- Attend and stay in school
- Earn income and move up in their work, free from job discrimination.

Moreover, women are still widely under-represented in decision-making at all levels, in the household and in the public sphere.

Addressing these inequities through laws and public policy is a way of formalizing the goal of gender equality. Legal changes, which most countries have now implemented, are often a necessary step to institute gender equality, but not necessarily sufficient to create lasting changes. Addressing the gaps between what the law proscribes and what actually occurs often requires broad, integrated campaigns.

UNFPA at Work

Effective advocacy requires partnership and coalition building. UNFPA alone is a relatively small agency, but when it works together with other international agencies and non-governmental organizations to address gender biases in laws and policies at the national level, it can be very effective. Formal international agreements, such as the ICPD Programme of Action and the Millennium Development Goals, provide key areas for policy changes. With its development partners, UNFPA advocates widely for legislation to advance gender equality, to eliminate all forms of discrimination based on sex, and to prevent gender-based violence and increase penalties for those who inflict it.

The Fund has established partnerships with parliamentarians in developing countries for political and legislative support for population and development challenges, of which the empowerment of women is central. Affecting changes in laws can require considerable patience and a deep understanding of the cultural context. In most countries, serious gaps still exist in available data on women's economic and political activity and decision-making ability. The Fund works to fill gaps in collecting sex-dis-aggregated data that is needed to put benchmarks on or monitor policy or programme effectiveness.

In many countries, UNFPA supports capacity-building for women's NGOs and for government to use the Convention on the Elimination of All Forms of Discrimination Against Women, because it provides a legally-binding basis for the realization of women's rights – political, economic, social and cultural in the 179 countries which have ratified it.

WOMEN EMPOWERMENT IN INDIA—DISTANT DREAM

Though India is developing economically and technologically by leaps and bounds, women here still continue to be discriminated. Census 2001 shows our national sex ratio as 921:1000 (921 females for 1000 males), and this will lead to detrimental social problems if not corrected. The main reason for this is female infanticide.

Gender wise abortions are on the rise. In economically developed states such as Haryana and Punjab the tendency is found to be more. A shocking study reveals that half of the world's malnourished children live in India owing primarily to the lack of nutritious food available to the mother. In all the critical stages, be it infancy, childhood, adolescence or the reproductive phase many women suffer malnutrition purely due to the discrimination and the narrow mindsets of the society. A shocking study reveals that half of the world's malnourished children live in India owing primarily to the lack of nutritious food available to the mother.

Dowry still remains the major reason for all the discrimination and injustice shown to women. Dowry has always been an important part of Hindu marriages. Not only among Hindus, its evil tentacles are now spreading to other religions also.

But despite all these measures there should be a strong determination among every man that every woman in this country should be honoured. Only then empowerment in its true meaning will be realized.

WOMEN IN HIGHER EDUCATION

Education in India especially higher education in India is indeed one amongst other elements which has captured the world's attention. The Vedas, Puranas, Ayurveda, Yoga, Kautilya's Arthasahtra are some of the significant traditional Indian knowledge system which even today, India can boast of. It is certainly not an overstatement to say that the history of higher education in India is long, pregnant with its copious past.

Higher education in India is defined as the education attained after the completion of 12 years of schooling. Higher education for women has gained a wider role and responsibility all over the world. Today, in the 21st century, one cannot afford to ignore the importance of higher education for women any longer. The reason for its need and urgency is that there is no biological difference in the systems of males and females. Need for higher education among women assumes all the more importance in countries like India where colonialism has remained a great force hindering education for the general masses and for the women in particular. Higher education of women in India is indeed necessary. Whether to provide society with competent men and women trained in agriculture, arts, medicine, science and technology and various other professions, or to strive to promote equality and social justice or whether to reduce social and cultural differences through diffusion of education, diffusing higher education of women in India is certainly that hidden key.

The objective of the Indian Society as has been laid down in the constitution is to achieve a democratic, socialistic and egalitarian society. In such a society women are supposed to perform their roles at par with men. Their status structurally needs to be equal with men and in the present scenario, higher education is certainly that factor which can actually support them to execute their role at par with men.

Higher Education may also be viewed in terms of the needs of its consumers. The term consumer is very wide and heterogeneous. It includes young and old of both sexes. Theoretically the need for Higher Education for both males and females is the same.

But it's sometime argued that males and females are different in their social and cultural needs. The basic argument which is given for women Higher Education is not that Higher Education for women is different from that of men. The main thrust is that in the field of Higher Education, women should also be equal partners. The commission on the Higher Education for women, University of Madras in 1979 has rightly observed: "for Women and men college education is necessary for character formation, ability to earn, creative self expression and personal development".

Main Factors Influencing Women'S Success/Failure in Completing Higher Education

Research has unveiled the fact that there are few influencing factors which supports in the success and failure in completing higher education in women.

Success :

- Women are strongly motivated to succeed in the education stream.
- The merit basis of the education system permits females to excel.
- Prejudice against women's education has been reduced. Higher Education has come to be considered equivalent to a bride's "dowry".
- Women's universities promote women's Higher Education.
- Women's expectations for education based employment are high.

- Some Higher Education courses provide scholarship facilities for women.
- Female students have been provided with residential facilities in some areas.

Failure :

- Female students have difficulties in access to transport facilities in general.
- Sexual harassment as well as occasional student violence hinder female students completion of higher education.
- Marriage in many cases leads to early withdraw.
- Gender stereotyping inhibits completion of studies.
- Financial constraints can cause withdrawal from the education stream.
- Part-time work to earn living interferes with studies.

6

Panchayati Raj System in India

This brief review of experience will be incomplete without some reference to the realty in the different states. This is a subject that has been extensively studied by many, in particular the Institute of Social Sciences, the National Institute of Rural Development and the Institute of Social Studies Trust. We can just note some major points that emerge from our general reading, meant only to give a flavour for further discussions in this conference.

It is only a few states that have experience over several electoral cycles with panchayati raj. For one thing, after the 73rd amendment, it is only now that the second round of election has become due. Thus, when we speak of such experience, it is that of states which experimented with PRIs before this amendment. Among them, West Bengal, Karnataka, Andhra Pradesh, Gujarat and Maharastra are the major ones. Kerala has much to offer in recent years, especially in involving people in the planning process.

But Kerala is exceptional in several ways—for example, in the high levels of literacy, in the history of political mobilisation, etc. In Kerala, the role of the party is critical, and there is apparently an overlap between party functioning and patriarchal attitudes. A recent study has shown that, in this state with high literacy, women who have held positions in the PRIs are not keen on contesting again. But it is still a new experiment. West Bengal has gone through several cycles of elections since

1978, when this system was introduced. A major reason for success here was the commitment of the Left Front government to these bodies. It has been argued that their strength comes from the fact that the cadres of these parties have now entrenched themselves in the PRI institutions. This is the charge made by the breakaway faction of the Congress, the Trinamool Congress led by Mamta Banerji. Be that as it may, the fact remains that these bodies have taken root, and work at the local level in this state is done through these bodies—and there has been an improvement over the centralised administration of the past. But this has also a flip side. For one thing, it has not meant that corruption has been eliminated—there are charges of much corruption. For another, NGOs have little space in West Bengal. They work in a hostile environment where PRIs are pitted against them. This can have a political base, but it is the reality. Overall though, West Bengal scores high on implementing Panchayati raj. About the role of women in PRIs, it is more difficult to say—but we would be inclined to hypothesise that the situation is better than most other states.

Andhra Pradesh is another state that took to PRIs in the 1980s, when N.T. Rama Rao was the Chief Minister. Here also the system started with hope. 9% of the seats were reserved for women but not the chairman positions. But the most important struggle that Andhra is known for—the anti-arrack agitation—came, not from women in the PRIs, but from women in the literacy programme in Nellore district. As a result of increasing literacy, and analysis stemming from the praxis methodology of Paulo Freire, women began to organise against the evils of drinking alcohol, and pushed for a policy of prohibition. This was, however, hijacked by the Telugu Desam Party, which rode on this slogan to power in AP. Once the state took over the demand of these women they became curiously disempowered. Prohibition became the hotbed of corruption. Women got trapped into a situation in which they had no control. Their organisation broke up. Little remains of the excitement of the literacy campaign days today.

Also, in more recent development, while the PRI system continues to exist, NTR's successor, Chandrababu Naidu, taking a leaf out of South Korean experience, introduced the Janmabhoomi programme for rural development. This is a programme run efficiently from the Chief Minister's office, by creating a bureaucratic edifice that is clearly accountable to him. The programme calls for contributions from local people for taking up projects that are of importance to them. This is done by selecting projects through discussions with the people in well organised meetings, attended by all the concerned officials, who have with them the authority to take decisions. Clear guidelines have been given for the patter of financing—how much will be matched in funds by the state government and for what purpose. Often shramdaan—free labour—is called for. The programme explicitly seeks to involve women in this process—in deciding upon what is to be done, how, and in monitoring the work. By all accounts, the programme has made a big difference to the implementation of projects in rural Andhra Pradesh. Even critics of the programme agree that it has made a big difference. Corruption has not been eliminated, but the percentages, we are told, are smaller. However, more work is being done, and so volumes make up for the difference.

The interesting thing about this programme is that it has many of the good points that are used for justifying local governance. But it achieves this end by marginalising the elected system of PRIs. That this is true is seen from the fact that elected Pradhans have recently gone on a fast in front of the Chief Minister's house.What is the lesson from Andhra Pradesh? Good work can be done outside of PRIs. But PRIs are a value we stand for—and so the managerial techniques of Janmabhoomi need to be welded into the PRIs. How this can be done is still an open question.

Madhya Pradesh is another interesting case. The Chief Minister realised its potential and decided to gamble his political career on it. He had two advantages. None of the major parties in MP were looking at decentralised governance—their attention was fixed firmly on urban areas and large contracts. He left these issues to his Cabinet. Two, the 73rd amendment had just been passed, elections had been held, and a large number of local elected representatives were looking for work and responsibility.

The state had just brought out the first state level Human Development Report in 1995. Among the finding was the paradox that, in a state where every village had a school, literacy levels were abysmally low. So were health and other social indicators. The Chief Minister made these his priority—he set up the Rajiv Gandhi Missions, which were coordinated from his office.

Putting together the expertise in his office with the energies of the local representatives, a *Lok Sampark Abhiyan* was organised. Each elected representative, accompanied by the local schoolteacher, conducted a survey of education and other conditions in his/her constituency. The Mission Office provided the technical support. As a result, each representative developed a good idea of what his/her constituency needed, and priorities were set which would be met through the Rajiv Gandhi Missions.

The finding for education was interesting. It was true that each revenue village had a school. But in MP, a revenue village consisted of several habitations—sometimes four or five, called *tolas*, which would be quite remote from it. Children in these tolas did not have access to school. Hence the low literacy was more due to problems of access than anything else.

The response was the Education Guarantee Scheme. Consider a village which had 40 children [25 in tribal areas] who wanted to go to school. If the panchayat met, decided to offer space where the school could be run, and to identify a "guruji" from the panchayat—or a neighbouring one—who had finished 12th standard, then the government undertook to set up a school within 90 days. In this time, the guruji would be trained in pedagogy, and materials would be provided. The power to sanction the school was vested in the janpad panchayat. Funds were transferred directly to the panchayat, which would supervise the functioning of the school. Within 2 years, over 20,000 such schools were set up—access to school is no longer a problem in MP.

Madhya Pradesh has made use of the panchayat system in an innovative way to meet social sector demands. Several of the Rajiv Gandhi Missions—all implemented through the PRIs—have done well, on an independent reckoning. Today, perhaps, it has the most progressive PRI system in the country. But here too, the support of the Chief Minister has been critical.

It is not power that has been demanded, but power that has been given. For all that, it is a positive development that must be built upon.

INDIAN PANCHAYATI RAJ SYSTEM

In spite of its status as the world's largest democracy, the vast majority of Indians, and particularly the 720 million people who live in rural villages, are largely dependent upon remote and unresponsive government structures historically characterised by bureaucracy, corruption and lack of transparency. In many parts of rural India, there has been a deep rift between the people and their government. Rural people rarely receive information about the plans and actions of government. They lack ways to influence policies, programmes, or resource allocations for development. Many have no effective means of participating in shaping their future, and government officials are not always accountable to the communities they purport to serve. It is no wonder that progress in improving the conditions of life in most parts of rural India has been slow to nonexistent.

As Nobel Prize-winning economist Amartya Sen has pointed out, "Democracy is not only the goal of development, it is the primary means of development". Only when every individual experiences greater freedom, voice and opportunity will each fully bring her or his creative powers to bear on solving the problems of the community. The challenges facing rural India can never be solved by top-down, bureaucratic interventions. The critical needs of communities in health, sanitation, clean water, education, family planning and income can only be met locally-through local responsibility, accountability and action-utilising local resources to the greatest possible extent. This truth, and the Gandhian principle of gram swaraj (village self-government), were recognised at the time of India's independence, but were not made a part of the constitution, never institutionalised and never fully put into practice.

Only in 1993, with the adoption of the 73rd amendment to the constitution, did India begin a process with the potential to create genuine democracy at the village level. It represents an historic opportunity to transform the face of rural India.

The 73rd amendment establishes panchayati raj: a system of local democracy through local councils known as panchayats. The amendment mandates that resources, responsibility and decision-making power be devolved from central government and placed in the hands of rural grass-roots people, with elections every five years.

The most revolutionary aspect of the amendment is that one-third of all panchayat seats are reserved for women. Rural women-who for centuries have lived in conditions of malnutrition, illiteracy and powerlessness-are now taking leadership roles in addressing these very issues.

Social and Political Elites

This revolution is not going unopposed. Social and political elites in many areas are seeking to undermine and nullify panchayati raj, since they perceive it as a threat to their monopoly on power and a challenge to their domination of society. The democratic process is held back by an entrenched patriarchal and feudal mind-set that insists that panchayati raj-and certainly women's leadership-will never work. The forces that oppose local democracy are the same forces that hold the subjugation of women in place. The destiny of the nation. For India to build a broad-based, solid foundation for economic and social progress, it must uproot the vestiges of feudalism and instil democratic values and practices. The people who live in India's 750,000 villages must become the authors of their own lives, and women must be respected and supported as equal partners in the process of development.

FACTS ABOUT PANCHAYATI RAJ

- *State Action.* The amendment required every state to pass or amend its own panchayat act by April 1994, and to hold elections by April 1995.
- *A Three-tier System.* The amendment created a system of local democracy at the village level (gram panchayat), the block level (panchayat samity, the lowest level of the government bureaucracy, encompassing 10-20 panchayats), and the district level (zilla panchayat, comprising 4-10 blocks).

- *Tradition*: Panchayats are an ancient form of local government based on the idea that when five (panch) elders come together, God will be present.
- *Gram swaraj* (village self-government) was a goal of India's Freedom Movement, although it was not originally enshrined in India's 1951 constitution.
- Until the 1960s, panchayati raj served as the foundation for rural development in India's first two five-year plans. As bureaucratic power increased, panchayati raj was allowed to die in most states.
- The passage of the 73rd amendment in 1992 by the Indian parliament became part of the constitution in April 1993 after many years of national discussion and debate. The late prime minister, Rajiv Gandhi, championed the rebirth of panchayati raj.
- *Gram Sabha*. To ensure that the panchayats themselves stay accountable to all the people of their constituency, they are required to hold village assemblies (gram sabha) several times each year, with a quorum of citizens attending.
- *Reserved Seats*. The 73rd amendment reserves seats for the most powerless members of society on a revolving basis, as determined by the election commission. One-third of all seats-including one-third of all panchayat presidencies-are reserved for women. In addition, seats are also reserved for members of scheduled tribes and scheduled castes proportional to their population.
- *Devolution of Powers*: The "11th schedule" of the amendment specifies 29 areas of responsibility, covering all key aspects of village life, which states may transfer to the panchayats-along with sufficient resources and decision-making authority. In practice, most states have transferred very little power and few financial resources to the panchayats.

AGENTS OF CHANGE

The greatest social experiment. The historic confluence of forces taking shape in India-the awakening of women and the emerging commitment to local democracy-have led to what is unquestionably the greatest social experiment in the world today: the transfer of decision-making power to one million elected women local government representatives. These women are not only the beneficiaries of change-they are the key agents for change.

Women and the Freedom Movement. Throughout India's long struggle for independence, women stood shoulder to shoulder with men. The Freedom Movement was their movement, and the battles were their battles. In fact, it was a woman-the Rani of Jhansi who fired the first shot that began the freedom struggle in 1857. While the women of India worked, fought and died for freedom, few have been able to share the fruits of that freedom. They remain subjugated, marginalized and disenfranchised, as they have been throughout history.

Today, their struggle is again the nation's struggle. Freedom for India's women means freedom for India to create a new future. Women face harsh opposition. The forces of patriarchy and feudalism that oppose local democracy also resist women's assumption of leadership roles in that democracy. Women who dare to contest and win local elections are often victims of manipulation, physical attack, violence and humiliation. A mind-set of cynicism pervades India-portraying elected women representatives as puppets of men. Yet, study after study has shown that once women come into power, the overwhelming majority exercise power independently.

Women are making a difference. Against all odds, women in panchayati raj are already making headway in areas of immediate concern to their families and their villages. These issues, often ignored by men, range from health and sanitation to campaigns against alcoholism and domestic violence. At the dawn of this new millennium, many of the entrenched social evils that have persisted for thousands of years are beginning to change.

Women are transforming the development agenda to address issues critical to village life:

- *Addressing Social Evils*: Women take action to address crucial social issues such as dowry, domestic violence, child marriage and child labour. They ensure that women know their rights and have access to information. They commit themselves to include traditionally excluded groups-the landless, scheduled castes and tribes.

- *Redefining Leadership*: Women are changing the nature of leadership, incorporating values such as honesty, openness, patience, collective support, inclusion and accountability.
- *Health*: Women-who are most often affected by poor health throughout their lives-take a stand for better nutrition, sanitation facilities, safe drinking water, and access to reproductive health care essential for healthy families and communities.
- *Education*: Women organise literacy courses for other women in the community. They ensure that schools are built for children, that teachers are held accountable, and that both girls and boys attend.
- *Income Generation*: Women form self-help groups and credit organisations among themselves to increase family income. Women leaders organise skills training for the women of the community.
- *Changing Village Dynamics*: In even the most conservative villages, women's leadership unleashes a process of change for the whole community. Women leaders empower other women to step out of the home, become literate and contribute to the community. They help to dissolve old prejudices, creating new partnerships with men.

CAMPAIGN IN PANCHAYATI RAJ

The Hunger Project in India is committing itself to ignite and sustain a co-ordinated, strategic campaign of action for women's leadership and the success of panchayati raj. The Hunger Project is beginning this initiative in four states where there has been strong official support for panchayati raj: Gujarat, Karnataka, Madhya Pradesh and Rajasthan. It intends to expand the campaign to all 11 states where The Hunger Project works.

Four-pronged Strategy: The Hunger Project's Panchayati Raj Campaign initially has four major components: alliance-building, leadership training, increasing media coverage and generating international support. The Hunger Project will identify additional high-leverage pathways for action as the campaign unfolds.

1. *Building Alliances for Advocacy and Action*: Women's leadership and panchayati raj are opportunities of such scale and importance that such a campaign can only be carried out by an alliance of organisations in each state committed to this issue. The Hunger Project is working strategically to build strong and active alliances among government agencies, NGOs, self-help groups, academics and media in support of women's leadership in panchayati raj.
2. *Leadership Skills Training*: India is blessed with many organisations providing training to equip women panchayat leaders with key factual information, such as the roles and responsibilities of panchayats, and details of government programmes. What appears to be missing-and what The Hunger Project is in a unique position to provide-is training for these women in fundamental leadership skills.

   Elected women representatives have grown up in an environment that tells them, day after day, that they-as women-are powerless. They have had precious few opportunities to develop their leadership skills. The Hunger Project has created a new Women's Leadership Workshop to enable women to have a breakthrough in their leadership skills, and to empower their leadership over time.

   Vision, Commitment and Action: In the workshop, women discover that they possess the power to actually change conditions they have considered both intolerable and hopeless. They generate their own vision for what they want to achieve, and learn how to inspire others to stand with them to achieve it. After a lifetime of doing only what they have been told, women discover their ability to create their own strategies and action plans. In the months following the training, participants come back together to support each other in achieving their goals.

3. *Increasing and Improving Media Coverage*: The Hunger Project has held workshops and press conferences to educate reporters about the untold success stories of women in panchayati raj. To enhance and expand this effort, The Hunger Project is launching the Sarojini Naidu Prize for Best Reporting on Women in Panchayati Raj.
4. *International Support*: India's pioneering work in panchayati raj sets an important example for countries around the world. People in both developed and developing countries need to know about and maintain support for these efforts. Through strategic communications and site visits, The Hunger Project is mobilising its global constituency to put and keep the international spotlight on this historic phenomenon.

The Sarojini Naidu Prize

For Best Reporting of Women in Panchayati Raj

Sarojini Naidu (1879-1949) was a poet of repute and an orator and was popularly known as the "Nightingale of India". A close associate of Mahatma Gandhi, she was a prominent leader of the freedom movement and was president of the Indian National Congress in 1925.

After independence, she became the first woman governor of an Indian state. The press plays a critical role in India. Throughout the twentieth century, India's media have participated in the Freedom Movement, generated response to famine and disaster, and strengthened Indian democracy. India's new constitutional commitment to women's leadership in panchayati raj is the next unfolding of human freedom and development in India.

It is time for the press to make another important contribution. Only through accurate and increased coverage of the historic process of women's participation in panchayati raj-including their battles to achieve hard-won successes-can the mind-set of cynicism be broken and the conspiracy to undermine panchayati raj be halted. Given the critical role of the press in this historic process. The Hunger Project is committed to supporting and encouraging the press to energetically and prominently report the breakthroughs and success stories of women's leadership in panchayati raj.

The Sarojini Naidu Prize will annually honour three journalists for outstanding reporting on women in panchayati raj. The awards will be presented in each of three categories:

- Best Hindi-Language Reporting
- Best English-Language Reporting
- Best Reporting in other languages

Cash Award: Each prize will include a Rs 2 lakhs cash award to enable the reporter to continue his or her work on this issue.

October 2: In recognition of the importance placed by Mahatma Gandhi on panchayati raj and the full participation of women in public life, the award will be presented on Mahatma Gandhi's birthday each year in New Delhi, beginning on 2 October 2001.

WOMEN TOWRDS FUTURE

Across India, The Hunger Project is seizing the historic opportunity of the election of one million grassroots women to local government. As women take office, they shift the agenda towards health, education, nutrition and family income. The Hunger Project has a four-prong strategy to empower these women leaders:

- Leadership Training for women representatives
- Making panchayats effective through mobilizing people's participation and advocacy to shift resources and authority to the local level.
- Alliance Building to support these women in achieving their vision
- Mobilizing the media to transform public attitudes
- LATEST NEWS: April 2007: THP-India Update to the Global Board
- March 6, 2007-Hunger Project plays leadership role in national celebration of International Women's Day

A COMPARACTIVE ANALYSIS

The concept "status of women" eludes precise definition and hence precise measurement. Status can be perceived in different ways: the extent of a woman's access to social and material resources within the family, community and society (Dixon, 1978), or her authority or power within the family/ community and the prestige commanded from those other members (Mukerjee, 1975), or her position in the social system distinguishable from, yet related to, other positions (Committee on the Status of Women in India, 1974), or the extent to which women have access to knowledge, economic resources and political power as well as the degree of autonomy they have in decision-making and making personal choices at crucial points in their life-cycle. The idea of status also connotes the notion of equality. There can be self-perceived status, group-perceived status or objective status, a situation which can lead to status inconsistency when a person is very high in one type of status and very low in another.

Women's Status in Retrospect

During the Vedic and Rigvedic periods (approximately 4000-1000 BC), women in India held equal status with that of men. The degradation of women started only since 300 BC. The patriarchal joint-family system, structure of property ownership, early marriage, self-immolation of widows (sati) or state of permanent widowhood, all became obstacles to the development of women. Since the late nineteenth and early twentieth centuries of the common era, several reformers fought against those aspects of the system that have resulted in the oppression of females. To them, women should labour under no dissatisfaction not suffered by man, and as a result of their efforts, independent India has adopted several rules and regulations to protect the rights of women and establish equality of status.

India is home to a diverse group of people characterized by different languages, customs, traditions, religions, life-styles or habits. Virtually each State has its own culture, which is very important in studying any aspect of this society including the status of its women.

Objectives and Indicators

Three types of comparison are attempted in this book:

(a) an inter-state comparison of the status of women,

(b) an intra-state comparison of the status of women vis-a-vis that of men in each State, and

(c) a comparison of status of women in relation to overall development.

This analysis of the objective status of women (as perceived by others on the basis of the outward manifestations of some selected characteristics) uses secondary data. Fourteen States having a population of 10 million or more are considered in the study, which together accounted for 313 million females in 1981 and 379 million in 1991. Some generally accepted proxies for "status" are identified and used within the constraints of data availability. Indicators such as a woman's control over resources and the laws of inheritance governing her right to property, perhaps would have reflected female status better, but could not be included because of the non-availability of data.

In all, 28 variables are considered; they reflect the status dimensions of education, employment, health, demographic situation and overall development. Owing to data limitations, the study relates to the early 1980s since most of the pertinent information is available only for that period rather than the current decade. However, this situation should not be of much concern in assessing a slowly changing society like India where drastic social changes normally do not occur in the short span of 10 years.

Employment

Remunerative employment is considered to be one of the major status-deciding factors. The common belief is that man's high status within the family is due to his position as bread-winner. It is argued that, if a woman's economic dependence can be reduced by her ability to earn an income outside the household, she would enjoy a higher status, which would be the case if there was not much difference in the nature of the work done by males and females (Lal, 1979). In this study, employment is represented by adult paid workers, modern sector workers and elected officials. Women's participation in paid employment has been found to be highly related to their status, because it shows the tendency among women to earn a living or to augment the family's income by working for others. Women's participation in modern sector work is a step ahead of any other type of paid employment. The modern sector is defined in this book as including all professional, technical, administrative, executive, managerial, clerical and similar work. Until recently, some of these occupations have been monopolized by males. Consideration of the indicator "elected officials" helps to show the extent of female participation in overall decision-making from the panchayat (village council) to the central Government levels.

Education

In order to create a sense of community among men and women at home and at work as fellow and equal human beings capable of playing many roles--many of them shared and interchangeable--women must be educated and allowed to participate in all activities (OECD, 1975). In India, the roles traditionally assigned for men and women are that of bread-winners and home-makers, respectively. Thus, the education of girls is not seen as an important requirement for preparing girls for their future role as "home-makers".

As such, in States where, besides economic need, the social and individual demand for education is also recognized, one would expect a higher rate of enrolment of girls in schools and a higher proportion of educated women in the population than is actually the case. In reality, women's creative and intellectual potentials are either ignored or underplayed in education in India. As a consequence, generally fewer women are found to have had the opportunity of gaining a higher level of education in India. This pattern of behaviour cannot be attributed to current attitudes alone; they have been molded over several generations. This particular aspect is represented by the percentage of educated older persons in each State.

Health

Infant mortality rate and expectation of life at birth are accepted indicators of the health situation of any population.

In societies where there is no discrimination between the sexes, women, on average, survive for a longer period than men. In view of this situation, female mortality should be either less than or equal to that of males. Where this is not the case, it can be argued that women do not receive adequate attention (reflecting low status), which leads to higher female mortality rates.2/Other things remaining equal, higher mortality of women would indicate low status compared with States where female mortality is lower.

Women, Marriage and Fertility

Marriage is practically universal in India and large families seem to be the norm even today after more than 40 years of implementing a family planning programme. Early marriage of girls, although illegal, is an accepted practice in many parts of the country. The majority of girls and women in India are infant not allowed by their parents to decide on either the age at which they would like to get married or their partners. This indicates that, in societies where a large segment of the population are poor and where the age at marriage is low, parents are transferring the burden of feeding their female children to someone else as soon as they possibly can.

Thus, it may be concluded that the status of females is comparatively lower in India than in societies where females marry at an older age. The singulate mean age at marriage and the proportion of ever-married girls in the 10-19 year age group are two of the three indicators used in this regard. The total fertility rates has been selected as the third indicator under the assumption that a high TFR indicates little control by women over their fertility behaviour owing to their low status.

Overall Development

The development indicators 16-28 are used to determine whether the differences in status, if any, are reflections of differences in the levels of overall development. The various development aspects covered here are urbanization, agriculture, manufacturing, electricity consumption, transport and communication, health and economic situation. In all, 13 variables are included.

PANCHAYATS IN RURAL DEVELOPMENT PERSPECTIVE

Panchayats have been the backbone of the Indian villages since the beginning of the recorded history. Mahatma Gandhi in 1946 had aptly remarked that the Indian independence must begin at the bottom and every village ought to be a Republic or panchyayat having powers. Gandhiji's dream has been translated into reality with the introduction of the three-tier. Panchayati Raj system to enlist people's participation in rural reconstruction in the 21st century village panchayats in india will be in the forefront of rural development towards this end, panchayats are to be given more powers finance and training panchayats growth, social development and facilitate good governance as well as sound micro-economic management.

The realization that people's participation is crucial for successful implementation of programmes like CD and NES was brought to sharp focus through the report of the team for the study of community projects and National Extension Service by Balvantrai Rai Mehta (1957). The committee observed that one of the least successful aspects of CD and NES work is its attempt to evoke popular initiative and recommended democratic decentralization.

The word 'Democracy' is derived from the green roots '*demos*' Meaning the people and '*krato*' meaning authority i. e. in democracy all authority originates from the people. Decentralization means distribution of functions and powers from a central authority to regional & local authorities democratic decentralization in the present context means that the government which has derived its authority from the people redistribute it to some extent to the people for decision and action at the local level. This is popularly known as PANCHAYATI RAJ in India. The policy of democratic decentralization envisages.

i. The establishment of elected and organically linked democratic bodies at the village blocks and district levels;
ii. The entrustment of all planning and developmental activities to these bodies;
iii. Transfer of adequate resources to these bodies to enable them to discharge duties.

Ashok Mehta (1978), in the report of the committee of Panchayati Raj Institutions (PRIs) indentified three phases of Panchayati Raj in India.

1. The phase of ascendency (1959-64)
2. The phase of stagnation (1965-69)
3. The phase of decline (1969-77)

THE CONSTITUTION SEVENTY-THIRD AMENDMENT ACT, 1992

To establish Panchayati Raj on firm footing, the constitution of India was amended, which may be regarded as a landmark in the process of democratic decentralization. The salient features of the constitutions Seventy Third AMENDMENT ACT, 1992 (Legislative Department government of India, 1993) were as follows the provisions of the act were applicable in all the states and union territories, except in some specified areas.

Constitutions of Panchayats-Panchayats shall be constituted in every state at the village, intermediate and district levels Panchayats in a state having a population not exceeding twenty lakhs.

Compositions of Panchayats-All the seats in a Panchayat shall be filled by direct election. The chairperson of the panchayats at the village levels shall be represented in the panchayats at the intermediate level or, in case of a level, in the panchayats at the district levels. The chairpersons of the panchayats at the intermediate levels shall be represented in the panchayats at the district levels. The M.Ps and M.L.As shall be represented in the panchayats at the intermediate and district levels. The members of the council of states and the M.L.Cs shall be represented at the intermediate and district levels. The chairperson of a panchayat at the village level shall be elected such manner as the legislature of a state may, by law provide. The chairperson of a panchayat at the intermediate level or district level shall be elected by and from amongst, the elected members there of.

Reservation of Seats

Seats shall be reserved for the scheduled castes (SC) and scheduled tribes (ST) in every panchayat. The number of seats so reserved shall bear the same proportion to the total number of seats to be filled by direct election in that panchayat, as the population of sc and st in that panchayat area bears to the total population of that area such seats may be allotted by rotation to different constituencies in a panchayat of.

- Not less than one-third of the total number of seats reserved under the clause shall be reserved for woman belonging to the Sc and ST.
- Not less than one-third (including the number of seats reserved for woman belonging to the SC and ST) of the total number of seats to be filled by direct election in every panchayat shall be reserved for woman. Such seats may be allotted by rotation to different constituencies in a panchayat.
- Not less than one-one third of the total number of offices of chairpersons in the panchayats at each level should be reserved for woman. The number of offices reserved shall be allotted by rotation to different panchayats at each level.
- Duration of panchayats-Every Panchayat shall normally continue for a period of five years.

Powers, Authority and Responsibilities of Panchayats

The legislature of a state may, by law endow the panchayats with such powers and authority as may be necessary to enable them to function as institutions of self Government and such law may provisions for the devolution of powers and responsibilities upon panchayats at the appropriate level, with respect.

- The preparation of plants fro economic development and social justice and
- The implementation of schemes for economic development and social justice as may be entrusted

Powers to impose taxes by and funds of the panchayats-

- The legislature of a state may be law, authorize a panchayat to levy, collect and appropriate taxes, duties, tolls and fees,

- Assign to a Panchayat taxes, duties, tolls and fees levied and collect by the state government;
- Provide for making grants-in-aid to the Panchayat from the consolidated fund of the state; and provide for constitution of funds for crediting all moneys received.

Constitution of Finance Commission

A Finance commission shall be constituted in each state to review the financial position of the Panchayat and to make recommendations.

Audit of Accounts of Panchayat

The legislature of a state may, by law make provisions with respects to maintenance of accounts by the Panchayat and the auditing of such accounts.

Elections to the Panchayat

The Superintendence directions and control of the preparation of electrol rolls for, and conduct of all elections to the Panchayat shall be vested in a state elections commission consisting of an election commissioner.

7

Political and Social Empowerment of Women in PRIs

The Constitution of India recognizes the political rights of women without any discrimination, distinction or qualification, to participate in the decision-making process at all levels. After five decades of strides in democracy and development, womens participation and their role in public life has not made the desired headway. The field reality is that womens constitutional right in decision-making at all levels, whether national or local is still marginal. The Lok Sabha general elections between 1989.1999 clearly showed that voting by women has declined. In the 1989 general elections approximately 71 per cent of men voted in contrast only 43 per cent of the women voted and in 1991 elections 52 per cent of men voted when there were 47 per cent women who voted. It would not be far from truth to state that no serious effort appears to have been made to mobilise women as an important political constituency by any political party.

Statistics indicate that the proportion of women contestants in parliamentary constituencies has not increased significantly over the years. Political parties seem reluctant to field women candidates. In the 1993 Lok Sabha there were only 35 women members in the house of 543 members and in the Rajya Sabha 28 women in the house of 245. The records of subsequent parliaments, also indicate similar trends. Generally speaking, the Indian society and its dominant culture over the centuries have downgraded the status of women, socially and economically depriving them of opportunities for development, participation and management. Women, who form the majority of country's illiterate, are underpaid or unpaid servants of society and family with no chance of expressing free opinions of their own. They are also objects of oppression or subjects of welfare. They are often relegated to the background and marginalised.

The process of empowerment will open a new vista of human resource development to them and bring them in the mainstream of social and economic development. The task that faces the government and society in setting right this inequality in sharing of power in a diverse and complex country with many religions and linguistic variations is how to overcome the attitudinal, institutional, cultural and social restrictions that have grown over the centuries. Women's progress has been painfully slow and even today they remain the poorest of the poor. In the emerging new economic order and liberalized world order the women who have lower level skills will get further marginalised. Almost 90 per cent women in employment work in the unorganised sectors and therefore outside the purview of protection. The provisions of the 73rd Constitutional Amendments and the Panchayati Raj Acts would give opportunities for their socio-political advancement. Guided and well-planned empowerment thus, can make them overcome the inferior status in the family and society and emerge as capable equal partners of men. Such equal participation will lead to a qualitative change not merely in womens lives but in the functioning of public institutions and nature of politics in our democracy.

AWARENESS

Knowledge is power. Deprivation of knowledge is reflection of their lack of awareness of various issues, agencies, procedures, schemes, projects and methods of management. Information on these and access to such information therefore becomes critical in their empowerment. The corner stone of the strategy to help women empower themselves is to facilitate various processes of action through which awareness can be generated. This will evolve dissemination of information and training in handling and using media appropriately. The identification of the training process and training needs of persons involved at different levels of Panchayati Raj and selection of training institutions is a major theme of empowerment.

POLITICAL EDUCATION

(a) Those women who have already entered panchayats through elections need to be politically educated and informed regarding the concepts and relevance of Panchayati Raj institutions, the functioning of state machinery, the Indian Constitution, the nature of Indian democracy and the policies and programmes for women and other weaker sections of the society.

(b) Women in the community who are by definition members of gram sabha who participate in election by way of contesting or voting would need training for campaigning in election or questioning the candidate. Political education can be imparted on the basis of concrete information, information on social issues, the current political development and trends, legislation, developmental schemes and other topics. Policy information and political mobilisation are mutually strengthening and would result in positive peoples movement for implementing many social-economic reforms which have had a tardy progress. Political training should aim at tapping their hidden potential and it should seek to build political awareness on the basis of collectively common interest and community development.

(c) Role of Catalytic Organisation Political action groups, the National Service Volunteers and woman study groups, agricultural extension institutions as well as agricultural colleges and universities, and social work departments can be mobilised as link organisation to play the role of catalyst. These institutions can provide necessary inputs for political education. Further, womens self-help groups, social activists, Mahila Mandals and grassroots level NGOs add positive vigour to the process. Networking and effective linkages open up new vistas.

ECONOMIC EMPOWERMENT OF WOMEN IN PANCHAYAT

The constitutionally mandated panchayats were visualised as institutions of self-governance. States would devolve power to the PRIs and give them resources and responsibilities so that they emerge as institutions of self-governance instead of remaining as agencies for developmental administration only. As the process of devolution is slow, it requires pressure from womens groups to force state governments to act fast and issue notifications to make it possible and practically brought to the field. Empowerment of women in political terms is a must to ensure this process.

The empowerment of powerless sections of society. women, Scheduled Caste/Scheduled Tribes (SC/STs). does not happen by merely giving them representation in the PRIs.

The 73rd Constitution Amendment promises that through a representative democracy, that is, by giving representation to socially and economically disadvantaged sections, PRIs will gradually be transformed from merely representative to participatory bodies. This, in fact, was implied in the provision of 1/3 representation to women. It envisages a shift from meeting the developmental needs of the people to enabling them to undertake developmental planning and bring about a change in development perspective. Democratic decentralisation presupposes that people not only have control over the resources but also have a perspective as to how to plan and allocate the resources at the local level.

DEVOLUTION OF POWERS BY STATE GOVERNMENTS A MUST FOR EMPOWERMENT

The 11th Schedule of the amendment of the Constitution specifies 29 areas of responsibility covering all aspects of village life, which states may transfer to panchayats along with sufficient resources and decision making authority. As mentioned, many states are yet to establish and accomplish this important task. Out of the 11th Schedule some of the areas that women members bear primary responsibility for are noted below:

(1) Agriculture, including agriculture extension
(2) Minor irrigation, water management and watershed management
(3) Animal husbandry, diary and poultry
(4) Fisheries
(5) Social forestry and farm forestry
(6) Minor forest produce. MFP
(7) Drinking water
(8) Fuel and fodder
(9) Poverty alleviation programmes
(10) Education, including primary and secondary schools
(11) Adult and non-formal education
(12) Health and sanitation, including hospitals and primary health centres (PHCs)
(13) Family welfare
(14) Women and child development,
(15) Social welfare, including welfare of the handicapped and mentally retarded, and
(16) Maintenance of community assets.

These indicate that there is an urgent need for State governments to issue notifications specifying devolution of administrative and financial powers to the panchayats.

SIDA'S COMMITMENT TO WOMEN EMPOWERMENT THROUGH ACTION PROGRAMMES AND RESEARCH IN RAJASTHAN: 1996

In 1996, with Sida support, ISS selected Rajasthan to launch an experimental project to take initiatives for action to empower elected women representatives of panchayats after the panchayat elections in 1995. What really motivated ISS is the basic recommendation given by the Conference on Panchayati Raj and political, social and economical empowerment of women held in April 1995.

For India to build up a broad-based, solid foundation for economic and social progress it must uproot the last vestiges of feudalism and instill democratic values and practices. The people who live in the villages of India must become authors of their own lives and become sensitive to the needs of women, and women must be respected and supported in the process of development.

Initially ISS selected three districts representing three distinct geographical regions of state (Alwar, Pali and Rajsamand). Each district is different in terms of agricultural patterns, socioeconomic development and history of peoples participation in the freedom struggle.

Zilla parishads, panchayat samitis and gram panchayats in the whole state. This also gives the total number of zilla parishads, panchayat samitis and gram panchayats selected for studies. The number of cases chosen for studies in the three districts were 3 zilla parishads with six women from them, 6 panchayat samitis with 18 women from them and 16 gram panchayats with 48 women from them.

SECOND STAGE OF PROGRAMME (JANUARY 1997 TO DECEMBER 2000)

Based on the experiences gathered in Rajasthan and the positive results observed, the Swedish International Development Agency (Sida) supported a three-year programme: Empowerment of Women through Panchayats in Rajasthan and Orissa., beginning January 1997.

The areas identified for implementation of this programme are three districts of Rajasthan (Alwar, Kota, Pali) and three districts of Orissa (Jagatsinghpur, Nuapada, Rayagada). The long-term objectives of this innovative project and action plan is to work towards political empowerment of women, that is, to prepare them fully to become effective partners in the decision making process, thereby leading towards the envisaged decentralised planning process.

The second objective is to bring about change in the patriarchal, caste-ridden hierarchical society into a more egalitarian and just society through making elected women representatives as agents of change.. Further, efforts should be made to generate a development process that is more gender-friendly, and finally, to strengthen the third tier of village level institutions including the Gram Sabhas, which are the lifeline of panchayat system.

Short Term Objectives

- to examine the nature and extent of womens participation in Panchayati Raj institutions in the light of their social background factors, class, caste, age, education, marital status
- and to identify the factors (both within the public and private sphere) which may hinder their participation in the political process and democratic institutions at different levels.
- to closely identify concerns and priorities raised by women in meetings and analyse the treatment meted out to them within the gender dynamics and background of the elected women representatives.
- to articulate, give expression to and find solutions to the problems and conflicts which women members might be facing in their work.
- to help them to take up issues with higher authorities.
- to instill confidence among women members by providing opportunities to meet their peers, share experiences and learn about their political rights and powers.
- to monitor performance of women panchayat members and to codify the lessons learnt for wider dissemination for the benefit of women in other districts in the same state as well as in other states.

Study Areas of the Project

The status of women in Rajasthan is very low, and this is reflected in zero female literacy rates in some villages, higher incidence of female infanticide, low female sex ratio and patriarchal society. In Rajasthan, the districts selected for the study are Alwar, Kota and Pali, which also represent divergent problems, caste, low female literacy and patriarchal society. On the other hand, in Orissa, the status of women is relatively high. However, a majority of the tribal population lives in abject poverty and ignorance, incapable of receiving the fruits of growth percolating down to them. The districts identified for the project (Jagatsinghpur, Nuapara, Rayagada) also represented varying sections of ethnic populations at different levels of socioeconomic development.

Among the non-tribal population in both States, the benefits of development reach women the last; where they do reach they reach slowly and haltingly. The development process for the past fifty years, both in Rajasthan and the coastal areas of Orissa, has created a middle class income population, but there is need for empowerment of women in these communities.

The panchayat elections in Rajasthan were conducted in February 1995 and after the expiry of the term, elections were held again in 2000. The project study was made for the panchayats elected for the term 1995.2000, even though the project could be started only in 1996.98. The newly elected members are being contacted by ISS. On the other hand, in Orissa, panchayat elections were held in January 1997 and they will in all likelihood continue in office till 2002. So the project districts in Orissa had the opportunity to study women who were freshly elected.

(a) Keeping the above parameters in mind, the ISS planned a programme of action in the six districts for the three years, i.e. 1998, 1999, 2000. The work related to monitoring the performance of elected women representatives in Panchayats was taken up in the initial programme. Questionnaires on womens participation in PRIs were prepared and distributed among the investigators. After compilation of data a thorough analysis was made and results were used for further intervention.

(b) A detailed book on the social background of the women panchayat members who are within the project was prepared and published as a source material for using during the training programme. These directories were found to be quite valuable and the women members regarded them as valuable possessions.

c) For the members of panchayats, a one-day training programme was organised. About 30 elected members, both men and women, from two panchayats underwent training simultaneously. This was done with a view that men also will be sensitised through their participation so that they can get a clear understanding of the role of women in Panchayats and in society.

The content and methods of the training undertaken by the ISS can be given as follows:

i) Interactive discussions instead of structural lectures;

ii) Role-plays.

iii) Simple learning materials in Hindi and Oriya were prepared and distributed and used extensively with required photographs and illustrations;

iv) Case studies of success and failures of women in panchayats were explained. There was reporting about the initiative taken by various members of panchayats who received training during the first stage of the project;

v) Rajasthan and Orissa Panchayat Acts were prepared in simple Oriya and Hindi as background materials and explained to the members in the interactive sessions;

vi) Video film shows were a strong and integral part of the training programme. Video film shows on womens empowerment and thereafter discussions were significant impact on the minds of the people, especially those who are illiterate world benefited maximum with this exercise. The ISS organised regular video shows to impress upon the Panchayat members about their role and the requirements of empowerment.

d) The directory of the women members under study (one page for each member with a passport size photograph, her address, and other important details) was prepared and distributed. This step provided information to the people in the Panchayats and other parts of the State about the elected members. It has enhanced womens status and boosted their self-esteem in the society.

e) Appropriate banners carrying messages such as Womens Political Empowerment is through Panchayats were displayed in the village streets, market places and other common public areas. Appropriate wall writings in the selected villages, blocks with an objective of creating the much needed atmosphere and awareness about panchayats and womens participation in it, were encouraged.

f) Two-day conferences at the inter-village panchayat, inter-block panchayat and district and state levels were organised. The conferences focused on issues such as the importance of grassroots level democracy, role of local government and development of society, womens participation in decision-making and many other relevant topics. Such programmes held in the panchayats boosted the morale of panchayat members, especially women, which otherwise got sidelined by vested interests.

g) Case studies and profile of women members were prepared. This included their struggle for success, difficulties in achieving their aspirations and their suggestions for rectification of the system.

The Institute was responsive to situations that arose from time to time. This approach facilitated maximisation of benefits to the target group as envisaged in the programme. The Institute is making an effort to make these districts into model districts from the point of functioning of the panchayats. The grant given by Sida was utilised in the broad framework of investing in people for creating much-needed social capital as well as institutions in order to build a society where women and men are equal partners.

PURPOSE AND SCOPE OF EVALUATION

The constitutionally mandated panchayat bodies were visualised as institutions of self-governance, and state governments are to devolve administrative and financial powers to the PRIs and give them resources so that these bodies reach the level of taking care of their affairs themselves. This process of devolution is slow but could be made faster if the elected members, specially the women, are empowered, and that empowerment of women in political terms is a must to ensure this process. It is also to be evaluated about a positive shift from meeting only the development needs of the people to enabling them to undertake development planning and bring about a change in development perceptive. How far the intervention through the activities and programmes of action brought out these changes.

The evaluation also envisages the nature and extent of womens participation in Panchayati Raj institutions in the light of their social background and factors such as class, caste, age, education, marital status and other identifiable factors, which hinder their participation in the political process, and democratic institutions.

Regional variances, differential economic development, availability of infrastructure and education levels indicate different priorities and issues for different areas and villages. The community and members of the panchayats have their own perceptions about their needs in terms of social and economic development. How far ISS interventions have made them (women) raise these issues at the panchayat level including the gram sabhas are to seen. Were there appreciable changes on the treatment meted out to suggestions and firm recommendation of women members? When the women members are brought to level of confidence which enables them to articulate and select suitable solutions to the problems and issues that they raise for the benefit of the common good, there is great need to prepare them for taking up various issues to the higher authorities including the zilla parishad, and in the governmental level to the BDO and collector.

Exchange of ideas with women members of other panchayats and sharing of experiences and learning about the progress made by them is a very important aspect of the objectives of the interventions. All these interventions would add to enhanced functional efficiency and completion of projects and programmes in the panchayat for imparting social justice. These achievements made by the women members through their own initiative and efforts are codified for larger exchange and wider dissemination for the benefit of women in other districts.

THEMATIC LEVEL-GRASSROOT LEVEL INTENSIVE CONTACT

The relevance of empowerment of women through the programme intervention adopted and introduced by ISS is well-focused taking into consideration how far these composite exercises introduced by ISS have given progressive shape to the overall objectives of the programmes.

(a) The first task of the programme was to make initial informal contact with the elected representatives important members of village and communities and express the intent of ISS on what exactly they were planning to introduce into the Panchayati Raj system. This was a difficult task which ISS could establish through a group of dedicated local level youth, both boys and girls, the more among them being girls. These investigators were motivated and trained with the specific tasks of interventions from time to time. A majority of the elected women ward members of the panchayats were illiterate only 10% of them had completed Class 10 and 70% attended school up to Class 5, the remaining had not received any formal education. Initially, very frequent visits were made by the investigators, block level coordinators and district level cordinators to ascertain the eagerness and willingness of these women members to take up the planned empowerment programme. During the course of field visits for evaluation it was strongly expressed by the village elders and the members of the civil society that elected members of the panchayat were very keen to get acquire knowledge about various aspects of the panchayat programme and its effective functioning. In the absence of any organised programme of this nature initiated by the government or any other body these women came very close to ISS field staff and started to open up and express their difficulties and grievances to get the required help and assistance. The transparency of the communication between these women and the investigators and coordinators was one of the most important composition of empowerment. Once the initial ice is broken the village communities come forward to support the investigators in their work of providing elected members with more information and training.

(b) Thereafter, workshops were organised in which 32 to 40 representatives participated and various subjects were introduced such as highlights of the Constitutional Amendment Act, powers of the panchayats, duties of the elected members, responsibilities of gram panchayats and conduct of Gram Sabha meetings. After this, periodical visits were made to oversee the performance of the elected members in discharging their duties as envisaged under the Act. Initially there were difficulties, but by gradual motivation and encouragement many of them shed their shyness and came out openly to express how they intended to solve the problems of the village community. After a period of three months, training programmes were organised with specific subjects introduced to them in a simple manner so that during these interactive sessions they could clarify their doubts about various aspects of their functioning. Local government officials from the development departments, prominent members of NGOs, college teachers dealing with social sciences also gave their valuable time and made efforts to be associated with these programmes. The most important and striking result of this is that the women members learn the art of effective articulation to make their suggestions and recommendations clearly and logically to the authorities. They felt very enthused when they acquired the skill of taking interview with senior block development officials to represent the case of the village in development.

(c) The above interventions made it possible to introduce to these members the importance of holding periodical Gram sabhas with well regulated agenda points and also explain to the members of other village the progress made in various socio-economic activities. Gram sabhas were at first attended very thinly; with the efforts of the investigators and active members the attendance grew in strength and the quality of participation improved. Many of these women members expressed their happiness that well coordinated and orchestrated gram sabha meetings brought out meaningful and useful suggestions for the composite planned development of the village. The minutes of these meetings were recorded with the help of investigators and sent to the panchayat meetings for their consideration and support. These efforts brought about an indirect pressure on the authorities of panchayat hierarchy to clear sanctions for the projects. Some of the panchayat women sarpanches were keen to take up these issues with the Block Development Officers for getting their genuine needs met. All these improvements were possible with the continuous efforts of the field staff working for the project. After a period of one year a district level convention was organised in which about 250 women representatives participated. This gave them the opportunity to exchange ideas and share information on the progress made in their respective panchayats. After this convention field level activities were intensified through field visits and maintaining of close contact by the field staff.

Observations of the field study on the impact of the programmatic interventions can be summarised as follows:

a) In the light of social background factors caste, age, education level and other factors the interventions by the ISS brought all these women representatives under one umbrella. Caste and class barriers narrowed down. Parda system, and shyness among village women started disappearing. They acquired courage to express their views both in formal and informal gatherings.

b) The women started showing keen interest to learn more about panchayat administration and community development.

c) These changes amongst the women brought respectability for them in the community.

d) With the help of the field staff they started taking initiatives to solve problems in the community.

e) The women acquired the confidence to share their experiences and also learn from their peers.

f) The women were encouraged to meet higher authorities of the government and represent their problems before them.

g) There is a wind of change in the panchayats as these women are acting as agents of change..

h) In the course of discussions they complained that the panchayats are not provided with adequate funds from the state government to meet their development needs.

i) They are getting slowly sensitised to the issues concerning social evils; they need more support to equip them for awareness and programme interventions in this area.

j) Great eagerness is demonstrated by the women to accomplish social justice for the marginalised and underprivileged.

k) A majority of them pleaded that they need more intervention for improving their awareness and functional capabilities.

l) They have started organising womens groups for income generating activities and thrift societies and need more support.

m) Initiatives are required for raising income from the Panchayats common assets, MFP sale, etc.

n) The secretaries to the panchayats have started co-operating better with woman sarpanches. This has improved the administration of Panchayats.

o) Block level officers are looking at the quality of change in the study area and then to expand the programme to other areas.

Periodicity and extent of the Gram Sabha meetings and improved participation of women voters in these meetings added a new dimension to the participatory approach of PRI. Minutes were prepared and sent up to Gram Sabhas. Gram Panchayat is acquiring the status of a neutral body to take care of the problems of the villages without any prejudice and extraneous considerations. This will improve the happiness and satisfaction of the Gram Panchayats as a whole. Even though ISS had made some arrangements to include male representatives in some of their programmes, it was observed that there is a need for introducing programmes for sensitising male members of the villages on gender issues and impressing upon them that women play as important a role as men in all activities of the community and that their potential must be used for development participation and management. This thematic change can be easily incorporated by ISS in their programmes without diluting the theme empowerment of women for social change..

Knowledge is power and its application brings about positive changes in the society. Awareness creation is an important area which requires emphasis for future interventions in the programme. Twenty-nine specific areas of responsibility covering all aspects of village life shown in the Amendments requires detailed introduction with such schemes under various Ministries and Departments. This will have to be prepared in detail by way of modules and effectively introduced to the panchayat. ISS will have to prepare necessary material for it as well as prepare the trainers.

THEMATIC CAPACITY OF THE ISS AND FIELD STAFF

Field Staff as a friend and philosopher ISS was founded in 1985 as a registered society to study contemporary social, political and economic issues, and problems that confront the country, in an inter-disciplinary perspective and make its findings and recommendations to the members of the decision-making organisations at various levels.

ISS has a highly qualified, motivated and experienced Director who is supported by research faculty consisting of senior fellows and senior research officers to add to its academic and research standard. Institute also seeks to build a large community of concerned scholars and activists engaged in ushering in a humane and just society. Recently the Institute has been permanently located in a building of its own in the prestigious institutional area of Vasant Kunj. The Institute provides high quality facilities for top class output. The Institute is capable of introducing the thematic of social relevance in an appropriate manner and gradually develop it as the programme progresses in spread and depth. So far the direction given by the ISS has had dramatic impact in the initial introduction of the theme empowerment of Women in the Panchayat.. in the most backward blocks of the underdeveloped districts. ISS has got the inherent capability to adopt and incorporate shifts for strengthening the programme and enlarging the scope. ISS Headquarters have assigned responsibility to two senior research officers to coordinate field programmes and report to the director. Dr. Ramesh C. Nayak is in charge of Rajasthan and Dr. Ms. Bidyut Mohanty is in charge of Orissa. Detailed discussion and interviews with these officers have left positive impressions of their capabilities, methodology and application for having taken this programme to an effective level and demonstrated visible results in the field. They are a great asset to the programme.

At the state level according to the availability of retired senior personnel from the government or NGOs state coordinators were assigned. In Orissa Shri Nirakar Beura was inducted into the project as State Co-ordinator since its inception in 1997. His experience, commitment and vision was demonstrated through the results which have reached into the far-flung areas of Rayagada and Nuapara districts. He was in constant touch with grassroot level workers, community elders, members of civic society and local government staff engaged in the developmental activities of the state. Since January 1999, Shri K.K. Patnaik, former Director (Panchayats) and Rural Development has been Regional Co-ordinator of ISS in Bhubaneshwar with his vast experience in the Department of Panchayats and Rural Development, he will be a great asset for the project. In Rajasthan the responsibility was given to Shri Kaushik the regional youth co-ordinator of Nehru Yuva Kendra Sanghatan. With his vast experience in working with youth and association with Mahilla Mandals and youth clubs, he could easily establish rapport with women members. Similarly, the contribution of the 6 district coordinators block coordinators and filed investigators have contributed immensely to the success of the project.

Block co-ordinators and district co-ordinators as well as village level investigators were all motivated to the level needed to accomplish the tasks assigned to them. Their responsibility is given below.

The job of the State Co-ordinator is:

1. To assist project co-ordinator in preparing literature for training.

2. To assist the project co-ordinator in organising workshops, state level conference, and training programmes.
3. To assist in preparing wall posters and cloth banners on Womens Empowerment through Panchayats..
4. Supervising the training and research work of district co-ordinators.
5. To report to the project co-ordinator every month.

District Co-ordinators

Each district is in charge of a district co-ordinator. These district co-ordinators are recruited from the respective districts. They are familiar with local needs and aspirations of the PRI members.

Their job is:

1. To coordinate research and training programmes at the district level.
2. To supervise the work of block co-ordinators.
3. To forward every months progress report to the state co-ordinator and project co-ordinator.

Job of Block Co-ordinator

The block co-ordinators are in charge of the block; their job is:

1. To co-ordinate research work and training progammes at block level.
2. To supervise the work of field investigators.
3. To accurately report every month.s progress to the district coordinator.
4. Organising Training and Awareness Programmes at Gram Panchayat level.
5. To assist in organising gram sabha meetings effectively.

Field Investigators

Field Investigators will work in the Gram Panchayat/village level under the guidance of block coordinators. These investigators will be recruited from the village level.

1. To report success and failure stories of Gram Panchayats and the women panchayat members to block/district coordinators
2. To suggest innovative ideas to the project co-ordinator regarding training/awareness programmes.
3. To motivate women to attend Gram Sabha meetings.
4. To assist block/district co-ordinators in organizing village level workshops, cultural and sports activities.

Apart from this, volunteers from among mainly retired technicians, bureaucrats, school teachers, and other such professionals can support the programme at the village level. They are paid only travel expenses. Being local they can be an asset to the project, when the project staff face problems.

During the course of field visits the field staff accompanied the consultant. Periodical discussions were made with them which give an insight into their commitment and interest in undertaking the task. Some of the female investigators and block co-ordinators who come from modest village backgrounds acquired quite good standard in their performance of the tasks assigned to them by associating with the project. In the light of the suggestions included in this report for thematic shift, appropriate refresher programmes will have to be arranged for these field staff. Advanced thematic changes need introduction of new techniques.

Training for the Elected Women Members

- Training is non-residential and for the day only.
- The medium of communication is the local language/ dialect.
- The master trainers are project staff and active women panchayat members,
- ISS provides all literature on panchayats to master trainers.
- All participants are provided with reading materials on Panchayats prepared by ISS in Hindi/Oriya.
- The emphasis is more on group discussions rather than on classroom teachings.

- Cultural programmes and sports activities for women are organised to motivate them for effective participation.
- All members are personally invited by field investigators to these programmes.
- The training date and course content are announced before hand.
- Loud speakers, banners, posters are used for gram sabha meetings.

Activities

i. National Conference on Womens Political Empowerment held on 24.26 April annually at New Delhi and since two years at state and district levels in study areas.
ii. State Level Conference
iii. Block level conference
iv. Regional workshops on womens participation
v. Cultural programmes and sports activities
vi. Awareness camps for women on panchayats/gram sabhas
vii. Training programmes
viii. Exchange programmes

The details of all the activities are to be fully reported.

SUSTAINABILITY OF THE INTERVENTIONS, BOTH STRUCTURALLY AND THEMATICALLY

The people who live in the villages must become authors of their lives and sensitive to the special needs of women and give support in the process of development. The main objective of the programme is to work towards the political empowerment of women, that is, to prepare them fully to become effective partners in the decision-making process, thereby leading towards a gradual decentralised planning process. Women empowerment will bring about change in the patriarchal, caste-ridden hierarchical society, making it into a more egalitarian and just society, through elected women representatives as agents of this change. To make the programme more effective and practical, there is need for slight shift in the thematics and there by structural adjustment in the existing staffing. This includes networking and involvement of civil society numbers in the process. Indeed, there will be sure necessity for enhanced financial allotment to meet the required changes in the programmes and the emoluments of the staff. The enhanced grants will be utilised in the broad framework of investing in people for creating vibrant social capital and responsive institutions to build a society where women and men are equal partners.

The sustainability of the programme cannot be organised by the people themselves as this involves resources such as finance, competent organisational backup and effective interlinking with governmental organisations working in the field. The support from international bodies, multinational and bi-lateral organisations would be necessary for a decade to cover the backward areas and establish credible standards of developed human resources among the elected members. When such models are placed on the ground, government will be induced to incorporate budget provisions for the purpose of empowerment of the elected members in the neglected areas. Sida should consider extending long-term support for this programme to establish workable models of the empowerment of women through Panchayati Raj.

It was observed that the interventions made by ISS have shaken up district administrations to evolve systems for organising gram sabhas; some of the BDOs have sought assistance from the ISS staff and are scrutinizing the thematics introduced by ISS for improving the conduct of gram sabhas. The emerging interest and sincere efforts from the government side would bring rapid changes to the progressive path of sustainability. Well-prepared and people-friendly models laid on the ground would inspire organisations and bodies to support these efforts.

OBSERVATIONS AT THE FIELD LEVEL

In order to economise on the administrative cost the field offices are established and run in a cost effective and austere way. In many places the district level co-ordinators and block level co-ordinators share the premises of the collaborating agencies. As indicated earlier, through modest training, motivation and the good standard of activities undertaken by them networking was made possible for them with other members of the village community, government agencies and other NGOs; these have added to their capacities for achieving good results. Further, structured refresher training with reserved thematics and added incentives by way of enhanced honoraria to meet the increasing costs of subsistence and travel will result in better implementation. There is a need for covering all the women elected representatives in the block/panchayats under study. Special attention should be given to women who are panchayat members working under male sarpanches. Men should also be included in the training programme for sensitising them about the importance of the participation of women members in the Panchayati Raj administration. This can be worked out by the ISS.

The potential impact of the training programme and interventions was visible in the study area. Womens participation in the gram panchayat meeting and suggestions and decisions have brought about substantial efficiency in the running of the programmes, completion of programmes, and extension of social justice to the needy. It is observed that the level of articulation and identification issues requires more guidance. This can be attained only through continuous training programmes and exposure to the areas of responsibility assigned to them as per the 11th Schedule.

The project structure and the leadership operating it is very effective-proper guidelines are issued periodical field visits and interactive sections held and motivational approaches held out to staffs. The consultant participated in three interactive sections with staff and observed the effectiveness of their perception and field work. These processes along with proper guidance have build up confidence among the staff. The staff at the field level is largely women who are very sensitive to the needs of women PRI members. Periodical travel of the representatives to the block, district, state, and New Delhi accompanied by volunteers have added a new dimension of confidence in them.

Project management was done through clear-cut guidance, field visits and inspections and reports received from lower functionaries to the state level co-ordinators. This gave the required information for monitoring the programme and the progress made in the identifiable goals. Perhaps it will be necessary to make detail planning regarding time-bound activities for the modified programmes.

RECOMMENDATIONS

There is a need for greater awareness generations in the panchayat community for which more NGOs and grassroot workers should be networked. The vision must be to develop PRIs to develop and to retain the character of the sub-governing institutions committed to public good with compassion and sharing with participatory character and approach. We have to make panchayats in to arbingers of an egalitarian and just society through making women elected representative into agents of change. Equal participation will lead to better functioning of public institutions and transform nature of politics in our democracy.

There is a need for slight shift in the strategy as far as the coverage is concerned.

a) As indicated earlier, male members to be brought under the scheme, incorporating them at appropriate levels.

b) Greater thrust to be given in equipping ward members and sarpanches for the administrative and developmental role they have to perform.

c) Introduce more traditional, cultural folk and sports competition to bring about cohesion among the village groups, especially the youth.

d) Prepare modules containing material narrated in simple regional languages as resource/training materials.

e) Awareness has to be built up through interactive discussions and distribution of simple understandable materials.

f) Evaluation of standard of performance of panchayat through local colleges and universities.

g) Intensify awareness campaigns in the colleges and schools about empowerment of women and ISS/Sida activities in this area.

h) In order to equip field staff organise training programmes at appropriate level at the initiative of ISS.

i) In order to bring about quick results in political empowerment, net-working should be done with the local NGOs, women study centre, Mahila Mandals, grassroots level workers, etc. The universities and colleges in the locations can play very effective roles.

j) Generation of self-employment through rural income-generating activities to supplement the income and also to occupy them profitably should be a priority area in the strategy.

Model programmes can be encouraged through the project staff. The vision approach adopted by ISS need not be renewed because of the fact that the programme itself is revolving round a vision of Women elected representatives as agents of change,. women as capable, equal partners of men, an opportunity to develop hidden potential of women for serving the community, and finally to restore rights and equality enshrined in the Constitution. The vision is to take women to reach to the higher echelons of democratic institutions at state and national level.

I) The immediate goals are to make women PRIs to be able to articulate their aspirations, issues of importance to village communities, and also to make them aware of developmental programmes. They must equip themselves with the knowledge of their rights and equalities.

II) Prepare elected gram panchayat members to know their duties, prepare them to effectively discharge their duties.

III) Sensitisation to the eradication of social evils.

IV) Implement the theme that education is basic for strengthening democracy and ushering in development.

V) Introduction of modern science and technology into village life.

VI) Communities, specially male members, should acknowledge the role of women in the community.

VII) Inculcate dignity of the human being and equality as the basic value of the society.

As mentioned earlier in the paragraph on thematic capacity of ISS and performance level of human resources available, there is no doubt that with required support and direction, ISS would be able to prepare the existing field staff to handle the shifts in strategies and introduce elements of upgradation to equip all concerned to reach the goals of the mission. The following suggestions are given in this regard.

- Taking into consideration the output of programme co-ordinators and the added responsibilities which will be thrust upon them, there is a need for upward revision of their emoluments. ISS could decide this upward revision and charge it to the project.
- Each of the programme coordinators may be given part-time secretariat service in preparation and compilation of reports.
- At present, state level co-ordinators are working on part-time basis and this arrangement may continue. They are managed well and motivated by the ISS headquarters. Taking into consideration the added responsibility which would be entrusted on them, there will be need to enhance honoraria paid to them.
- Most important and significant field staff management pertains to the motivation level and training of field staff so as to envisage better output through them at the field level. There is a need for an enhancement of honoraria and travel expenses on par with other voluntary organisations working in the field. These training programmes and upgradation of capability would make the field staff more committed and motivated. ISS has ample capacity to take up to this task.

Financial management of any programme is very vital for the successful achievement of the goals. Swedish International Development Agency was liberal in releasing grants for the programmes which started in 1996, thereafter in the second stage 1997.2000. Annexe. 3 give percentage break-up of the programme (Budget heads). It can be observed from the budget heads that for the period 1996.1997, the following are the details.

i) salary for the programme coordinator and field investigator;
ii) travel for field work;
iii) questionnaire, books, stationary, infrastructure facility, work consultation.
iv) and meeting and overheads.

But for the subsequent period 1998.2000, training programme budget head was added along with literature, background materials and stationery. An additional head for reports and publication was also added. The major expenditure was for salaries for programme coordinator and honoraria for field staff which consumed on an average 35 per cent, travel and field visits 15 per cent training programme expenditure 12.5 per cent, meetings and workshop and consultations varied between 25 per cent to 30 per cent, literature and background materials and stationary 5 per cent, reports and publications 2 per cent, and an average overhead expenditure between 5 to 7.5 per cent. For the period January 1998 to March 2000 consisting of 27 months, the total expenditure is about Rs. 43 lakhs. This indicates average project cost for each state per annum works out to be an average of Rs. 10 lakhs. Under the restructured and enhanced programme content there is a need to raise this financial allocation to Rs. 15 lakh average for each state covering about 25 panchayats. This would mean that for a block period of 2 years the allocation would come about Rs. 60 lakhs to cover both states. The proposed budget heads suggested:

1. Salaries for programme co-ordinators and field staff honoraria = 35 per cent
2. Travel and field visits = 15 per cent
3. Meetings, consultations and exchange visits = 17 per cent
4. Preparation of back ground materials and stationary = 5 per cent
5. Reports and publications and media = 5 per cent
6. Overhead including publicity = 5 per cent
7. Training programme including material = 18 per cent.

Details of minor heads will have to be prepared by ISS. It would be necessary to work out details of expenditure on training programmes meetings and consultations and rationalise it by using facilities available in the districts and other austere measures.

Empowerment of women in the Indian context is to bring about gender equality. Thematic approach to structural planning of the entire programme address the question related to gender equality. When 1/3 of the sarpanches in block are prepared well to manage the affairs of the gram panchayat and take decisions as per rules and regulations, chairing the meeting is one of the achievements reaching towards gender equality. Male ward members in the villages patiently listening to their female sarpanches will definitely bring about gender equality. ISS has very thoughtfully structured their approaches to remove the hurdles in a most gentle way by using interactive sessions, group discussions and other community actions. During the course of the visits in Rajasthan it was a pleasant surprise to listen to the achievements and experiences narrated by the former sarpanches and upa-sarpanches. They were full of confidence and hope about the full gender equality. Some of them have not attended formal schools, but the interventions through this programme have brought out their inner talents which changed their personalities and made them ready to serve the community. Some of them have sufficient calibre to be assigned as trainers for the future generation of elected members.

EXERCISE OF PRI EMPOWERMENT

One of the major areas of concern in the exercise of PRI empowerment is the critical state of the panchayat finance. So far, most of the states have in their possession at least two reports of the SFCs constituted by them.

a. The recommendations of the SFCs are expected to lay the foundations of a sound system of local finance, promote regional balance in respect of basic services and thus be an important step towards effective decentralisation. How do you think the state governments can be made to act on these reports? How will you react if the transfer of Union finance commission grants for local bodies and other devolutions are made conditional on the achievements made in respect of devolution to the PRIs?

b. The state governments have, by and large, failed to adopt definite policies on allocation of funds to the PRIs. Should it be made mandatory for the states to frame legislation in this regard clarifying a definite formula for such devolutions?

c. One of the important tasks of SFC is to determine the size of the divisible pool taking into account the functional domain of the state government and that of the local bodies. The issues are: (i) Should the divisible pool include sharing of only tax revenue or both tax and non-tax revenue? (b) Should central revenue devolution be included? (iii) Do the local bodies have a claim on the central kitty?

d. In order to synchronize the periods covered by the SFCs and the Union Finance Commission, it is necessary to amend Article 243I (1) by inserting the words 'or at such earlier time as the Governor considers necessary' after the words 'at the expiry of every fifth year' to bring it in conformity with Article 280. Such synchronization is considered necessary for making the SFC reports relevant to the period covered by the Union Finance Commission. What is your view?

e. The status of resources raised by the PRIs from own sources is highly unsatisfactory in most of the states. The gram panchayat is the only institution among the PRIs that enjoys revenue raising powers. Do you support the view that intermediate and zilla panahcayats should also have revenue raising powers? Should the state transfer of funds to the panchayats be made conditional/ incentivised (through a prize scheme or through a grant of matching funds) upon the performance of the local bodies in generating local resources?

f. Apart from the already assigned revenue raising powers on (i) land & buildings; (ii) entertainment taxes; (iii) vehicle tax on non-motorised vehicle;

(iv) advertisement and hoarding tax, (v) pilgrim fees, (vi) market fees, (vii) cattle registration fees, (viii) parking fees, (ix) grazing fee, what other taxation areas could be assigned to PRIs.

g. Do you think the state government's power to give tax concession (without consulting panchayats) in lucrative tax sources such as large industries in rural areas is justified?

h. In view of the weakness of the panchayat functionaries in estimation or collection of taxes, what measures do you suggest for their capacity building?

i. In view of the growing importance of PRIs, is there a need to create a permanent SFC cell at the state headquarters to collect data continuously and make them available to the SFC as & when constituted?

j. The 12th Finance Commission recommended Rs. 20,000 crores as block grants to panchayats for 2005-10 (just 4% of the central transfers). A jump of Rs. 8,000 crores over the recommendation of the 11th FC. In 2002-03 the expenditures incurred at the local body level where just about 1.8% of the GDP and constituted about 5% of the total government expenditure. The 12th FC recommended these transfers to be used for water supply and sanitation. Is this quantum of grant adequate? Secondly, will it be more useful to make such transfers unconditional or continue with the present system of specific purpose transfers?

k. What could be the mode of transfer of funds for the central schemes? Should it be rooted through the consolidated funds of the states or given directly to the PRIs?

l. What could be the possible measures to insulate such transfers from the ways & means problems of the states?

m. What other measures would you suggest for enhancing/ improving the resource base of the PRIs?

n. Is there a need to have a baseline standard on accounting and auditing for PRIs?

o. Instead of multiple transfers, should there be cross sectoral convergence of allotments into block funds such as anti-poverty fund, a water security fund, the public health fund, an education fund, a family welfare and child development fund, a housing fund and a rural connectivity fund.

p. Should the state widely publicise such transfers on public domain or otherwise?
q. On the basis of activities assigned to panchayats should each state government create a panchayat sector line item in the budget to emphasise such allocations?
r. Similarly do you suggest similar action on the part of union government ministries?
s. What are the implications if the funds allocated and transferred to panchayats are made no lapsable?
t. Should the hierarchical procedure for furnishing technical/administration sanction for a project be done away with? What alternative models could be tried in this context?
u. Do you agree that a fiscal responsibility regime with details on timing and periodicity of fiscal transfers to PRIs and preconditions for release of funds is required?

REFORMS FOR PANCHAYAT

Capacity Enhancement

a. There is a general feeling that the State Institute of Rural Development (SIRDs) are not given due care and attention in all the states. What are the steps needed so that the SIRDs are adequately strengthened and dedicated fully for building the capacity of the elected members of the PRIs and the officials attached with them?
b. What are the implications of transferring/outsourcing the functions of the SIRDs to competent NGOs/ educational institutions including the universities both in the public and the private sectors?
c. It is quite often seen that for every centrally sponsored scheme (CSS), a new capacity building (CB) arrangement is made, probably because this service is not seen as a continuous process, but as an external, temporary and

a time bound input. Will it be rational to dovetail the individual capacity building elements of various CSSs into the continuous process of CB of the PRIs through the permanent institutional arrangements, namely the NIRD, the SIRDs and similar other institutions?

d. Should the NGOs/other civil society groups be involved in capacity building of the PRIs?
e. What should be the special arrangements to build the capacities of the representatives from among women and other weaker sections of the society, especially in the context of the rotation system?
f. Do you think there is a necessity to set up a composite extension centre at the level of each delivery panchayat so as to cater to the training requirements of all PRI falling in that areas?
g. Is there a need to have a formal certification course for the secretariat and technical staff working with panchayats through institutions such as IGNOU?
h. Since many of the elected represented of the PRIs are not sufficiently educated/trained on issues of governance both administrative as well as technical, will it be desirable to have a short training course for such representatives immediately after elections?

Personnel Management

- What should be the human resource policy for the panchayats to discharge their functions in the assigned areas effectively? Should there be cadres specifically earmarked for Panchayats both at the district and the state levels? If so, what are the implications of the same?
- What should be the best mode for staffing of PRIs? Should the staff on contract or on permanent basis?
- How will career progression be ensured for permanent staff of PRIs?
- Should the personnel policy of the panchayats allow lateral as well as inter panchayat movement? Should there be convergence of cadres at some level?

- What ideally should be the relationship between the panchayat Chairperson and the CEO? Should the appointment of CEO remain confined only to the IAS? What could be the alternatives?
- Should the PRIs be allowed to outsource some activities to civil society groups?
- What are the measures needed to be taken to ensure administrative control of the PRIs over the state government functionaries dealing with the subjects listed in the XI schedule of the Constitution?
- Some state governments have faced difficulty in placing the services of the concerned government staff to the PRIs consequent upon devolution of certain activities or institutions. In this context, should there be an enabling provision in the constitution permitting the state legislatures to make, by law, provisions that would empower the state governments to depute their staff to the panchayats and to enable the latter to exercise full power of administrative and functional control over such staff?
- Do you think there is a need to have a continuous scheme of programmes and training for PRIs officials? Should these training programmes have a basic curriculum common to all panchayats across the country? What could be the contents of this curriculum?
- In the spirit of decentralization envisaged in the 73rd amendment what are the measures needed to simplify the process of technical scrutiny of schemes at various levels of hierarchy? Should the criterion remain based on financial outlay and not on the technical complexity of the schemes?
- What are the measures needed to redraft technical codes in order to make them citizens friendly so that the projects could be taken up with participation and involvement of the people and civil society groups?
- At present the state PWD and in some states other technical departments provide technical sanction/ scrutiny/guidance to projects, what are the measures needed to liberalise the system and involve private

technical bodies, retired technocrats and civil society institutions having technical wing in providing technical support services to panchayat project?

- Should panchayats be entrusted with the task of monitoring the attendance of village level staff of different departments?
- At present gram panchayat grade C employee of the district administration. In view of the gradual empowerment of this structure in terms of both volume of work as well as their financial outlay, is there a need to upgrade a post to grade B level or at least to a senior grade C status with appropriate qualification and experience requirement?
- Should the PRIs be encouraged to take up ventures where people/stakeholders make a part contribution with the government making available the balance amount? Is there a need to monetize shramdan (voluntary working) in such works?
- Apart from institutional monitoring through standing committee of the PRIs, what could be other forms of an effective monitoring regime?

Grossroot Participation

Planning from below:

a. In many State Acts, planning has not been made a mandatory task of the panchayats, particularly at the levels of gram panchayats and intermediate panchayats. Is this not unconstitutional? What amendments are necessary in these Acts to make 'planning' a mandatory task of all the tiers of panchayats?

b. Most panchayats cannot undertake planning function, because of paucity of untied funds, among other things. Despite recommendations of many State Finance Commissions, most state governments fail to provide substantial funds to the PRIs in untied form, presumably because they face serious financial constraints.

   In the circumstance, what are the initiatives needed on part of the central government to create a pool of resources drawing funds from various sources including the federal Finance Commission grants and channellise them to the PRIs to enable them to prepare local level development plans under broad guidelines to be given by the respective State Planning Boards?

c. (i) Should the Planning Commission take initiatives in creating a framework for institutionalising panchayat level planning and for integration of panchayat plans with the state and national plans? (ii) What are the initiatives the Planning Commission can take to activate the State Planning Boards so that they become a catalising centre providing directions, advice and support to PRIs for preparation of participatory panchayat level plans?

d. The Planning Commission has emphasized that implementation of grassroots level planning by PRIs. What specific initiatives can the Planning Commission take?

e. Comprehensive and workable methodology for preparation of plans at different levels of panchayat has not been developed by most states. What could be done to ensure this?

District Planning Committee

The District Planning Committees (DPC) have failed to emerge as effective institutions. Some states have not formed the DPC. A few states tried to make it more powerful than the PRIs. In most states they are not functioning. Moreover, the concept of 'district plan' has not yet taken a concrete shape. There are many issues surrounding DPC and the 'district plan' that need to be addressed.

(a) Under Articles 243G and 243W, panchayats of all three tiers and the municipalities will prepare plans for their areas. These plans are not draft plans, but are final and actionable plans. But the district plans to be prepared by the DPC under Article 243ZD are draft plans. How to remove this anomaly and reconcile Articles 243G/ 243W with Article 243 ZD?

(b) Article 243ZD gives two tasks to the DPC, namely to integrate the panchayat and municipal plans and to prepare a consolidated district plan. This means that the district plan goes beyond consolidating the individual plans of local bodies. It is expected to address certain issues, which are beyond the capacity of individual panchayats and municipalities. Are these things restricted to sub clause (a) of clause (3) of Article 243ZD, namely rural-urban integration, environmental conservation, balanced and sustainable use of natural resources and financial or other kinds of resources? Whether the district plan should have a larger scope, for example, inclusion of programmes of various line departments on subjects/activities not devolved to the local bodies? Is it possible to suggest an alternative model for integration of PRIs/ULBs at the district/urban level for preparation of a composite development plan and for effective delivery of services in their areas?

(c) Legitimacy of the DPC – In view of the existence of Zilla Parishad as the apex elected PRI at the district level, is there a need to create a separate constitutional body DPC to prepare the draft plan for the district under Article 243Z (D)? What in your opinion justifies this special constitutional recognition to the DPC, when neither the national planning commission nor the state planning boards have been given this status?

(d) Do you find weight in the view that the DPC, being a stand-alone committee outside the PRI-Municipal system, a body of indirectly elected and nominated members, will have no accountability either to the local bodies or to the local people?

(e) Expanding the role of district panchayat – Keeping in view the overall pattern of democratic decentralization envisaged under the 73rd and 74th constitution amendments, do you think the task given to the DPC can be performed by the District panchayat itself? In that case will the district Panchayat be the government for the entire district, including the urban areas? The task of preparing the district plan for the entire district can then be given to this body and there is no necessity of a separate constitutional body like DPC. What are the possible implications? What are the constitutional amendments and institutional arrangements needed to create such an enlarged/empowered district panchayat (taking care of both PRIs/ULBs)?

f. If the above is accepted, is there a need to have an advisory body of officials/technical experts/scholars to replace the DPC which will advise the district panchayat in preparing a district plan or to coordinate the planning exercises at the local level or to examine the local plans for, among other things, prevention of overlapping and duplication of schemes/projects at the inter-panchayat level.

g. When the district level panchayat represents both rural and urban population, it has to become the district government in which case the chief Executive Officer of the district government will automatically become a key functionary at the district level. What will be the possible implications of merging the present post of Collector/Deputy Commissioner with that of the CEO?

SOCIAL EMPOWERMENT OF WOMEN

Education

Equal access to education for women and girls will be ensured. Special measures will be taken to eliminate discrimination, universalize education, eradicate illiteracy, create a gendersensitive educational system, increase enrolment and retention rates of girls and improve the quality of education to facilitate life-long learning as well as development of vocational/technical skills by women.

Reducing the gender gap in secondary and higher education would be a focus area. Sectoral time targets in existing policies will be achieved, with a special focus on girls and women, particularly those belonging to weaker sections including the Scheduled Castes/Scheduled Tribes/Other Backward Classes/ Minorities.

Gender sensitive curricula would be developed at all levels of educational system in order to address sex stereotyping as one of the causes of gender discrimination.

Health

A holistic approach to women's health which includes both nutrition and health services will be adopted and special attention will be given to the needs of women and the girl at all stages of the life cycle. The reduction of infant morality and maternal mortality, which are sensitive indicators of human development, is a priority concern. This policy reiterates the national demographic goals for infant Mortality Rate (IMR), Maternal Mortality Rate (MMR) that are set out in the National Population Policy 2000. Women should have access to comprehensive, affordable and quality health care. Measures will be adopted that take into account the reproductive rights of women to enable them to exercise informed choices, their vulnerability to sexual and health problems together with endemic, infectious and communicable diseases such as malaria, TB and water borne diseases as well as hypertension and cardiopulmonary diseases. The social, developmental and health consequences of HIV/AIDS and other sexually transmitted diseases will be tackled from a gender perspective.

To effectively meet problems of infant and maternal mortality, and early marriage, the availability of good and accurate data at micro level on deaths, birth and marriages is required. Strict implementation of registration of births and deaths would be ensured and registration of marriages would be made compulsory. In accordance with the commitment of the National Population Policy (2000) to population stabilization, this Policy recognizes the critical need of men and women to have access to safe, effective and affordable methods of family planning of their choice and the need to suitably address the issues of early marriage and spacing of children. Interventions such as spread of education, compulsory registration of marriage and special programmes like Balika Samridhi Yjana should impact on delaying the age of marriage so that by 2010 child marriages are eliminated.

Women's traditional knowledge about health care and nutrition will be recognized through proper documentation and its use will be encouraged. The use of Indian and alternative systems of medicine will be enhanced within the framework of overall health infrastructure available for women.

Nutrition

In view of the high risk of malnutrition and disease that women face at all the three critical stages viz, infancy and childhood, adolescent and reproductive phase, focused attention would be paid to meeting the nutritional needs of women at all stages of the life cycle.This is also important in view of the critical link between the health of adolescent girls, pregnant and lactating women with the health of infant and young children. Special efforts will be made to tackle the problem of macro and micro nutrient deficiencies especially amongst pregnant and lactating women as it leads to various diseases and disabilities. Intra-household discrimination in nutritional matters vis-à-vis girls and women will be sought to be ended through appropriate strategies. Widespread use of nutrition education would be made to address the issues of intra-household imbalances in nutrition and the special needs of pregnant and lactating women. Women's participation will also be ensured in the planning, superintendence and delivery of the system.

Drinking Water and Sanitation

Special attention will be given to the needs of women in the provision of safe drinking water, sewage disposal, toilet facilities and sanitation within accessible reach of households, especially in rural area and urban slums. Women's participation will be ensured in the planning, delivery and maintenance of such services.

Housing and Shelter

Women's perspectives will be included in housing policies, planning of housing colonies and provision of shelter both in rural and urban areas. Special attention will be given for providing adequate and safe housing and accommodation for women including single women, heads of households, working women, students, apprentices and trainees.

Environment

Women will be involved and their perspectives reflected in the policies and programmes for environment, conservation and restoration. Considering the impact of environmental factors on their livelihoods, women's participation will be ensured in the conservation of the environment and control of environmental degradation.

The vast majority of rural women still depend on the locally available non-commercial sources of energy such as animal dung, crop waste and fuel wood. In order to ensure the efficient use of these energy resources in an environmental friendly manner, the Policy will aim at promoting the programmes of nonconventional energy resources. Women will be involved in spreading the use of solar energy, biogas, smokeless chulahs and other rural application so as to have a visible impact of these measures in influencing eco system and in changing the life styles of rural women.

Science and Technology

Programmes will be strengthened to bring about a greater involvement of women in science and technology. These will include measures to motivate girls to take up science and technology for higher education and also ensure that development projects with scientific and technical inputs involve women fully. Efforts to develop a scientific temper and awareness will also be stepped up. Special measures would be taken for their training in areas where they have special skills like communication and information technology. Efforts to develop appropriate technologies suited to women's needs as well as to reduce their drudgery will be given a special focus too.

Women in Difficult Circumstances

In recognition of the diversity of women's situations and in acknowledgement of the needs of specially disadvantaged groups, measures and programmes will be undertaken to provide them with special assistance. These groups include women in extreme poverty, destitute women, women in conflict situations, women affected by natural calamities, women in less developed regions, the disabled widows, elderly women, single women in difficult circumstances, women heading households, those displaced from employment, migrants, women who are victims of marital violence, deserted women and prostitutes etc.

Violence against Women

All forms of violence against women, physical and mental, whether at domestic or societal levels, including those arising from customs, traditions or accepted practices shall be dealt with effectively with a view to eliminate its incidence. Institutions and mechanisms/schemes for assistance will be created and strengthened for prevention of such violence, including sexual harassment at work place and customs like dowry; for the rehabilitation of the victims of violence and for taking effective action against the perpetrators of such violence. A special emphasis will also be laid on programmes and measures to deal with trafficking in women and girls.

Mass Media

Media will be used to portray images consistent with human dignity of girls and women. The Policy will specifically strive to remove demeaning, degrading and negative conventional stereotypical images of women and violence against women. Private sector partners and media networks will be involved at all levels to ensure equal access for women particularly in the area of information and communication technologies. The media would be encouraged to develop codes of conduct, professional guidelines and other self regulatory mechanisms to remove gender stereotypes and promote balanced portrayals of women and men.

8

Training Modules of Participatory Local Development

INTRODUCTION

The training modules are meant to cover gaps in existing training programmes that were identified by a broad-based training needs assessment among stakeholders. The focus is on two key *Panchayati Raj* institutions-the *Gram Sabha* including all registered voters at village level and the *Sarpanch* (head of the lowest elected tier of *Panchayati Raj* institutions-the *Gram Panchayat*). The main issues here are lack of participation of the rural poor and the lack of preparedness of local elected officials. Hence the need for training for good local governance. Although tailored to the training needs of *Panchayati Raj* functionaries in India, the modules provide guidance on core issues in institutional capacity-building for local development planning, which are, to a large degree, similar in other developing countries within the region.

Objectives

1. To equip trainers with the means to enhance the awareness and skills of *panchayat* functionaries, including women, in order to increase their confidence in their capabilities to address the core issues of day-to-day local governance. In many cases, the *Sarpanch* is a woman who is least prepared for her new role.
2. To familiarize trainers with participatory training tools and to assist them in acting as facilitators, offering

alternatives/new methods to tackle problems/issues faced by elected *panchayat* functionaries.

Structure

The modules cover the different stages of participatory local governance ranging from social mobilization to participatory community monitoring and evaluation. An additional module explains the use of the different participatory training tools. Reference information and case studies/examples relevant to the training are also included in the annex.

TRAINING MODULE ON PARTICIPATORY PLANNING AND MANAGEMENT

Participatory planning

Participatory planning is a process by which a community undertakes to reach a given socio-economic goal by consciously diagnosing its problems and charting a course of action to resolve those problems. Experts are needed, but only as facilitators. Moreover, no one likes to participate in something which is not of his/her own creation. Plans prepared by outside experts, irrespective of their technical soundness, cannot inspire the people to participate in their implementation.

However, the training on participatory local planning and management of the three million newly elected local government Panchayati Raj officials, one-third of them women, is a major challenge.

The handbook module on this topic is intended to be utilized by NIRD and State-level government and non-government agencies to build awareness of both government officials and grassroots representatives, elected to district, mandal and local village-level councils, including the village head, called the Sarpanch, who is often a woman.

Awareness building on principles of participatory planning

1. Development should be seen more as a change from the bottom up than from top down.
2. The development process should be managed as a natural organic process rather than according to plans, goals, objectives, targets and schedules, implying that

goals and targets may change and, therefore, their timing should be tentative and flexible to make room for adaptation to local conditions.

3. Development programmes should aim to strengthen local organizations and not state and central government bureaucracies. New programmes should be chosen according to their ability to increase local development management capacity. Start with a few schemes to solve some immediate local problems to build local confidence and experience.
4. The development process is supported by local institutions with village panchayats, primary cooperatives, religious, youth, community-based users' and self-help groups playing a lead role. It is more important to make sure that the development process is rooted in a strong local institution than ensuring that local institutions have a grasp of all the finer technical points. It is comparatively easy to arrange technical services from outside than to bring about social involvement and willing popular participation in the development process. Strong local institutions are necessary as support posts quite independently of whatever technical skills and other background they may have.
5. It follows from the above that the development process must be based primarily on confidence and learning rather than on experts and training. It is more important for the people who will take decisions at the local level to have full confidence of the people they represent, than to be trained experts. This also implies that technical staff of departments should work in tandem with local institutions rather than sit on judgement on the plans prepared by these institutions.

Simple is practical

The participatory planning process has implications for the working methods of a conventional local development planner. Current decentralized planning techniques often keep people out of the planning process, which severely limits their ability to deliver the intended results at local level and reinforces the centralizing tendencies in decision-making. The basic issue of whether people or planning techniques should be changed first, has not yet been answered. As a facilitator of local change, the development planner will have to shed much of the planning jargon and simplify his planning techniques so that these are widely understood. In view of the training needs of the three million newly elected local decision-makers and the limited local expertise, there is an urgent need for training material on the introduction of simple local planning methodologies and techniques that can be used at the village level, with minimal need for external assistance.

How to initiate participatory planning

(i) Identify local needs, particularly of rural poor families

- The best way to find what people need and what they see as possible solutions to their problems is to ask them directly. This also creates awareness and willingness among the people to take part in any action that will follow.
- But before asking what they want, it is necessary to establish a common ground of understanding with them. There are bound to be conflicting interests within a community. Special skills and sincerity are needed to build consensus.
- It is important to ensure steadfast community support for a pro-poor development initiative. Local officials, CBOs, field workers of voluntary organizations, teachers, women, and retired people, must be involved in the consultations and discussions.

(ii) Collect basic data

- Once local contacts are established, the next step is to collect, with the people's help, basic data about the community, characteristics of the area, resources situation, socio-economic status and other relevant facts.
- The aim is to get a factual baseline picture which will help in setting goals and measuring changes brought about by the project at a later stage.

- It is helpful at this stage is to associate with local officials and NGO functionaries in collecting and verifying facts from different sources.
- To seek people's cooperation, it is important to respect their ideas and abilities. The focus should be on the community as a whole and seeking its commitment to helping the poor.
- Participatory rural appraisal (PRA) is a practical tool for participatory data collection and analysis.

(iii) Formation of working groups

- It is helpful is to form working groups that include local officials, to prepare status reports and develop perspectives.
- The aim of the working groups is to analyse and compare data, draw inferences and identify priority areas for intervention. This is aimed at greater clarity and strengthening of participation of local people, particularly the rural poor, by giving greater local planning responsibility and establishment of good working relationship between technical planning experts and the local people. Importance is to be given to detailed specification of the roles of participant individuals, groups and committees in carrying out the tasks.
- Conflicts and disagreements may arise in the process, which are not in themselves a negative factor, but have to be properly resolved and managed at every stage of decision-making.

(iv) Formulation of the objectives

- The first step in participatory local planning is to define precisely what specific objectives are to be achieved, which should be stated in concrete terms, e.g. increasing i) incomes of identified households, ii) production of certain crops and iii) literacy among locally elected women officials.
- The objective may not always be quantifiable, particularly when it involves attitudinal changes. Its still helps to be as specific as possible so that people can see how much change has taken place.

(v) Deciding the strategy

- This is the most difficult part of participatory local planning as it involves assessing and mobilizing needed resources and choosing the planning methods. It is important to specify: a) resources that are locally available and those needed from outside. (people with skills, funds, raw material inputs, etc.); b) if resources are available when needed; and c) who should be approached, who will approach and with whose help to secure these.
- Consider alternative local planning methods and approaches such as (i) whether to contract a job to private individuals or to do it on a cooperative basis; ii) whether to focus on several small household-based units or one big unit; and iii) whether to train local people as trainers for the jobs or to hire trained personnel from outside.
- Once a course of action is chosen, it should be explained and specified in clear terms to avoid confusion and misunderstanding among the local stakeholders.

(vi) Ensuring feasibility

- The working groups at this point should consider whether the objectives are realistic. It is important to ensure that: i) assumptions and stipulations regarding the availability of resources, managerial competence and technical expertise are realistic; ii) proposed activities are economically viable; and iii) local market can absorb the expected outputs.
- It is important to identify potential project beneficiaries and check how the benefits would flow to them.

(vii) Preparing the work plan

- This is a blueprint for decentralized project management drawn up by the project implementation committee, specifying the 'what, who, when and how' of local project implementation.
- The work plan should contain the following information in simple tabular form: (i) all activities for implementation of the project; (ii) names(s) of the

person(s) responsible for each activity; (iii) starting and completion time for each activity; and (iv) the means to carry out the activities.

- It should also define the outputs expected from each activity to measure performance during implementation or on completion of the project, for effective monitoring and evaluation.

(viii) Preparing the budget

- The material and human resources must be given a monetary cost, which form the project budget.
- The cost is further broken down in terms of each period of time and also in terms of availability-whether locally available or to be secured from outside.
- External resources can be government grants or loans from financial institutions, etc.

STEPS IN IMPLEMENTATION OF LOCAL DEVELOPMENT PROJECTS

1. Appointing a project coordinator

- After hiring staff and technical persons for different jobs according to the schedule, the organization/agency in charge of the project should appoint a coordinator for the project.
- The coordinator can be hired from outside or someone from within the community with the commitment and demonstrated leadership qualities can be chosen for the job.

2. Setting up a project implementation and monitoring committee: This is made up of the project coordinator, representatives of the local community and a representative of the funding agency. Its role is to supervise implementation on a day-to-day basis and to work as a crisis management group.

3. Staff training: This is needed to reorient project planning staff for the jobs to be performed.

4. Transparency

- Important for retaining community interest and support for the project to ensure its smooth progress. Maintain total transparency in procurement and use of resources. Project details, budget and sources of funds can be displayed publicly at different places in the project area.

- Involve more and more local people in various activities with daily/weekly briefings to inform community leaders about ongoing activities and problems, if any. Care is needed to ensure the quality of inputs procured and used.

5. *Anticipating obstacles:* The project coordinator should be aware of likely difficulties, be able to anticipate obstacles and take preventive action. Advance action is needed to ensure timely availability of workers, especially technical people. Plans should be ready to deal with any contingency.

6. *Timely release of funds*

- Implementation is often delayed by the non-availability or inadequacy of funds. Various bureaucratic formalities, postal delays, etc. may delay commencement.
- If there is more than one source of funding, it is all the more necessary to ensure that no mistake is made in completing formalities of Terms and Condition (T&C) documents and also in submitting timely progress reports, which are needed for timely release of fund installments.
- The project coordinator should ensure that there are enough funds for the activities as well as for paying project staff salaries.
- It is important to be prepared for delays by having flexibility in project design for such eventualities. Sticking to the guidelines and instructions of funding agencies and adherence to the project schedule are the best way to ensure timely releases of fund instalments.

Monitoring

This is important for timely and proper project implementation. Monitoring provides feedback so that necessary adjustments can be made in the work plan and budget. Therefore, monitoring schedules are often based on the project work plan. It is essentially a tool that helps both project-implementing and funding agencies.

1. Monitoring parameters

- Time schedule
- Cost
- Process

These are already specified in the work plan. Monitoring reports must be reviewed by the project implementation committee, focusing on information about delays-the extent and implications, needed corrective action and the person or agency responsible for it. This not only points out the source of the fault but also protects project management from blame for the delay.

2. Integrity

- It is important for the implementing agency to maintain a high level of financial credibility, which is closely watched by funding agencies.
- Monitoring, therefore focuses on cost-flows and wherever there is under or over-expenditure, this should be brought to the immediate attention of the funding agencies. It should be discussed frankly with them in order to reach agreement on the best course of action.
- Implications of delay or cost-overrun can also be discussed with the village community to explore possibilities of mobilizing local contributions to compensate for the extra cost. Integrity pays in the long run.

Contributed by B. P. Maithani, Professor and Head (CIBT), National Institute of Rural Development (NIRD), Hyderabad, India.

TRAINING MODULE ON SOCIAL MOBILIZATION

Social mobilization enhances participation of rural poor in local governance

Social mobilization is the cornerstone of participatory approaches in rural development and poverty alleviation programmes. It is a powerful instrument in decentralization policies and programmes aimed at strengthening human and institutional resources development at local level. Social mobilization strengthens participation of rural poor in local decision-making, improves their access to social and production services and efficiency in the use of locally available financial resources, and enhances opportunities for asset-building by the poorest of the poor.

Role of Gram Sabha *and public information in social mobilization*

The Constitution's 73rd Amendment has made the village council, the *Gram Sabha*, into a very powerful tool of social mobilization. Many types of neighbourhood groups, health and literacy programmes, *Mahila Mandals* (village women's groups) and the mass media-newspapers, radio and TV-also play a vital role in social mobilization at the community level. Social mobilization of rural poor at community level will be successful if directly linked with issues affecting their livelihoods. For successful social mobilization of the rural poor, there is a need for improved access to public information on local development issues directly linked with their livelihood interests. An effective way of doing this is by facilitating free access to public information on local development programmes and activities, which has been a critical factor in the success of *Panchayati Raj* in the States of Kerala and Andhra Pradesh.

Examples of successful social mobilization

Total sanitation programme in Avanur Gram Panchayat, *Kerala, India*

This example of successful mobilization of the entire community by a gram panchayat to meet a basic need has been widely recognized. It has brought national honour and a cash prize of Rs 1.2 million to the panchayat. In 1996, a survey held by the Avanur Gram Panchayat in Kerala State found that over 2 000 of Avanur's 5 000 households were too poor to afford basic sanitation facilities. The Gram Panchayat President convened a series of awareness-building meetings for all families below the poverty line.

As an outcome of these meetings it was agreed that the Gram Panchayat would provide all these families building material for a sanitation unit, with the condition that each beneficiary family would complete 20 percent of the work on its own. The meetings focused on awareness-building of women as main beneficiaries. Much to the surprise of all, the campaign was successfully completed within three months. The Gram Panchayat spent only 20 percent of allocated resources because 80 percent of the work was done by the beneficiary families themselves. In this way, a total of about Rs 12 million in assets could be mobilized for the poorest families.

Total housing scheme in Avanur Gram Panchyat, Kerala State, India

The Avanur Gram Panchayat used the cash award of Rs 1.2 million to start a Total Housing Scheme for families below the poverty line. This led to 500 houses being built during 1997-2000. The Gram Panchayat gave each family an amount of Rs 20 000 in three stages, as a grant. The beneficiary families contributed their own labour and material worth Rs 30 000 for each unit. The scheme created assets worth more than Rs 25 million.

The Gram Panchayat has also successfully implemented a drinking water scheme and neighbourhood units in Avanur, and was declared the 'Best Panchayat' in Kerala for its innovative work.

The Janmabhoomi programme in Andhra Pradesh: a learning model for capacity-building for participatory local development planning

Janmabhoomi was inspired by South Korea's Saemaul Undong programme and launched in January 1997 as a mass mobilization effort to involve people in rural development planning and decision making through PRIs in Andhra Pradesh.

It aims to take the administration closer to the people, make it more responsive to their felt needs and to promote transparency and accountability in public affairs. It is also directed against the caste system. It has specific programmes for disadvantaged groups like women, the Scheduled Castes and Tribes and people with disabilities to integrate them into the mainstream of development.

Janmabhoomi has activated the Gram Sabha, which is convened every three months and presided over by the Sarpanch, the Mandal president, the ward member and government officials.

Janmabhoomi objectives/methodology

Objectives

- Bring governance nearer to the people
- Participation of people, especially weaker social sections, in development process
- Responsive, transparent governance, accountable to people
- Through above, achieve goals of poverty alleviation and equity.

Methodology

- Large-scale information dissemination
- Formation of self-help groups (SHGs) of stakeholders in key sectors of the rural economy to promote mass mobilization. Development funds routed through SHGs, which are statutorily recognized.

Institutional arrangements

- *Gram sabha* at the habitation level
- Habitation committee at the habitation level
- Nodal team at the *Mandal* level
- *Janmabhoomi* volunteers' team
- Social animators
- District level committee (Collector as its Chairperson)
- State level committee (Chief Minister as its Chairperson).

Local development planning

The programme has so far completed 13 rounds of participatory decision-making in local development. The most important impact has been to generate public awareness, galvanize the administrative machinery and open up access of rural poor to local governance.

Janmabhoomi has also developed a strong community spirit among the people and improved transparency in administration.

Social mobilization programs as part of decentralization

In Nepal, a citizens' charter has been prepared and district development councils (DDCs) organized under the Local Self Government Act (LSGA) with subject-wise sections (for e.g. on agriculture & livestock), each equipped with computers and accessories. Job descriptions of the section have been prepared and staff trained in different areas to become more professional. Institutional reviews to identify DDC capacity gaps have been initiated and an internal communication system established.

Local development fund (LDF) bylaws have been approved and the LDF made operational from July 2002. The LDF has developed pro-poor policies with at least 50 percent credit capital earmarked for the poorest of the poor. The repayment period and credit activities are defined according to the local poverty profile and first priority for seed grant utilization is given to the poorest of the poor.

District development plans are published annually and all village development committees have prepared and published five-year plans. There are regular meetings, interaction and coordination and initiation of different development activities with line agencies, I/NGOs and private sector. Development activities, income and expenditure are published regularly in district bulletins. Internal revenue increased from NRs3 328 882 in 1997 to NRs12 281 500 in 2001. External resources are mobilized from various international donor agencies.

Decentralization programmes in Nepal emphasize social mobilization as an instrument for the more efficient allocation of local resources. As an example, community organizations in the country's Kavre district identified the poorest of the poor on the basis of consensus, which facilitated their participation in village development programmes.

For example, the local women's group built a community centre without outside help. They organized weekly meetings for members of their group, who contributed only five rupees each, every week. Yet, this enabled the women's group to mobilize NRs 48 000 and invest NRs 85 000. This example was followed by village men, who established 34 men's groups, which met every Saturday, with each member contributing NRs 15. These local women's and men's groups were able to save and invest their capital for the construction of a bridge near the centre of the village at a total cost of NRs 140 000, which is a sizeable contribution from the local poor.

The core elements in the strategy for social mobilization and capital formation among the poorest in the Kavre District, are self-governance; institutional development of community organizations (COs); social capital development; skill and enterprise development; micro-finance activities; and infrastructure support.

Local capacity has also been developed and strengthened by human resource development, strategic management, organization structure and culture financial and information management.

The guiding principles are sustainability, a participatory approach, gender equity, good governance, decentralization and human rights.

TRAINING MODULE ON ENHANCING WOMEN'S PARTICIPATION

Main objectives of the training module for women local council members

1. To explain the 73rd Constitutional Amendment to newly elected women *panchayat* members.
2. To make women local council representatives aware of laws protecting women's rights.
3. To make women council members aware of their roles and responsibilities in local development.
4. To enhance participation of women members in development planning within *panchayats*.
5. To develop women's leadership and communication skills for enhancing social mobilization.
6. To make them find ways and means to interface with other layers of local self-governance within the State and claim the *panchayat*'s entitlements.
7. To familiarize them with rural/women/child development programmes to reduce poverty

8. To empower them to identify and break cultural barriers and improve their social-economic condition.

The 73rd Constitutional Amendment Act strengthens women's participation in local development planning

- Provides for reservation of seats in favour of Scheduled Castes and Scheduled Tribes in proportion to their population and for *reservation of one-third seats for women at all levels.*
- Provides for *reservation of the office of Chairperson at all levels in favour of* Scheduled Castes and Scheduled Tribes and *women.*

Women in participatory local development planning

Systematic awareness-building and training is needed for enhancing rural women's capacity to take up their new responsibilities as local legislators and decision-makers under *Panchayati Raj.*

The local government bureaucracy is also in urgent need of sensitization to women's problems and issues linked to gender bias in local development planning. The panel responsible for formulating the training agenda should include elected women representatives besides local development personnel.

The training of women *panchayat* members should be based on their own local experiences and elicit their involvement in preparing a framework that will enable them to analyse and understand their roles and responsibilities in accordance with the 73rd Constitutional Amendment.

Design of a training programme for women village council members and *Sarpanch*

- Training should be both for trainees and trainers.
- Training programme should have a focus area and relevant content areas.
- Framework should be flexible and flow according to the participation of members and their viewpoint.
- Process of training should not be fluid but tailored to the needs and expectations of the trainees.
- The content should not be lecture-oriented, but based on interactions and discussions.

- Resource persons could function as catalysts to help local women council members understand roles and responsibilities.
- Local experts should have working knowledge of the local language and training methods and material should take into account sensitivities of women council members.
- Trainers should use participatory training methods and tools, which meet women trainees' expectations in the area of decentralized rural local governance, both in method and design. Field visits should be an integral part of the training programme for women council members.
- The training material should be, wherever necessary, pictorial.

Training module for women local council members

Empowerment

- Institutional empowerment; empowerment of different segments of rural society
- Empowerment of PRIs empowers different segments of society
- Political, economic and social dimensions with special reference to SC/ST, BC (backward castes) and women
- Socio-cultural milieu and women's empowerment

Leadership

- Meaning and importance in any institution or organization
- Context of leadership *in Panchayati Raj*, its significance
- Women leadership, male leadership, leadership among other weaker sections-SC/ST & OBC (other backward castes)
- Leadership-socio-economic and political profile of the state in the context of PRIs.
- Capacity building of *Panchayati Raj* representatives/ leaders
- Qualities of a good leader for good governance
- Leadership and ethics

- Developing systemic thinking abilities

Communication skills

- Confidence-building
- Capacity and awareness-building
- Access to information through Information Technology
- Ability to communicate in any language

Stress management

- Coping with day-to-day affairs
- Group interactions and discussions
- Consultations for remedial measures
- Ability to resolve conflicts at the local level

Gender sensitization

- Sex and gender issues in the process of development, specifically rural development
- Socio-cultural and related factors leading to gender discrimination, analysis of rural society
- Awareness and capacity-building in PRIs
- Gender considerations in the process of local planning
- Gender issues and problems, capacity-building of women representatives in *Panchayati Raj* especially their role in decision-making coupled with different centrally and state-sponsored programmes for women's development and empowerment.

Women council members

A quick appraisal of the trainees before the start of the training will help the trainer in designing the training programme. This can be done by: i) obtaining a brief bio-data of the participants and ii) SWOT (Strengths, Weaknesses, Opportunities and Threats) analysis. Since the training is for elected women members at all three PRI levels and for officials dealing with PRIs, it will not be difficult to obtain their personal particulars. Who are the women trainers/trainees?

- Core women trainers from national training/research institutes/department of personnel & training/training and development cells/university teachers/NGOs.

- Women master trainers from state training/research institutes/department of personnel & training/training and development cells/university teachers/NGOs.
- District/divisional level women trainers from regional training centres/college teachers.
- Sub-district/divisional women trainers from extension training centres (ETCs)/college teachers.
- Elected women representatives at *mandal* or block level and women local development officials.
- Women elected as village council members.
- Retired women teachers/officers.
- Women staff in NGOs/CBOs.
- Women government/bank officials.

What are the requirements for women trainers?

- It is important for the trainer to be in constant touch with the trainees. *Not much can be accomplished if 'trainers' suddenly appear on the scene, conduct 'training' and vanish. This should be discouraged. It is necessary to be one among them.*
- Trainers can build rapport by residing in the field for some period while conducting the training.
- Links with established voluntary organizations with clear knowledge of the field is essential.

Capacity-building programmes for elected women council members

Karnataka: use of satellite broadcasting, computers and promotion of social safety nets for women

The experimental programme launched by the Government of Karnataka was the second of its kind in the country. It used one-way video and two-way audio satellite broadcasting technology developed by ISRO (Indian Space Research Organisation) to beam programmes to 17 districts of Karnataka. The Department of Women and Child Welfare beamed programmes for elected women gram panchayat representatives. It is possible to organize video-conferencing among women panchayat members in villages, taluks and districts, and with anybody anywhere in the country. In the Bellandur village Gram Panchayat, 30 km from the Karnataka State capital Bangalore, women panchayat members can access administrative data for five villages with the click of a computer mouse such as size of family land holdings, taxes due from them and the number of beneficiaries under various housing and employment schemes.

The status of applications for power and water connections can also be seen on the two computers at the Panchayat office.

Set up in 1977, the Women's Welfare Society, Belgaum, has been working to assist women in distress and children from poor families. Over the years, it has expanded its work in Belgaum city and to nearby rural areas like Hidkal, Hunnur and Aralikatti.

Sangathi, a family counselling centre started by the Society in 1993 in Belgaum, has helped settle matrimonial disputes amicably in some 900 families.

Women in distress can get immediate assistance from Santwana, a 24-hour help-line. The Society has also established a short stay home at Hidkal in Hukkeri taluk for women and girls in distress, which offers food and accommodation free of cost. It also provides vocational training, like tailoring. Two printing press units in Belgaum and another in Hidkal, teach women composing, printing and book binding, to start their own ventures. The Society runs seven creches for children of working women.

Its Urban Family Welfare Centre at Vadagaon in Belgaum provides health check-up and family planning services to the people. The Society is also providing education to slum children and has organized campaigns on AIDS awareness.

Project expenses are met from public donations and assistance from organizations like the Central Social Welfare Board, the Department of Women and Child Development, the Directorate of Health and Family Welfare Services, the Karnataka State Women Development Corporation and Nehru Yuva Kendra. The society has about 700 staff. Its efforts won the Society the 1996 State Award and the Rani Kittur Chennamma Award in 1999.

Exchange programme for women council members

The Centre for Rural Management in Kerala State and the Institute of Social Sciences, Southern Regional Centre, Bangalore, organized an exchange programme for women panchayat members in the two states. It enabled Panchayati Raj functionaries to understand and gain first-hand experience of panchayat functioning in states other than their own. Stressing the vital role of training and education in preparing effective and dynamic women panchayat leaders, the field visits also developed bonding with counterparts in other states, adding to their self-confidence. Unlike formal training programmes, exchange programmes are more responsive to specific local training needs.

Women's group enterprise development

Bindu Mahila Sangham of Srirangam village in Nizamabad mandal saved Rs.17 000, got a revolving fund of Rs. 25 000 and 80 000 from the National Bank for Agricultural and Rural Development (NABARD). Anjaana Mahila Sangham and Sai Mahila Sangham make ready-made garments. Rudramma Mahila Sangham of Yedapally village makes leaf plates and earns at least Rs.10 000 in two months.

The groups use a marketing network set up with the help of the Mandal Development Officers. Similarly, Arvind Mahila Sangham was able to sell 200 000 rupees worth of soft toys at the annual industrial exhibition held in Hyderabad. Arvind Mahila Sangham of Dharmavarm village also successfully marketed their goods at the bazaar arranged by the state government.

The Baba Mahila Sangham of the Lambda's is an interesting case. Located in Ausali Thanda, a hamlet of around 40 houses, two SHG groups made Bnjara garments and assorted ornaments made from German silver.

Women's group enterprise development in Kushadevei village, Kavera District

The female community organization (FCO) in Kushadevei village, Kavera district of Nepal is a classic example for the study of social mobilization. The Kushadevei FCO initiated individual economic enterprises as well as collective, village enterprise development schemes. The self-rule adopted by the FCO is the backbone of their achievement.

At least eighty percent of the members actively participate in the meetings conducted regularly at settlement level. Each member regularly saves the amount decided by the CO. The manager takes decision on the basis of consensus on the agenda presented in the meetings.

The CO keeps account of the savings and investment, which are examined at every meeting. Members put forward suggestions on development initiatives and improving their settlement, which are subject to intense discussion during the meetings. The CO members have jointly undertaken some activities for the community through their own resources without any external support.

Women panchayat leaders as effective local development managers

A large number of women grassroots leaders across India are disproving the perception in a section of the media that women panchayat representatives are merely proxies for their male relatives who do not take active interest in the affairs of their panchayats. The following examples demonstrate that women can run panchayats successfully:

1. Struggle against corruption
   - Pushpa Rana, Pradhan of Atakfarm panchayat in Dehradun district, Uttaranchal State strongly resisted the officials' demands for bribes. Although this created a lot of delays and other problems, she finally had her way.
   - Sojar Bai of Ramtek panchayat in Harda district, Madhya Pradesh State went one step ahead and got the corrupt official, who was demanding a bribe, suspended.
2. Efficient use of resources
   - Alka Chauhan taught a lesson in public finance to government engineers. A support wall built in her Nalapani village in Dehradun district at a cost of Rs 42000 had collapsed and a junior government engineer

estimated it would cost Rs 45 000 to rebuild. But Chauhan organized the villagers to build the support wall at a cost of only Rs 25 000, and the money thus saved was spent on other development works.

- When Suraiya Begum became chairperson of Sultanpur Chilkana Nagar panchayat, it was burdened with debts. Even some of her supporters feared that new development works would not be taken up till old debts were cleared. But by the time she completed her five-year tenure, a record number of development works worth Rs 8 million had been completed.

3. Resolving disputes
   - Suraiya Begum has helped resolve many family disputes. Pushpa Rana prevailed upon villagers to settle all disputes among themselves before approaching the police, saving them the money they had to spend on bribing the police and middlemen.

4. Fighting alcoholism
   - In Gazidipur village of Sharanpur district in Uttaranchal State, panchayat member Kamia confronted the Pradhan who favoured setting up of a liquor shop in the village and successfully organized village women to get it removed.
   - On being elected Pradhan of Bhilangana block of Tehri Garhwal district in Uttaranchal State at the young age of 23, Veena Sajwan began mobilising local women against the sale of liquor that was promoting alcoholism among local men. She even met the State Chief Minister and reminded him of his promise to curb the liquor menace.

TRAINING MODULE ON SOCIAL AUDIT

Basis of social audit

Social audit as a term was used as far back as the 1950s. There has been a flurry of activity and interest in the last seven to eight years in India and neighboring countries. Voluntary development organizations are also actively concerned. Social audit is based on the principle that democratic local governance should be carried out, as far as possible, with the consent and understanding of all concerned. It is thus a process and not an event.

What is a social audit?

A social audit is a way of measuring, understanding, reporting and ultimately improving an organization's social and ethical performance. A social audit helps to narrow gaps between vision/goal and reality, between efficiency and effectiveness. It is a technique to understand, measure, verify, report on and to improve the social performance of the organization.

Social auditing creates an impact upon governance. It values the voice of stakeholders, including marginalized/poor groups whose voices are rarely heard. Social auditing is taken up for the purpose of enhancing local governance, particularly for strengthening accountability and transparency in local bodies.

The key difference between development and social audit is that a social audit focuses on the neglected issue of social impacts, while a development audit has a broader focus including environment and economic issues, such as the efficiency of a project or programme.

Objectives of social audit

1. Assessing the physical and financial gaps between needs and resources available for local development.
2. Creating awareness among beneficiaries and providers of local social and productive services.
3. Increasing efficacy and effectiveness of local development programmes.
4. Scrutiny of various policy decisions, keeping in view stakeholder interests and priorities, particularly of rural poor.
5. Estimation of the opportunity cost for stakeholders of not getting timely access to public services.

Advantages of social audit

- Trains the community on participatory local planning.
- Encourages local democracy.

- Encourages community participation.
- Benefits disadvantaged groups.
- Promotes collective decision making and sharing responsibilities.
- Develops human resources and social capital

To be effective, the social auditor must have the right to:

- seek clarifications from the implementing agency about any decision-making, activity, scheme, income and expenditure incurred by the agency;
- consider and scrutinize existing schemes and local activities of the agency; and
- access registers and documents relating to all development activities undertaken by the implementing agency or by any other government department.

This requires transparency in the decision-making and activities of the implementing agencies. In a way, social audit includes measures for enhancing transparency by enforcing the right to information in the planning and implementation of local development activities.

Appropriate institutional level for social audit

The most appropriate institutional level for social audit is the *Gram Sabha,* which has been given 'watchdog' powers and responsibilities by the *Panchayati Raj* Acts in most States to supervise and monitor the functioning of *panchayat* elected representatives and government functionaries, and examine the annual statement of accounts and audit reports. These are implied powers indirectly empowering *Gram Sabhas* to carry out social audits in addition to other functions. Members of the *Gram Sabha* and the village *panchayat*, intermediate *panchayat* and district *panchayat* through their representatives, can raise issues of social concern and public interest and demand an explanation.

The *Gram Sabha* should have the mandate to: inspect all public documents related to budget allocations, list of beneficiaries, assistance under each scheme, muster rolls, bills, vouchers, accounts, etc., for scrutiny; examine annual statements of accounts and audit reports; discuss the report on the local administration of the preceding year; review local development for the year or any new activity programme; establish accountability of functionaries found guilty of violating established norms/rules; suggest measures for promoting transparency in identifying, planning, implementing, monitoring and evaluating relevant local development programmes; and ensure opportunity for rural poor to voice their concerns while participating in social audit meetings.

Social audit committees

Social audit can also be used for auditing the performance of all three PRI tiers with a social audit committee at each level. These committees should not be permanent, but can be set up depending on the nature of programmes/schemes to be audited.

Social audit committee members can be drawn from among programme stakeholders. It is advisable to use the services of retired functionaries of different organizations, teachers or persons of impeccable integrity living in the *Zilla Panchayat*/ Block *Panchayat* / *Gram Panchayat* jurisdiction. Both facilitators and social audit committee members can be trained by social audit experts.

Steps in social audit in local bodies

1. Clarity of purpose and goal of the local elected body.
2. Identify stakeholders with a focus on their specific roles and duties. Social auditing aims to ensure a say for all stakeholders. It is particularly important that marginalized social groups, which are normally excluded, have a say on local development issues and activities and have their views on the actual performance of local elected bodies.
3. Definition of performance indicators which must be understood and accepted by all. Indicator data must be collected by stakeholders on a regular basis.
4. Regular meetings to review and discuss data/information on performance indicators.
5. Follow-up of social audit meeting with the *panchayat* body reviewing stakeholders' actions, activities and

viewpoints, making commitments on changes and agreeing on future action as recommended by the stakeholders.

6. Establishment of a group of trusted local people including elderly people, teachers and others who are committed and independent, to be involved in the verification and to judge if the decisions based upon social audit have been implemented.
7. The findings of the social audit should be shared with all local stakeholders. This encourages transparency and accountability. A report of the social audit meeting should be distributed for *Gram Panchayat* auditing. In addition, key decisions should be written on walls and boards and communicated orally.

Key factors for successful social audit

- Level of information shared with and involvement of stakeholders, particularly of the rural poor, women, and other marginalized sections.
- Commitment, seriousness and clear responsibilities for follow-up actions by elected members of the *Gram Panchayat*.
- Involvement of key facilitators in the process.

How to enhance local capacities for social audit

- Organization of a mass campaign to increase public awareness about the meaning, scope, purpose and objectives of social audit.
- Establishment of a team of social audit experts in each district who are responsible for training social audit committee members (stakeholders).
- Implementation of training programmes on social auditing methods-conducting and preparing social audit reports, and presentation at *Gram Sabha* meetings.

Social development monitoring (SDM): a social audit process

SDM is a periodic observation activity by socially disadvantaged groups as local citizens who are project participants or target beneficiaries. It could also take the form of action intended to enhance participation, ensure inclusiveness, articulation of accountability, responsiveness and transparency by implementing agencies or local institutions, with a declared purpose of making an impact on their socio-economic status.

Conclusion

To sum up, the following proposals can be made to make social audit a regular and effective institution to promote the culture of transparency and accountability through the *Gram Sabha.*

1. States should enhance *Gram Sabha* powers to make them effective instruments of participatory decision-making and ensuring accountability of PRIs in local development planning.
2. An agency like the Ombudsman can be set up to look into complaints of local maladministration.
3. Development functionaries found guilty of violating established norms for local development planning should be punished.
4. It is important to ensure that rural poor are given due protection when they wish to stand up to speak against any misconduct.

9

Women's Participation at Grassroot Level

A democratic polity involves the decentra-lisation or deconcentration of power in a way that the affairs of the local people are managed by means of their positive participation. It implies the extension of democracy at the grass-root level in view of the fact that the people's participation signifies the constitution of a democratic government not merely at the top but also at the foundation level of the political system. Thus, democratic decentralisation or Panchayati Raj aims at making democracy real by bringing the million into the functioning of their representative government at the lowest level. The philosophy of Panchayati Raj is deeply steeped in the tradition and culture of rural India and is by no means a new concept. 'The rationale behind the concept is to involve the public in local planning, identification of beneficiaries, decision making and proper implementation of policies and programmes of the people as described by them. Panchayati Raj Institutions (PRIs) have today the basic commitment towards rural development.' Panchayati Raj, as a system of governance, has had its ebbs and flows in the Indian polity ever since Indian attained independence. Various committees headed by Balwant Rai Mehta, Ashok Mehta, V.P. Naik, P.B. Patil, G.V.R. Rao, L.N. Singhvi overhauled these institutions which gave necessary impetus to the 73rd Constitutional Amendment Act.

The Panchayati Raj, an enigmatic and elusive concept, has undergone topsy-turvy changes in its role, shape and function after the 73rd Constitutional Amendment Act, 1992 which came into effect from April 24, 1993.3 With the passage of the 73rd Amendment, India is at a crucial juncture in the evolution of PRIs—the Indian brand of rural local self-government. It has envisioned people's participation in the process of planning, decision-making, implementation and delivery system.

Gender equality and gender equity are emerging as major challenges in the global development debate. Social scientists and development activists are giving increasing emphasis to these fields in their agenda for research and development. As Noble Prize-winning economist Amartya Sen has pointed out, "Democracy is not only the goal of development, it is the primary means of development." Women's participation in political processes is important for strengthening democracy and for their struggle against marginalisation, trivialisation and oppression. Emergence of women as a strong group would change the prevailing political practices, the nature and content of debates in the legislature and women's issues can be taken care of from the feminist perspective both in policy formulation and implementation.

Although the new Constitution through various Articles (Art. 14, 15, 23, 29, 30, 42, 45 etc.) did guarantee equal rights for women, Indian women continue to remain oppressed and struggle over everything from survival to resources. While women have made considerable progress in some areas such as education and employment, they continue to be subjected to the influence of the existing patriarchical attitudes in Indian society. The dilemma for Indian women today is that despite the liberal provisions of the Constitution and various laws, serious inequalities remain. In fact, right from the days of the freedom struggle the Indian women have been consistently encouraged to take part in active politics. But due to the vitiated political milieu, resulting from increasing politicisation and criminalisation of politics, the level of political participation of women has been adversely affected despite the fact that there has been a marked increase in the level of literacy and political awareness among women.

This kind of constitutional provision (73rd Amendment) has created a scope for accomplishing development with social justice, which is the mandate of the new Panchayati Raj system. There can be no real progress if women of a country are not made partners in this process of development. 'Mahatma Gandhi also believed that full and balanced development of the nation and establishment of a just society is possible only when women participate actively and fully in the political deliberations of the nation. The Balwant Rai Mehta Committee on Panchayati Raj System emphasised that rural women should not become mere beneficiaries of development but should be made equal partners in its affairs as contributors.'

India is perhaps the first country to recognise this social fact underlined by Lenin on the International Working Women's Day in 1921,8 and to have taken concrete measures to draw women into leadership positions and thereby into politics by giving them one-third reservation in what may now be called the third tier of governance—the Panchayati Raj. The constitutional amendment providing one-third representation to women in elected bodies as well as reserving one-third of the offices of chairpersons for them will have far-reaching consequences in Indian political and social life. Article 243D(3) of the Constitution (Seventy-third Amendment) Act, 1992, reads:

Not less than one-third (including the number of seats reserved for women belonging to the SCs and STs) of the total number of seats to be filled by direct election in every Panchayat shall be reserved for women and such seats may be allotted by rotation to different constituencies in a Panchayat.

And Clause (4) has the following provision: ...not less than one-third (including the number of offices of chairperson reserved for women belonging to the SCs and STs) of the total number of offices of chairpersons in the Panchayat at each level shall be reserved for women: provided also that the number of offices reserved under this clause shall be allotted by rotation to different Panchayats at each level.

Now, some general observations can be made regarding the role of women in grassroot level governance. It has come to the notice that the percentage of women at various levels of political activities has increased formally. The general trend is that those in politics are women belonging to the younger age-group between 25-45. It is also revealed that women take up political career as an extension of their domestic role. While women have been active in mass movements, their presence is not felt in decision-making. The influence of the husbands and close relatives is quite palpable. This tendency is due to lack of confidence. This dependency is a stumping block in their empowerment. 'Another positive impact of the grassroot level experiment is the increase in the female literacy rate. Studies reveal that after two years of their election to PRIs, many women demanded literacy skills and also felt the need to educate their daughters.

Issues in which women representatives generally take interest are drinking water supply, primary health, child care, public distribution system and environmental protection. One quality observed among women representatives is their patience to hear the problems of the public. They also work in adverse circumstances. It has been observed that women representatives are honest and accurate in presenting issues to the decision-making bodies and authorities. Women would bring new ideas in local governance. They believe in a sustainable development and their emphasis is on natural resources management. Women representatives working at the grassroot level also believe that communal harmony is an important element of development and they strive to achieve this objective. Another promising fact is that they do not indulge in corrupt practices.' Under this system, in many parts of the country, the elected women have exhibited their leadership in solving some of the local problems and creating facilities for betterment of the rural society.

Women are considered an extremely pivotal point in the process of change in the rural areas. Women's participation in panchayats provided opportunities to women to participate in the decision-making process. Women's participation proved to be the most effective instrument in bringing about a change in their way of life in terms of economic well-being and adoption of new technology. Women's entry into PRIs, both as members as well as heads of Panchayats, has pushed them into the policy-making and policy-implementation process in a very big way. Whether their husbands, fathers, brothers or other relatives compelled them to take up these roles, or whether they assumed these roles as dummy incumbents, one thing is certain: they crossed the rigid boundaries drawn through their households by the same male relatives.

PROBLEMS OF QUALITATIVE WOMEN PARTICIPATION

Prior to the reservation bill, statistics regarding women's participation in PRIs were significantly lower (between four and five percent). Today 33 per cent of candidates participating in the PRIs are women. 'In general, participation at local level can be viewed from two angles—quality and quantity. As far as the qualitative aspect is concerned, there are three levels of quality of participation: passive participation, active participation and decision-making participation.'

But women representatives lack this aspect of qualitative participation. A constitutional provision is only a necessary step which should be followed by effective measures for women's upliftment in the rural areas. To make women's participation in society and politics a reality, enormous work remains to be done, given their present socio-economic conditions.

Despite reservation for women, effective participation in PRIs have failed due to misuse and manipulation by the local power-brokers. Ignorance of women about their rights and procedures and about their potential and responsibilities have kept them far behind men in the local bodies. It is very much doubtful that mere increase in the number of reserved seats for women in local bodies is likely to increase the participation of women. Unless structural changes are brought about, a sincere effort is made to educate women and the power structures existing in rural areas are neu-tralised, nothing much can be achieved. Women representatives often run into barriers (especially of family and society) and are hindered from participating effectively. They feel inhibited to speak especially when they are in large male dominated assemblies. Those who muster up enough courage and strength to speak receive very little respect or attention. It has been observed that women are invited only to complete the quorum. Further, the officials also pay heed to the needs of upper class women in preference to the needs of peasant women. The rights of women thus get systematically nullified by the local bureaucracy.

The family, community and the state (represented by the officials) have together created a situation wherein elected women representatives are facing many operational constraints while playing their roles and discharging their functions in the PRIs. 'Women representatives have some individual weaknesses:

- Illiteracy and low education levels of the majority of the women elected to the PRIs.
- Overburdened with family responsibilities.
- Introversion due to the lack of communication skills.
- Poor socio-economic background with which the women have come into the system and poor capacity building.
- Patriarchical system indirectly controls and directs their participation.'

There are some other limitations regarding women's qualitative participation in PRIs:

- Male family members and also leaders from the caste group/community come in the way of the affairs of the Panchayats.
- Indifferent attitude and behaviour of officials working in the system.
- Misguidance by the local bureaucracy.
- Apprehension of no-confidence motion by the other elected members of the system.
- Mounting pressure from the political party which has vested interests in the gender reservation for positions in the PR system.

Women representatives face problems at every stage of their participation—from the Gram Sabha to Zilla Parishad. 'In an Open Forum organised by the Rural Litigation And Entitlement Kendra for 300 elected women representatives of PRIs of Uttar Pradesh, the following observations were made by the participants:

- Government orders on devolution of powers to PRIs were a mockery.
- There was a blatant practice of 'commission' demanded by Block level staff.

- Women were branded as 'incompetent' in the eyes of villagers and were forced to quit through the passing of no-confidence motions.
- Undue interference by the husband (post sarpanches) of women representatives, treating them as mere dummies.
- Widespread use of corrupt practices among the male members and local bureaucrats.'

It is clear that mere reservation is not enough because a woman representative lacks qualitative participation due to both internal and external factors. Woman's empowerment is not something which can be handed over to women only. This is a process which involves sincerity, earnestness and capacity and capability on the part of both men and women. It is a challenging task in village India as even today she cannot take any independent decision. She feels subordinate to her husband and even to her son.

STEPS TAKEN BY THE GOVERNMENT

In keeping with its past and present policy objectives, the government has launched a number of programmes focused on empowerment of rural women. 'In 1998, a scheme was started that aimed at empowering women in rural areas. It was called Swashakti—the Rural Women Development and Empowerment Project. In 2001, the government launched Swayamsiddha—the Integrated Women Empowerment Scheme that aims at holistic empowerment of women through awareness generation. In 2002, Swadhar was launched to make rural women economically strong. Under the Ninth Plan (1997-2002), 'Empowerment of Women' became one of the nine primary objectives of development. India has heralded the New Millennium by pronouncing the year 2001 as Women's Empowerment Year.' Under the provisions of 'The Women (Empowerment for Equal Participation) Bill 2005, it is stated that reservation for women in local bodies like village panchayats, municipalities etc. is not enough. They should have equal participation in the governance of the nation—legislative, executive and judiciary on the basis of their numerical strnegth.' One of the admirable steps of the government is that now girls are entitled to equal property rights along with their brothers. Recently, 'with the efforts of the Ministry of Women and Child development, the Domestic Violence Act, 2006 has been passed and come into force from October 26, 2006. The Act covers abuse or threat of abuse, whether physical, sexual, verbal, emotional or economic and it also covers both houses and work places.' This Domestic Violence Act will certainly help the rural women representatives who suffer from physical or psychological threats/violence from male members of PRIs.

SUGGESTIONS

There is a need to empower rural women to enhance their quality of participation. The awakening of women in India towards a society where justice and brotherhood prevail, can best be achieved by woman-to-woman contact. The cultural patterns of Indian society are such that social progress among women can be promoted effectively though the medium of personal relationship among them. It is women who can inspire confidence and offer stimulus for social change especially among their sisters in the rural areas.

Hence, effective leadership among women must come from the ranks of women themselves. Their qualitative participation can be achieved through training besides of course the literacy educational programmes. Mahila Mandals could be activated for this purpose where women could learn skills and acquire confidence. Links have to be strengthened between the village and the bureaucracy at the lower level. Special programmes on the role of women in PRIs, on rights of women and procedures should be prepared and highlighted through the mass media so as to make women aware and improve the quality of their participation in the socio-political system. The commitment to political empowerment must be supplemented by a new conceptualisation of women's role in the economy of India. The government (Ministry of Women and Child Development) should take the responsibility to make the rural women aware about their rights and responsibilities.

There should be a remedy for each problem of rural women participation. It should be followed by comprehensive empowerment policies and programmes. Some problems and their remedies are as follows:

- 'Low Status and Morale: Need of Upgradation—Most of the women in rural areas feel inferior to male members of family/Panchayats. This attitude needs to change to make women as part and parcel of the family as well as Panchayats. They should retain their confidence level.' There is another major problem with the women representatives. Women hailing from SC and ST categories may find it difficult to mix with representatives of general categories. To cope with this problem, it is necessary to inculcate confidence among them and to bring attitudinal changes through training in the psyche of the upper classes. Stern action should be taken against such persons who foment communal feelings.
- 'Dependence upon Men since Childhood: Need of Independence from Early Stages—In Indian villages, girls remain dependent upon the father, brother or cousin and this very feeling continues in their married life. We must give capacity building training to girls in schools to be independent.' The programmes of free universal education upto the age of 14 should be vigorously implemented. The courses of studies should inculcate the values of gender equality, self-respect, courage, independence etc. which would help to develop the personalities of girls/women. 'In all kinds of public participation, the primary responsibilities of women for looking after home and children always come in the way; unless arrangements are made for child care and other domestic responsibilities, sustained participation of women in the public sphere is not possible.'
- 'Women Elected Representatives of PRIs Give Way to their Menfolk: Need of Taking Independent Decision—Women representatives in PRIs must be trained in the art and science of decision-making so that they are not influenced by extraneous factors. They must develop leadership qualities. They should discuss among other women and take their opinion.' All women members of

Panchayats and other executive bodies must be trained and empowered to exercise their authority. Particular attention must be paid to the development of inter-personal communication skills among the community leaders. Efforts are required to elicit participation of women by establishing links between the elected representatives and the development functionaries. The prevailing male dominated power structure in the village is not ready to accept women as chairpersons (Sarpanches, Pradhans of Block Samiti and Chairperson of Zilla Parishad) of the Panchayats. This problem can be solved by persuading women to come forward to assume responsibilities. This requires special orientation camps for the rural elite.

- Lack of Interest and Knowledge: Need of Enthusiasm and Training—'Women lack interest in PRIs on account of the lukewarm attitude to PRIs by the Union and State governments. They must generate enthusiasm within themselves by making a goal and attach themselves to the altar with a spirit of dedication and reverence.' 'The women participants must be mutually able to communicate in order to be able to exchange ideas. They should be given proper training in the working of the politico-administrative institutions. It is also suggested that PRIs prepare publicity material in local languages. Audio-visual and print media can contribute significantly by the dissemination of information on women related issues and prospects.'
- 'No Forum to Exchange Ideas: Need for All Women Forum—Elected women representatives of three tiers should meet once in three months and formulate integrated plans. In this way, they would be more participative while deliberating on important issues.' The empowerment process requires social change by organising and mobilising the women's groups for struggle. Mahila Mandals should be formed in all the villages and get the full support of the National Commission for Women (NCW) and other women's welfare-based NGOs.

- 'Women MLAs and MPs do not take Interest in them: Need of Motivation by their own Examples—Women MLAs and MPs should visit frequently the elected representatives of PRIs to solve the problems faced by the rural women members. They should encourage them to take decisions independently.' The national and regional political parties can play an important role in making them aware about the process, values and working of democratic institutions.

Empowerment has multidimensional focus and its success depends on environmental forces in a given society. For that, a healthy environment is a must for women's empowerment at the grassroot level. Drawing lessons from experiences and case studies at the local, national and international levels is important.

In the end, it can be said that 33 per cent reservation for women in PRIs is a good step but it should be supplemented with effective measures that ensure the qualitative aspect of women's participation. As the India Panchayati Raj Report 2001 reveals: "Women's expectations and hopes for a greener, cleaner, responsive and representative politics have gone up. They will send out more clearly and energetically the message of women's empowerment and social development. For that reservation needs to be accompanied by considerable amount of affirmative action programme." To influence and lead effectively, women representatives must develop and use legitimate power (authority). To empower is giving women the capacity to influence the decision-making process by integrating them into our political system. Hence empowerment of rural women can be made possible not only through reservations but it also requires removal of the causes of disempowerment whether social, political or psychological.

TOWARDS MORE PARTICIPATORY GOVERNANCE

A democracy works when all citizens including the most marginalised people have the capability to ask questions, seek accountability from the state and participate in the process of governance. The quality of the democratic process depends on the capability and integrity of the organs of the state, institutions of governance and the extent of people's participation in governance. How can the impact of these factors be increased in India, and what are the major constraints to better governance?

These questions were the focus of the session on governance and panchayati raj at the National Conference on Empowering Livelihoods organised by the PACS Programme on October 24-26, 2005, in New Delhi.

Among the issues highlighted were:

- Challenges faced in panchayati raj.
- How the RTI Act can be used to strengthen panchayati raj.
- The potential of the National Rural Employment Guarantee (NREG) Act.
- Increasing the role of women.
- Improved governance in the context of food security.

CHALLENGES FACED IN PANCHAYATI RAJ

The panchayati raj system, introduced through the 73rd Constitutional Amendment, is the most definitive step towards re-energising democracy in the history of independent India.

'Panchayat' traditionally refers to the five elders in a village who mediated conflict and spoke on behalf of all the residents of a village. The word has been retained by the 73rd amendment to the Constitution, but it now refers to a body elected according to law. The same word is used for the three tiers of local administration brought in by the amendment — the highest being the district or zilla panchayat. The lowest is the gram panchayat that may cover several villages. All citizens of these villages constitute the gram sabha, which becomes the basic unit of democracy.

Panchayati Raj Institutions (PRI) cover more than 96% of India's rural population, where gram sabhas act as platforms for people's participation, to raise demands and to ensure transparency and accountability in the responses of panchayats. Panchayati raj can lead to local economic development with social justice — PRIs can be given the power to implement schemes like the Sarva Shiksha Abhiyan and Employment

Guarantee Scheme (EGS). However, a number of daunting challenges face PRIs today. Across all states there is a lack of genuine devolution of funds, functions and functionaries in panchayati raj. Added to that are social challenges that work against the emergence of leadership from marginalised sections of society, such as women, dalits and tribals. Further, as Sudha Pillai, additional secretary, panchayati raj, Government of India, pointed out, there is a lack of role clarity among gram panchayats, block panchayats and district panchayats.

The Panchayats Extension to the Scheduled Areas (PESA) Act of 1996 is one of the most potent legislative measures in recent times. It recognises tribal people's modes of living, aspirations, their culture and traditions. But, more than eight years after the Act was adopted, the enabling rules are still not in place. This clearly shows that state governments are reluctant to operationalise the PESA mandate.

How the RTI Act can be used to strengthen panchayati raj

Participation in any process presupposes the existence of knowledge about the process itself, its operation and its inputs as well as outcomes. The Supreme Court recognised the right to access information, as implied in the fundamental right to freedom of speech and expression, way back in 1973. But it took a quarter of a century for the first access to information legislation to be passed in India in Tamil Nadu.

The story of unlettered labourers in a remote village of Rajasthan demanding the right of access to muster rolls during the mid-1990s has become an unforgettable part of the history of the right to information (RTI) movement in India. This and other movements launched for food security, environmental protection, consumer rights, protection of habitats from illegal mining and justice for people displaced by development projects finally resulted in the framing of comprehensive RTI legislation applicable throughout the country.

The RTI Act, enacted by the central government in June 2005, became fully operational on October 13, 2005. Under this law, any citizen can seek information from any public office starting with that of the President down to the gram panchayat.

RTI movements across the country have, even in the absence of a central RTI law, unearthed mismanagement of public funds. The RTI Act provides strength to redouble these efforts, and empowers the taxpayer to question the manner in which public authorities spend the money he/she pays in the form of taxes. But the Act needs to be seen as an opportunity not just to unearth corruption but also to prevent its occurrence.

Use of the RTI Act can ensure that gram sabhas and the elected bodies of panchayats at the intermediary and district levels plan and prioritise development properly. The Kerala model of involving people in the planning process at the village level needs to be replicated in every panchayat in the country; the RTI Act provides the tool for ensuring that this happens.

This effort will not make headway, however, until awareness is built about the RTI Act in every village. State governments are mandated to educate people, particularly disadvantaged communities, about their rights under the Act. But this duty is subject to the availability of resources. It is now the responsibility of civil society organisations to ensure that they themselves learn the various provisions and implications of the Act and then spread this knowledge in a missionary mode.

The potential of NREG

Another important milestone is the National Rural Employment Guarantee (NREG) Act, which has the potential to improve the livelihood of millions of rural poor. Work undertaken under this Act could help reverse the recent neglect of rural infrastructure and be a crucial part of regenerating the rural economy. Providing employment would have a beneficial impact on health, education and other determinants of social welfare by breaking the cycle of rural poverty.

There may also be indirect benefits if more women are given the opportunity to work, as higher levels of female labour force participation are associated with lower infant mortality rates and higher primary school enrolment rates. The revival of rural employment opportunities would also reduce migration to urban centres.

NREG rights would also give greater bargaining power to traditionally disadvantaged groups and lead to greater mobilisation of the rural poor. By using the RTI and NREG Acts, people in remote villages will be able to identify the most needy and underprivileged, provide for their needs in development plans, monitor the implementation of development programmes and evaluate outcomes on the basis of actual improvements at the ground level.

Enhancing the role of women

The process of political participation is complex. In particular, unless specific conditions are met, women face multiple hurdles and find it difficult to participate in the political process that has hitherto been a male bastion.

Recognising this limitation, India has passed laws that make it mandatory for local governments to include women. One-third of the seats in local bodies, gram or village panchayats, municipalities, city corporations and district bodies, are reserved for women. This first step has brought around 13 lakh women into the political process. But elected women representatives have experienced and continue to experience hardships, and their participation in governance has generally been met with scepticism and cynicism.

There is, therefore, a need for several interventions to ensure that women's participation in politics leads to a substantive change. The politics of presence, or of recognition, does indeed lead to a politics of outcome or redistribution as well. However, within a deeply unequal socio-economic system, other supportive and enabling conditions will need to be provided.

What has been established is the presence of a critical mass of women in the political process at the local government level. The evolution of women's participation in governance needs to be facilitated and fostered, and the decisions of mahila sabhas need to be honoured by gram sabhas. Equally important is reservation for women in parallel systems — for example watershed development management bodies and others.

There also needs to be an overall willingness on the part of the state machinery to incorporate gender agendas as well as officers sensitive to women's issues and women's rights. The presence of a vibrant and sensitive media is also critical in providing visibility to struggles and helping create pressure. PRIs as grassroots democratic governance institutions are a necessary, but not sufficient condition for the transformation to a better social order. Enabling women's participation through reservations is a first and important step. Much more will be needed if gender justice is to become the norm. And it will take time. Meanwhile, it is important to support the fledgling first step of women's reservations in every way we can.

IMPROVED GOVERNANCE IN THE CONTEXT OF FOOD SECURITY

While poverty in India is falling, concerns over food security are increasing. Almost 204 million people in India do not have enough to eat — they do not get two meals a day throughout the year — and this number is more than the number of hungry people in all of sub-Saharan Africa. Around 39 million people in India suffer from transitory food insecurity, with the highest incidence found among the scheduled tribes (STs) followed by scheduled castes (SCs). It has been estimated that almost 30% of children in the country have a birth weight of less than 2.5 kg, and 53% of children below five years are underweight. About half the women in the age-group 15-49 years, and three-fourths of children, have been found to be anaemic.

The prevalence of malnutrition is not only due to lack of access to food but also the absence of safe drinking water, sanitation, environmental hygiene, primary healthcare and awareness.

The state of governance in India in relation to food-related schemes is very poor. Even decentralisation through PRIs has not helped much in the poorer states. In this regard, Professor Ramesh Sharan, Department of Economics, Ranchi University, said: "There is a need for active participation of civil society organisations in policy formulation especially drought mitigation and famine relief codes."

Good governance is critical for enhancing food security. Gram sabhas need to be empowered to monitor the implementation of various schemes and have access to information regarding the selection of beneficiaries and disbursement of benefits. Gram sabhas should be entitled to conduct a social audit of all food and employment schemes. Harsh Mander, social activist, writer and former civil servant, said that it is equally important to reduce vulnerability towards food insecurity by creating awareness about existing welfare schemes. There is a need for dissemination of the Supreme Court orders on food security, preparing and sensitising the poor for social audits and exercising the right to information and right to employment.

Conclusion

Poverty and deprivation in large parts of the country need to be tackled by addressing larger issues of governance. Good governance would include the following:

- A responsive political and bureaucratic system that ensures that entitlements reach the poor.
- Appropriate policies for the poor, and adequate allocations for state-sponsored schemes.
- Participatory, decentralised and efficient implementation of pro-poor programmes in a transparent and accountable way.
- Quick and fair justice, at low cost, for the poor.

10

Women Reservation Policy in Panchayats

In 1993 one of the most important step for the empowerment of women and increasing their participation in decision making was taken by reserving 33% seats for women in panchayat raj institutions. This paved the way for election of around one million at the village, block and district level. By now most states with a few exceptions like Bihar have completed at least one five year term. What has been the experience of around 7 to 8 lakh women during their first tenure? What lessons can be learnt for the future from this experience? Given the chance, they excel: It is easy to point out numerous examples of women who have worked entirely according to what they were told by their husbands or other male members of their families. In some cases elected women remained at home while their husbands attended the panchayat meetings and carried out official transactions on their behalf. Some of the elected women were approached by men only when their signatures (or thumb impressions) were needed.

All this is true to a substantial extent, but this is not the whole picture. In our male dominated society it is easy to hear jokes about the subservient role of several elected women, and some fierce arguments based on this that reservations for women has failed. Nothing could be further from the truth. In order to realise the greater potential created by these reservations, we should look at several other examples in which women got an opportunity to play an independent role. In such situations time and again, we see them making remarkable achievements for development of their village and quite often resisting the presence of vested interests with a lot of grit and determination.

They bring new perspectives: The yearnings of several women to assert their independence and make a significant contribution to the welfare of the people is visible in many such examples. In many cases they have been helped by volunteer organisations and people's movements active in their region. In some cases enlightened family members, including husbands, have also encouraged them to realise their potential of initiating meaningful social change.

From such examples it is quite clear that when conducive conditions exist for women to play a leading and active role in the decision making of the village, the entire village community benefits. This increased participation of women is often associated with better utilisation of financial resources, increased harmony in village and prioritisation of some important but neglected aspects of development such as girls' education and sanitation. Social reform measures such as reduction in alcohol consumption and domestic violence clearly get more prominence when women come to the forefront in rural communities.

Corruption has been one of the main problems of panchayat raj institutions. Interviews in several villages confirm that when women representatives function in an independent way, possibilities for corruption are lesser. Even if a pradhan or sarpanch is honest, there is the other threat that government officials refuse to release money and do not cooperate in other ways unless a certain commission is paid to them. There have been numerous examples of women sarpanchs resisting these demands of officials. In fact one hears of such resistance from women more frequently than from men. This opposition to the demand for commission has been strongly voiced by several women pradhans at their open meetings and training programmes.

Specific cases: Pushpa Rana, pradhan of Arakfarm panchayat in Dehradun district strongly resisted the bribe demands of officials. Although this created a lot of delays and other problems, she finally had her way. Sojar Bai of Ramtek panchayat [district Harda in Madhya Pradesh] went one step further and got the corrupt official [who demanded a cut from her] suspended from his job.

As for the careful use of scarce funds, Alka Chauhan provided a lesson to government engineers. A support wall that had been built in her village Nalapani [district Dehradun] at a cost of Rs. 42,000 had collapsed. A junior government engineer estimated that it will cost Rs.45,000 to rebuild the wall. But Alka Chauhan mobilised the villagers to build the wall at a cost of only Rs.23,500 and the money saved in this way could be spent on other development work.

When Suraiya Begum became the chairperson of Sultanpur Chilkana Nagar panchayat, it was saddled with debts and even some of her supporters feared that new development work may be hindered by the need to first clear old debts. But she managed the situation in such a way that by the time she completed her first five year tenure, a record number of development works worth Rs.80 lakhs had been completed.

More women leaders

As Rehana, a social worker of Sultanpur says, "Women are known to use money very carefully at home and somehow manage the family budget even when income is low. Women show the same abilities when they manage the village funds." Her colleague Shaheen adds, "When men are in-charge of development works, they indulge in a lot of wasteful spending in inaugurations and completion ceremonies. Women know how to be frugal and concentrate on the real work." Women representatives have shown the capacity to increase the panchayat income to make the development work more self-reliant. Many elected women have been closely involved with the promotion of self-help groups in villages. Urmila Yadav, sarpanch from Kosli village [Haryana] first took a step to clear encroachments on panchayat land and then built some shops on it. The rent from these shops can provide a regular income to the panchayat.

Women are generally known to have a greater capacity for resolving disputes. When she was the chairperson Suraiya

Begum's door always remained open for many victims domestic violence. She helped to resolve many disputes. Pushpa Rana prevailed upon villagers to first settle all disputes locally and go to the police only if village level efforts failed. The result was that the money people had to spend on paying bribes to the police and middlemen was saved.

Many elected women representatives have made an effort to reduce liquor consumption and to remove liquor vends. In Ghazidipur village of Saharanpur district, a panchayat member Kamia confronted the pradhan who supported the location of a liquor vend in the village and successfully mobilised village women for the removal of this liquor vend.

Battling the male empire

It is hoped that greater participation of women will result in better implementation of water, sanitation, girls education, women's health and maternity. Chandravati Singh made a detailed survey of where exactly hand pumps were needed in her panchayat. [Garchapa in Chitrakut district, UP] which is spread over a wide area. This led to maximising benefits from the limited budget at her disposal for drinking water schemes. Some women elected members have prioritised toilets for ladies at bus stops, a clear need which had been ignored earlier by men pradhans.

In Sirmaul panchayat of Indore district, the sarpanch Kiran Kanchal not only set up a maternity home but also set up a committee to run it on a viable basis without raising the service charges too high for villagers. Madhu Semval [Nathuvala panchayat, Dehradun district] helped to check the spread of a cholera epidemic. Natho Begum [pradhan of Enfield gram panchayat, Dehradun district] was so devoted to promoting the education of girls that she donated her own land for this purpose, even though she herself belongs to a poor family.

Some women have overcome heavy odds to accomplish very commendable work in panchayats. Sudha Patel [sarpanch of Changa village, Anand district of Gujarat] is blind, but her work with the help of a friend has won widespread praise. Rajjo, a Dalit woman is completely illiterate and comes from a very poor family. However her work in Sultanpur Chilkana as deputy chairman was so good that almost the entire village adores her.

Some women have resisted efforts of vested interests to harass and dislodge them with a lot of courage and firmness. So many efforts were made to dislodge Ramali Behn from Ahmedabad Zilla panchayat by powerful vested interests, but she survived them all by her transparent way of functioning and by establishing direct relationship with people. When efforts were made to implicate Savita Behn Bharat Singh Pasaya [sarpanch of Pandra, Dohod district, Gujarat] and her family members in false allegations, she proved her innocence before a large gathering of villagers and officials.

All round progress

When women succeed in overcoming heavy odds to achieve good results in panchayats and also face vested interests with courage, it has an exemplary impact on a large number of other women. They also want to come forward to participate more actively in village affairs and contribute to the welfare of the community. Apart from this, it is also quite evident from the examples given above that the more active role of women in village often contributes to the welfare of the entire community and several important areas which were neglected earlier, now get prioritised. Thus it is in the interests of not just women but the entire village community to encourage the further empowerment of women in village affairs. The 33% reservation for women in panchayat raj institutions is an important part of this empowerment of women. To further strengthen the effort of elected women representatives, the government should provide greater security to women from the anger of powerful vested interests who try to harm and harass them in various ways. Voluntary organisations should also play a crucial role in helping and training elected women representatives.

WOMEN'S RESERVATION BILL

The 73rd and the 74th Constitutional Amendments have provided for 33% quotas for women's representation in all local self-government institutions.

Prior to these Constitutional Amendments the state of Karnataka had reserved25% women's quota in Panchayati Raj

Institutions and the state of Maharashtra has also passed 30% reservation for women in urban-local and rural self-government institutions and more recently Bihar has in its new Bihar Panchayati Raj Act 2006 stipulated a 50% reservation in its Panchayats for women. Ratifying the 73rd and 74th Constitutional Amendments by the parliament in 1993 bolstered all National Political Parties to announcing 33% reservation for women in Parliament. This is known as the 81st Constitutional Amendment or Women's Reservation Bill which was tabled in 1996. It has been met with a great deal of resistance and has not been passed since then even though it has been tabled many times. It is to be mentioned here that on May 2004 General Elections out of the total 539 Legislators only 49 women legislators were elected

WOMEN'S SUFFRAGE MOVEMENT: A BRIEF HISTORY

Women traditionally the marginalized community in society has found it difficult to bring about positive change for themselves within the political processes.

Women through time have always been at the fringes of governance and political processes. It was only after the Suffrage Movement started that women were looked as equal citizens of society. In effect the Suffrage Movement began as a movement in the 1800's across the world to guarantee voting rights to women which were denied to them before. Most countries after a great deal of struggle by its female populace, were given the voting rights but with severe restrictions such as women could only vote but not stand for elections or since women were traditionally homemakers they would only vote for issues relating to the home.

It was only in the last century that the movement picked up and more and more electoral rights and privileges were granted to them. India granted its female electoral community the right to vote as early as 1947 but many countries like Switzerland granted voting rights to women as late as the 1970's. Sadly; the Middle East has not yet completely given voting rights to its women as yet. To be able to vote is not only the ability to participate in political processes but it also recognizes women as equal citizens of society and of the Nation-State. The right to vote translates into the recognition of the fact that women are not only caretakers of home but do have their own issues and concerns which needs to be addressed.

BACKGROUND ON WOMEN LEGISLATORS – INTERNATIONAL COMPARISON

The women's Suffrage movement has come along way from just demanding Right to Vote. This movement in the last century has produced many female world leaders and Legislators who have taken countries to new levels of progress and prosperity. President Srimavo Bandarnayake was the first politically elected head of state of Sri Lanka in 1960 followed by Indira Gandhi OF India, Golda Mayer of Israel, and Margaret Thatcher of Great Britain ,ANGELA Merkel of Germany to name a few influential women leader.

The former British Prime Minister Margaret Thatcher (1979-1990) is known for pulling Great Britain from the throes of Economic Depression and making it the Super Power it is today. Known as the 'Iron Lady" a name given to her by the soviets, she took tough decisions that have helped bring about the economic boom that England experienced under her. She also deftly handled the Falklands Crisis bring a victory for Great Britain. Prime Minister Thatcher was also prudent enough to change her stance on the Soviet Union during the Cold War heralding the end of communist regime in USSR

The INTER PARLIAMENTARY UNION has mentioned that the number of women in Parliament is so less that many more years are required before equality of the sexes is achieved in Legislatures across the world. Most women legislators in developing and developed countries have faced and face many problems in first getting elected and if elected, then to carry out their office term without too much male influence. Most countries have inscribed in their constitution or Legislation some kind of the positive measures for women and there are about 50 countries where the political counties have introduced quotas or other measures in their statutes. Sweden has the Zipper System whereby every other candidate in the electoral process has to be a woman. Positive action has seen immediate results, some countries like Rwanda seen an increase in the number of women legislators who now stand to be 48.8 %.(Dahlerup 2006)

Women in western countries are slightly better placed than their developing country counterparts as women legislators face fewer stigmas and are also easily accepted. Whereas women in developing countries have to be from the political elite class to be part of the legislation process. There are very few exceptions to this occurrence like Mayawati and Uma Bharti. Women in any developed country look at politics as a viable career option whereas women in India and developing countries join politics mostly at the behest of the male relatives to safeguard their political bastions.

Highlights of the Reservation Bill

1. As nearly as may be one-third of all seats in Lok Sabha and State Legislative

   Assemblies shall be reserved for women.
2. Reservation shall apply in case of seats reserved for Scheduled Castes (SCs) and Scheduled Tribes (STs) as well.
3. Seats to be reserved in rotation will be determined by draw of lots in such a way that a seat shall be reserved only once in three consecutive general elections.

CRITIQUE TO THE WOMEN'S RESERVATION BILL

1. Rotational reservation. Rotational reservation of one-third of the seats exclusively for women would lead to a grave uncertainty for sitting male MPs eroding their meticulously developed political base and leaving them no scope to pursue politics as a life long career.
2. The Bill also ignores an important recommendation of the Joint Parliamentary Committee on the 81 Amendment Bill about extending reservation to Rajya Sabha and Legislative Councils that was incorporated in the Clause 21 of its Report
3. The Bill turns women's quota into a zero sum game where women would get seats only if male MPs were removed from one third of the constituencies.

4. Reservation for Minorities within Women's Reservation Bill.

Infact most political parties have cited flaws in the present bill. The Samajwadi Party (S.P.) and the Rashtriya Janata Dal (RJD) want separate quotas for Other Backward Classes (OBCs), Dalits and minorities within the seats that will be reserved for women in Parliament and the State Assemblies. The Janata Dal (United) is also in favour of quotas within the quota for women.

This has led to forming a deadlock and for the past many years and there do not appear any signs of breakthrough.

ALTERNATIVES TO THE WOMEN RESERVATIONS BILL

Since the first introduction of this bill these has been a great deal of debate on what would be the best alternatives to the present bill. Senior Feminist Scholar Madhu Kishwar has in her paper advocated nominating 33% of women as opposed to reserving the constituencies for women also known as the M.S.Gill formula. Rami Chhabra's proposal emphasize converting 50% constituencies into dual member constituencies.

A proposal for *Dual Member Constituencies* has been propounded by Dr.M.M.Joshi who convened a four party meeting in which the proposal for Dual Party Membership was put forth.

The highlights of the proposal are:

1. Current 543 Lok Sabha constituencies would be grouped into three lots of 181 each. In each election, one of these lots would be converted into dual-member constituencies, each electing two Members of Parliament-a male and a female.
2. This would increase the number of elected Lok Sabha members to 724 (362 + 181 + 181) from 543 Lok Sabha constituencies.
3. The dual-membership would rotate after each election to the next lot of 181 constituencies.
4. The proposal would also apply to State Assemblies and to SC and ST constituencies.

Another alternative would be to wait till 2026, when the existing freeze will be lifted on the Lok Sabha and the population will stabilize itself. It would be feasible to then increase the size of the house and to fix an appropriate number of candidates. Secondly, it has been suggested that 33% of the constituencies can be converted into dual member constituencies in which one man and one woman can be elected.

These are few proposals which can change the content of the Bill but still keep the spirit of the bill and also be true to the demands of women groups who want a more active say in governance.

The 73rd and the 74th amendments to the constitution give reservation to women in all Panchayati Raj Institutions. This has lead to unprecedented rise in the number of women in these institutions increasing it to 43% of the total seats. When the Women's Reservation Bill is passed in parliament in whatever form it will herald a change in the way 50% of the population of society (women) is looked at.

11

Equity to Women with Disabilities in India

INTRODUCTION

Women with disabilities are multiply disadvantaged through their status as women, as persons with disabilities, and majority numbers as persons living in poverty.

In May 2002, ESCAP adopted the resolution "Promoting an inclusive, barrier-free and rights-based society for people with disabilities in the Asian and Pacific region in the twenty-first century". The resolution also proclaimed the extension of the Asian and Pacific Decade of Disabled Persons, 1993-2002, for another decade, 2003-2012.

"There are currently some 5.6 billion different people in the world. Some have a difference called disability." —Disability Dimension in Development Action: Manual on Inclusive Planning, United Nations. The 1970s marked a new approach to disability. The concept of human rights for disabled persons began to become more accepted internationally. The Declaration on the Rights of Disabled Persons, adopted by the General Assembly on 9 December 1975, encouraged national and international protection of the rights of the disabled. Recognition was given to the fact that disabled persons were entitled to the same political and civil rights as others, including measures necessary to enable them to become self-sufficient. The declaration reiterated the rights of disabled persons to education, medical services, and placement service. It further recognized their right to economic and social security, to employment, to live with their families, to participate in social and creative events, to be protected against all exploitation, abuse or degrading behaviour, and to avail themselves of legal aid. Realizing the need to promote the full participation of the disabled in the social life and development of their societies, on 16 December 1976, the General Assembly declared the year 1981 International Year of Disabled Persons (IYDP), stipulating that it be devoted to integrating disabled persons fully into society.

"Around the world, women make up just over 51% of the population. Women with disabilities are the most marginalized in Indian society. They are deprived of political, Social, Economic, and health opportunities. The problems of women with disabilities become very complex with other factors such as social stigma and poverty. Women with disabilities have been largely neglected when it comes to research, state policies, the disability and women's movements, and rehabilitation programmes, and this has become a widely accepted fact in recent years. Also, "due to numerous societal standards, they continue to be left out of the decision-making processes. This reality is especially true of women with disabilities in cultures where the role of wife and mother is considered to be the primary role for a female." Irene Feika, Deputy Chairperson of Underrepresented Groups, Disabled People International.

Although this may seem to be of minor importance, the pattern of ignoring and isolating disabled women is repeated throughout national and international publications and websites of people with disabilities.

Education

Women with disabilities do not form a homogeneous group. For example, the mentally ill and mentally retarded, the visually, hearing and speech impaired and those with restricted mobility or with so-called "medical disabilities" all encounter different barriers, of different kinds, which have to be overcome in different ways.

Throughout the Asian and Pacific region, public attitudes are changing regarding the value of educating and training women with disabilities. The prejudice surrounding their ability and value continues to perpetuate the view that educating them is futile. Opportunities for girls with disabilities to receive an education or to attend training courses are available to only a few. For example, the then International Council on Education of the Visually Handicapped estimated that only two per cent of visually-impaired children in developing countries receive any formal schooling. In China, where there are some 5 million disabled children aged between 7 and 15 years, only 6 per cent are enrolled in schools. It is reasonable to expect that the number of girls included in those estimates is significantly less than half.

One report on women with disabilities in the Raichur district of Karnataka State, India, indicated that the literacy rate of such women was 7 per cent compared to a general literacy rate for the State of 46 per cent.

Traditionally, schools for disabled children are most commonly segregated institutions for those with visual, hearing and intellectual impairments. Girls with extensive physical disabilities have even less opportunity for schooling. The few special schools, concentrated in large cities, have residential facilities; the residential system discriminates against access by girls. So long as education for people with disabilities is largely confined to a segregated system, only a few disabled girls and women will be benefited.

Evidence also indicates that a predominantly segregated school system for disabled children is unlikely to be adequate and accessible for this group of children, and that it is also educationally inferior. A study of disabled girls, both in special (usually residential) schools and in regular schools, found that those in special schools were less proficient in basic literacy and numeracy skills, had lower expectations about their own capabilities and lacked confidence in social settings. Thus, it is obvious that mainstreaming girls with disabilities into society must begin at school.

Education is the key to the advancement of women and girls with disabilities as it provides access to information, enables them to communicate their needs, interests and experiences, brings them into contact with other students, increases their confidence and encourages them to assert their rights. Without a basic education, their chances for employment are almost nil. Hence, there is an urgent need to consider policies and programmes that will place greater emphasis on the participation of women with disabilities in the mainstream education system. Certainly the challenges are great. *In the year 2003 Ministry of social justice and empowerment has introduced novel scheme of providing scholarships for people with disabilities to pursue higher education. The important feature of this programme is it reserves 50% of scholarships for women with disabilities.*

Employment

Women in general face discrimination in employment. For women with disabilities, this discrimination is far greater. In situations where there is high unemployment, opportunities for remunerative work tend to be severely limited. When disabled women do find jobs, they receive considerably lower wages. For example, even for an industrialized country, studies have shown that a disabled woman working full-time earns only 56 per cent of the salary of a full-time employed disabled man. In fact, disabled women earn the lowest wages compared to disabled men or non-disabled women.

Furthermore, in addition to the prejudice and discrimination barrier, the inaccessibility of the physical environment (e.g., buildings, roads, transport and toilet facilities) is a serious obstacle to disabled women working outside their homes.

Since the lack of mobility limits disabled women from obtaining raw materials and marketing their products themselves, engaging in piece-work is the most common form of income-generation available to them. Examples of piecework by disabled women and girls include labour-intensive and poorly paid activities such as weaving, sewing, basket making, the assembling of toys and production of handicraft items.

The materials are delivered to their homes and finished products are collected by agents. There is no legal or social protection. Disabled women and girls may be exposed to unsafe materials and subjected to excessive hours of work under harsh conditions. Even where disabled women have jobs, their rights as workers may be overlooked. Faced with discrimination, little job mobility and few skills, disabled women workers may be forced to endure oppressive working conditions.

Social exclusion

Women with disabilities, especially from rural areas, are likely to be left out of family interactions and community activities. In addition, they are exposed to social stigma and stereotyping within their communities, which leads them to feel devalued, isolated, and ashamed.

A study conducted demonstrated culturally appropriate form independent group living to have a beneficial impact on the women's levels of sociability and their confidence to venture out in public or to social functions.

Living among other women with disabilities and in a non-judgmental environment helped in raising self-esteem and in developing social skills. All of the women who resided in the group house felt accepted, sociable, and confident to venture. Together, confidence in their abilities was strengthened and they could carry out their business with mutual support. Thus, independent group living helps in Social Development (Increased sociability, public confidence and ability to support) and Personal Development (improved self-image, independence and professional motivation)

Despite the most optimistic outlook for change in employment opportunities for women with disabilities, the present reality is that the best hope for productive work may lie in self-employment or group employment probably on a cooperative basis. While numerous projects exist which provide skills training for disabled women, they frequently fall short of meeting the ultimate goal of providing a means of adequate income.

A critical need remains for programmes such as credit schemes, entrepreneurial skills training and advisory services for disabled women and to develop a niche in the market for the goods and services they can offer. For women with disabilities in rural communities more attention has to be paid to developing options for productive and remunerative work, and the requisite training.

Incest is very common in India. Women with disabilities are the easy prey for the exploitation within the family. We also do not discuss these issues in public. The large demand of parents of mentally retarded daughters for compulsory sterilization speak volumes. There is a need to tackle this issue by creating awareness and strengthening the existing laws to punish the offenders severely.

Abandoning girls with disability is another issue that needs strengthening. The measures required are to prevent abandoning by creating awareness and to improve homes for them, which are often the centres of exploitation.

Adoption of children with disabilities is another issue, without which these children stay homeless. There is a need to start SOS homes for these children instead of allowing them stay in orphanages forever.

Apart from economic independence, work is an essential means of enabling a person to develop a sense of identity and self-esteem. Thus, gainful employment is an important means of promoting the social integration of disabled women. *From the perspective of the State, investing in the education and training of women with disabilities, and promoting opportunities for their employment, is sound economic and social policy. Gainfully employed women with disabilities contribute actively to the economy*

Health

Health problems of older women will become an increasingly important issue in developing countries partially because of the sheer increase in absolute numbers. Today, two out of three of the world's 469 million women older than 50 already reside in developing countries. By 2020 three out of four will reside in developing countries, an absolute increase of 408 million.

It is imperative to keep in mind the heterogeneity of developing countries. Aging and disability have close association. Older women constitute a distinct population that requires interventions very different from a population of younger women, who need an emphasis on maternity care. Obviously health problems of women are not homogeneous and cannot all be addressed through the traditional maternal and child health services. The pattern of the health problems older women face reflects to a large extent the level of development of their region and country. Additionally, a woman's well being is a result of all her previous experiences, including factors such as urban or rural residence, marital status, number of children, education, income, and nutrition. Furthermore work has a tremendous influence on women's physical and mental health. Indeed, occupational health problems are emerging as a result of the increased number of women in urban industrial jobs.

Two other issues that emerge as critical, but that are rarely discussed by disabled women's groups are terrorism/riots and its impact on disabled women and AIDS among disabled women.

AIDS poses a bigger threat to disabled women. It is estimated that as much as 10 percent of the population in many Asian countries is already infected by AIDS. Given the extremely poor health care and lack of appropriate AIDS prevention information received by women with disabilities all over the world, the AIDS rates are expected to be very high.

Policy directions and programs towards prevention of mortality and morbidity among women older than 50, and major causes of disease burden are required.

Advocacy

In general, the burden of work for women with disabilities falls squarely on the shoulders of disabled women themselves so that disabled women's issues can be addressed and information and resources shared. Women with disabilities have been an integral part of the history of movements for disability rights. In spite of their contributions, however, disabled women's issues were largely ignored and their accomplishments minimized.

In addition, within disabled women's organizations the focus seems to be on organizing and advocating for women with physical or visual disabilities. There is very little attention paid to women with other disabilities such as women with mental retardation, cerebral palsy, and mental illness even to the point of lack of access to these organizations. With the realization that their future lies firmly in their own hands, women with disabilities around the world are focusing on their enormous strength and emerging resources to directly change the picture. Since the beginning of this current movement for Independent Living, women with disabilities have been active organizers and advocates for the rights of all people with disabilities.

A BBC report states that "War, poverty, lack of health care and lack of decent working conditions and safety regulations are the fundamental causes of most disabling impairments. The problem is circular: poverty means few resources; few resources perpetuate poverty at the same time as they cause disability."

Disabled women in India face numerous challenges. "In the absence of well coordinated government policies aimed at integrating disabled people in mainstream activities, disabled women live under extremely difficult conditions, for not only are they women but most of them are in the rural areas. The women with disabilities in India are discriminated against equality. Discrimination deprives disabled women of vital life experiences, and therefore by denying them the opportunity to participate fully in community affairs they are deprived of equality of opportunity."

Without effective remedial action, the consequences of disability will add to the obstacles to the development of women with disabilities. Hence it is essential that we include immediate, adequate and appropriate measures for the equalization of opportunities for girls and women with disabilities in the following areas:

Some of the key areas of concern to disabled women include:

- Awareness: to highlight the plight of women with disabilities, especially in rural areas
- Education: Disabled girls are less likely to attend school than disabled boys.
- Training: Professional and Vocational-limited access into training programmes.
- Employment: Disabled women are less likely to be granted loan facilities or be employed
- Violence: Women and girls with disabilities are particularly vulnerable to violence, especially within the home situation. Sexual abuse is quite common,

especially among women with mental and/or hearing disabilities. Abuse by physicians and caregivers, e.g. forced sterilization, is common.

- Health services: Refusal of health workers to advise disabled women and girls on appropriate family planning services and methods
- Empowerment

Some of the needs to be addressed:

- Public education and awareness programmes to promote positive perceptions on the potential of disabled women in society
- Career-oriented education for disabled women
- The right to control their own fertility
- Legislative provisions to promote and protect the human rights of disabled women
- Accessible, well-equipped resource centres and clinics that will provide information on issues affecting disabled women
- Provisions in the social security system that will deal specifically with the needs of disabled women, especially young disabled mothers
- Development of specific measures to redress the social and economic exploitation of disabled women in rural areas and informal settlements.

Among approximately 40 countries in the Asia and Pacific region, 25 countries already have self-help organizations of disabled persons. Twenty of these organizations are nationwide cross-disability organizations.

One Indian disabled woman frames the situation this way: "The issues of women with disabilities are same as other women in India plus more [complex] as they lack access to education, resulting in all the problems linked with illiteracy such as poverty, lack of decision making power and lack of available options. Because of disability they are not considered to be women who can fulfil the traditional roles of Indian women. The concept that a woman has rights is well adopted by the women in India, however not by women with disabilities."

An Indian disability activist says: "In a society where the practice of gender inequality has become a convention, disabled women are the most isolated and marginalized. After years of struggle, disabled men have succeeded to some extent in making their voice heard. A special initiative is required to make sure that disabled women are also heard."

Tools for Empowerment

Non-governmental organizations can play a powerful role in counteracting the cycle of oppression through which disabled women are denied access to support and resources that would empower them to reach their potential and contribute to the community.

The need for funding support presents a critical challenge for women with disabilities. One survey respondent summed it up: "there is much to be done and not enough resources to do it with."

Some of the recommendations to NGOs to more effectively include women with disabilities:

- Disability organizations, leadership training projects and independent living services must collect data on involvement of women and girls with disabilities and conduct specific outreach efforts to include women with disabilities.
- Mainstream organizations must support and work in partnership with organizations led by women with disabilities.
- Women with disabilities must be involved in all policy and decision making processes, and at every level of the projects: as staff, volunteers, participants, and evaluators.
- Education, vocational training and rehabilitation programs must include women with disabilities, to prepare women and girls for careers and gainful employment.
- Rehabilitation and adaptive technology must be available for women with disabilities, and women with disabilities must be involved in the development and production of adaptive devices.

- Health service personnel must be trained to offer informed and sensitive service and education addressing the health needs of girls and women with disabilities.

Non-governmental organizations must work with women with disabilities to pressure governments to effectively implement the recommendations, which have been made over the years by various UN bodies and non-governmental organizations, particularly at the Fourth World Conference on Women in Beijing in 1995.

- Entrepreneurship development cum pre vocational training cum Vocational Training cum placement multipurpose centres to promote self and group employment (with a cross disability approach) for women need to establish at least one in each Taluk/block level with hostel facilities. After successful training and placement in the open employment/self or group employment independent living houses need to be supported by the government. Such houses should be identified from the government housing projects and houses in the ground floor with accessibility should be provided in addition to providing loans to purchase accessible taxi/auto rickshaw/cycle rickshaws for commuting to the work place. NGO's who are interested in building such housing facility for workingwomen with disabilities need to be supported with grants.
- Women with disabilities working in the agriculture related work needs extra support.

Other Recommendations

Aligning with the Biwako Millennium Framework for action: towards an inclusive, barrier-free and rights-based society for persons with disabilities in Asia and the Pacific

The Commission has to set the following targets

- By 2005, Governments should ensure anti-discrimination measures by forming special task forces to protect women with disabilities.
- By 2005, self-help organizations adopt policies to promote full representation of women with disabilities,

- By 2005, women with disabilities should be included in all the policy making bodies from panchayath to parliament levels
- Set up state wise task force to prepare white paper on the quality of services available for girls/women with disabilities and all the institutions managed or supported by the government and other donors.
- The Commission should insist on 50% Reservations for girls with disabilities in schools and colleges (out of the existing quota) as well as 50% of the total of job opportunities, reserved for persons with disabilities, ranging from a minimum of 30% and to a maximum of 50% as per the PWD Act, 1995.
- In order to improve the quality of life of women with disabilities in the rural and urban India, district CBR Societies for women with disabilities should function in cooperation with CBR societies for persons with disabilities at the district level, with the District Commissioner as the Chairman of the and the Deputy Director, Women & Child Development as the Secretary. All organizations working for women with disabilities and all organizations of women with disabilities and Self-Help Groups of Parents of adolescent girls with disabilities should become members of the society. A sample of the By-laws of the District CBR Society for persons with disabilities is enclosed and By-laws for district CBR Society for Women with Disabilities need to be developed.
- In urban areas in addition to the reservation, women with disabilities are finding it extremely difficult to get hostel facilities. Therefore, a 3% reservation should be made in all existing women's hostels for women with disabilities.
- There is a need for a scheme to support Self help mutual aid groups of women with disabilities on the lines of Stree Shakthi in Karnataka and the DFID Velugu programme in Andhra Pradesh for women with disabilities and this should include a seed money to start both self and group employment. In addition to

promoting self and group employment, there is a need for EDP programmes, both rural and urban, for women with disabilities to start their own cooperatives on the lines of SEWA, both in Khadi Commission and all the poverty alleviation programmes. Industrial development corporations. Women's development cooperatives should provide skill development, financial support and marketing linkages. In all the shops and malls owned by government or cooperatives or quasi government, out of the 3% reservation, 50% reservation should be made for women with disabilities and it should be allotted at 50% of the cost.

- Finally, about movies and media, initiatives should be taken to regulate the media, which are mainly focusing on women's external beauty to promote the brands and nothing beyond. We can promote this on the lines of the Erikson Company, Finland which states women with disabilities should also promote the popular brands. This will help to fight for the age-old image about women and help people to appreciate inner beauty.
- Under Sarva shisha Abhiyan a special programme for the inclusion of girls with disability in ICDS and elementary schools should be launched on the lines of Joyful inclusion and Udisha Portage programme launched by the Women and child Development Department, Government of Karnataka in cooperation with CBR NETWORK (South Asia)
- The existing practices of discrimination based on degree of disability or econominc criterion should be removed for children with disability up to the age of 0-14 years for the educational purpose to scale up the access to basic educational services.

CLASS, CASTE AND GENDER-WOMEN IN PARLIAMENT IN INDIA

Recent reports in India indicating that many women politicians are finding it difficult to participate in politics, let alone equalize the gender gap that exists, point to an increasing need to analyse the role that women play in Indian politics. The latest elections, with its saga of violence and conflicting rhetoric, further support this need.

A recent "Times of India" report (February 1998) corroborates much of what has been discussed in this handbook: namely that "domestic responsibilities, lack of financial clout, rising criminalization of politics and the threat of character assassination" are making it increasingly difficult for women to be part of the political framework. Moreover, women politicians point out that even within the political parties, women are rarely found in leadership positions. In fact, "women candidates are usually fielded from 'losing' constituencies where the party does not want to 'waste' a male candidate".

In this section we examine the results of a study of women parliamentarians in India during the Tenth Parliament (1991-1996). The discussion focuses on three main areas: the social profile of women parliamentarians; the routes they have taken to get to their political position; and the public policy areas in which they were involved.

THE INDIAN POLITICAL SYSTEM

India is a bicameral parliamentary democracy, with a strong multi-party political system. The lower house is called the Lok Sabha (Peoples' Assembly) and has 545 members. The upper house is called the Rajya Sabha (States' Assembly) with 250 members. In 1991, women constituted 5.2 per cent of the membership of the Lok Sabha and 9.8 per cent of the membership of the Rajya Sabha. This was lower than the preceding 1989 parliament. The election results in 1996 showed a further decline in women's representation. This trend is worrying given the recent state-led initiatives to ensure women's representation in political institutions.

One of the reasons for this decline may be the strength of the party system itself, which can lead to the marginalization of issue-based politics, or to an expropriation of movements that are based on single issues. The women's movement in India has had to confront this issue. Indian political parties are, however, organizationally weak and dependant on local elites. This might be a second factor for the resistance to implementation of gender-sensitive political initiatives.

Women's Movement and the Issue of Representation

The demand for greater representation of women in political institutions in India was not taken up in a systematic way until the setting up of the Committee on the Status of Women in India (CSWI) which published its report in 1976. Before this the focus of the growing women's movement had been on improving women's socio-economic position. The CSWI report suggested that women's representation in political institutions, especially at the grass-roots level, needed to be increased through a policy of reservation of seats for women. In 1988, the National Perspective Plan for Women suggested that a 30 per cent quota for women be introduced at all levels of elective bodies. Women's groups insisted that reservation be restricted to the panchayat (village council) level to encourage grass-roots participation in politics. The consensus around this demand resulted in the adoption of the 73rd and 74th amendments to the Indian Constitution in 1993.

In 1995, the question of quotas was raised again, but this time the focus was women in parliament. Initially, most political parties agreed to this proposition. But soon doubts surfaced. When the bill addressing this issue was introduced in the Eleventh Parliament in 1997, several parties and groups raised objections. The objections focused around two main issues: first, the issue of overlapping quotas for women in general and those for women of the lower castes; second, the issue of elitism. Most women's groups felt that the caste issue was a divisive one for women. Also, many felt uneasy about giving special privileges to elite women by ensuring seats for them in the parliament, while they had previously supported quotas for women at the grass-roots level of the panchayats. To date, the amendment has not been passed by parliament. However, the current government of the Hindu nationalist BJP has committed itself to introducing another quota bill for women in parliament.

PROFILE OF WOMEN IN THE INDIAN PARLIAMENT

The 39 women representatives in the 1991-1996 Indian Parliament were mostly middle-class, professional women, with little or no links to the women's movement. A significant number of them accessed politics through their families, some through student and civil rights movements, and some as a result of state initiatives aimed at increasing representation from the lower castes.

Gender and Caste in Parliament

Caste has been an important feature of Indian public and political life. Most of the women MPs in the Tenth Parliament were members of the higher castes. For example, there were six women from the Brahmin caste. This represents a sizeable 17.14 per cent of the women MPs, while Brahmins comprise only 5.52 per cent of the population. However, it is important to guard against making an easy correlation between caste and political representation. For example, of the six women who are Brahmins, two are MPs from the Communist Party of India. In both cases the caste factor is less important than their privileged class backgrounds. Further, both were products of political movements, the nationalist struggle and the anti-emergency movement.

The number of women who are able to avail of India's caste-based reservation system remains small. While 22 per cent of the parliamentary seats were reserved for the Scheduled Castes, women occupied only 4.1 per cent of the reserved seats. Two women MPs were from what are called the Scheduled Tribes. However, out of 39 women MPs in the Tenth Lok Sabha (representing seven per cent of the total), 14 per cent were from the Scheduled Castes. Two women MPs belonged to the "backward" castes and represented open constituencies. Caste, therefore, affects the profile, loyalties, and work of representatives in the Indian Parliament.

Class, Social Position and Gender in Public Life

Out of the 39 women MPs in the 1991-1996 Lok Sabha, 32 had postgraduate qualifications; in the Rajya Sabha 14 out of the 17 women were graduates. The class position of these women is obviously more important to their educational levels than caste. Only one out of the seven lower caste women MPs was not a graduate, and the one Scheduled Caste woman MP in the Rajya Sabha had postgraduate education. The levels of education are also reflected in the professional profiles of these women. Thirty per cent of women MPs in the Rajya Sabha for example were lawyers, and 25 per cent in the Lok Sabha were either teachers or lecturers.

Most of the women MPs (about 65 per cent) were between their late 30s and 60s, and therefore did not have the responsibility of bringing up a young family. Given the almost universal marriage pattern that exists in India, the figure for unmarried MPs is extraordinarily high, and indicates the social pressures on women who join public life. For those who are married, the pressures of public life are eased a bit by their class situation. Most MPs are able to afford paid help in the home. In many cases the joint family system, or at least strong family support also helps. However, the constraints of family life continue to be real concerns even for privileged women.

Women have different strategies to cope with these constraints. If the family has accepted a woman's career in politics, she can negotiate with her family. This is more likely if the family is an elite political family with more than one member participating in politics.

If the woman was already active in political life before she married, she can face tremendous pressures from her husband's family to conform to a traditional role that allows little scope for pursuing an active political career. A woman politician's options in this case are either to conform to the expectations of the family and retreat from public life, or to leave the family in pursuit of an uncertain future in party politics. In the latter case, the lack of family support and the stigma of divorce are a clear disadvantage for a woman in politics.

Class also mediates the influence of religion. With only one woman Muslim MP in the Rajya Sabha and one in the Lok Sabha, Muslim women are significantly under-represented. Dr. Najma Heptullah, who was also the Deputy Speaker of the Rajya Sabha, is from an elite class and educational background, and enjoys support for her work from both her natal and marital family. Margaret Alva, a Christian, and then Minister of State, and Founder Chair of the National Commission for Women of India, is from a similar background. In both cases the families were involved in the national movement, were influenced by liberal ideology, and were highly educated.

Thus, the majority of women in the Indian Parliament are elite women. While their public role challenges some stereotypes, their class position often allows them far greater range of options than are available to poorer women.

ACCESSING THE SYSTEM

Surprisingly, active participation in the women's movement has not been one of the entry routes into formal party politics for women MPs.

Kinship or more?

"Male equivalence" has been a dominant explanation for how women access political life. The assumption here is that women access political life with the support, backing and contacts of the family, in particular that of the husband. In the sample of 15 women surveyed, 1/3 of the women MPs, for example, have "family support" in the background. However, in a well-argued critique of this theory, Carol Wolkowitz points out that "male equivalence" is an inadequate conceptual framework. First, because it is the public sphere (e.g. state institutions, press, and political discourse) that has to be negotiated if the family decision to put forward a woman in politics is to succeed; it is not a private, but a public matter. Second, in many cases the husbands do not support the candidature of the wife at all. It is the pressure of party political bosses that forces the issue in many cases. The centralized system of distribution of seats in mass political parties helps in this context. A party's concern with levels of representation of certain groups within its ranks, and consequences for legitimacy of the party among the under-represented groups might be the motive for including women.

Social and Political Movements

Together with "kinship link" and state initiatives, an important factor impacting on women's access to political life seems to be social and political movements. These movements have created windows of opportunity and some women have been able to take advantage of these opportunities to access political life. For example, the national movement was an important mobilizer of women. Gandhi's contribution to bringing women into politics is well-documented; the left movement also mobilized women. Women's organizations were constituted under the umbrella and control of the party - the Mahila Congress and the All India Women's Federation (CPI). However, none of the women interviewed in this survey had strong links with the women's wing of their party prior to their entry into parliamentary politics.

The civil rights and anti-emergency movement led by Jaiprakash Narayan (JP) in 1975-1977 was an important political movement that brought students to the forefront of national politics. Many women, both on the right and on the left wing, joined this movement and continued on in politics. Finally, in the context of current politics in India, fundamentalist and communal parties are mobilizing women. One of the most charismatic woman MP's is Uma Bharti, the product of the rise of Hindu militancy in Indian politics. She is the member of the Vishwa Hindu Parishad, a mobilizational wing of the BJP and a "preacher" of Hindu texts by profession. She was in the forefront of the movement that brought down the Babri Mosque in Ayodhyaya.

Political Leadership and Quotas

The influence of individual national leaders is also an important factor that militates against the "male equivalence" theory. While Indira Gandhi, for example, did little to promote women's representation in politics, Rajiv Gandhi accepted the principle of reservation of seats for women. He initiated measures that had a direct impact on the inclusion of women in politics, e.g., the 1993 provision for reservation of 33 per cent of elected seats on village panchayats for women. As we have mentioned, who is able to take advantage of such reservations is mediated by class, ethnicity and caste. However, the support of the state and state/political leaders can be important to women who want to access the political system. Quotas for women as a strategy for accessing the political arena has growing support among women MPs, despite the fact that very few have accessed the system through that route, and are firm believers in the meritocratic argument. Most women MPs have supported the 81st Amendment, which would ensure a 33 per cent quota for women in parliament, even though party discipline has not allowed them to vote for this. This issue highlights the constraints that the party system poses for women politicians.

GENDER AND PUBLIC POWER

Out of the 20 Congress women MPs in the 1991-1996 Lok Sabha, none was a Cabinet minister; two were Ministers of State; and two were Deputy Ministers of State. In the Rajya Sabha, out of seven Congress women MPs, one is a Minister of State. The portfolios of these Ministers included, Human Resource Development, Civil Aviation and Tourism, Health and Family Welfare, and Personnel and Public Grievances. All these are generally regarded as "soft portfolios"; this does not, however, take away from the responsibility that these women ministers have. One Congress woman MP is the Deputy Chairperson of the Rajya Sabha. At the level of the party, one MP was on the disciplinary committee of the party, and one was the President of the Mahila Congress. Among BJP women, the one Rajya Sabha member was the spokesperson on the economy and general political line of the party. Of the 10 members of the Lok Sabha, one was one of the vice-presidents of the party, and two were on the National Executive Committee of their party.

The system of institutional incentives and disincentives at the level of the party and parliament impact on the issues that women espouse in parliament. Most women MPs interviewed did not have women's issues high on their list of interests. Rather, they wanted to be on committees relating to economy, international relations, and trade. As ambitious women these MPs want to be where power and influence converge.

The Accountability Question

One of the important issues for any discussion on gender and representation has to deal with the constituency that women represent. As there are no "women's only" constituencies, women MPs are not accountable to women as women. And yet, when issues regarding women are raised in the parliament, these women are expected to, and do participate in the debates. Issues such as the welfare of women and violence against women are particularly important in uniting women MPs. These issues are discussed in the "ladies room" in the parliament.

However, as all the MPs questioned made clear, they are "party women first"; party whip is rarely flouted.

Some women MPs are also asked by the party leadership to get involved in the women's wing of the party. While the women MPs do not necessarily see this role as an enhancement of their status within the party, some have made a success of this role and as a result gained influence with the leadership of the party.

As "party women" with political ambitions, women MPs respond to the institutional incentives and disincentives that are placed on them. All these factors limit the potential of these women MPs representing the interests of Indian women across a range of issues.

As a result there seems to be little regular contact between women's groups and women MPs. The exception here is of course the women's wing of political parties that do liaise with women MPs. This does allow the possibility of women MPs becoming conduits between the party's leadership and its women members. They are also consulted from time to time by the party leadership on issues regarding the family, and women's rights. But non-party women's groups do not seem to approach women MPs.

Women's representation in the parliament, while important on the grounds of social justice and legitimacy of the political system, does not easily translate into improved representation of women's various interests.

While we cannot assume that more women in public offices would mean a better deal for women in general, there are important reasons for demanding greater representation of women in political life. First is the intuitive one - the greater the number of women in public office, articulating interests, and seen to be wielding power', the more the gender hierarchy in public life could become disrupted. Without sufficiently visible, if not proportionate, presence in the political system - "threshold representation" - a group's ability to influence either policy-making, or indeed the political culture framing the representative system, is limited. This fact is confirmed by the various other contributions in this volume. Further, the fact that these women are largely elite women might mean that the impact that they have on public consciousness might be disproportionately larger than their numbers would suggest.

Second, and more important, we could explore the strategies that women employ to access the public sphere in the context of a patriarchal socio-political system. These women have been successful in subverting the boundaries of gender, and in operating in a very aggressive male-dominated sphere. Could other women learn from this example? The problem here is, of course, precisely that these women are an elite. The class from which most of these women come is perhaps the most important factor in their successful inclusion into the political system. We can, however, examine whether socio-political movements provide opportunities for women to use certain strategies that might be able to subvert the gender hierarchy in politics. Finally, we can explore the dynamics between institutional and grass-roots politics. As this study demonstrates, the "politicization of gender" in the Indian political system is due largely to the success of the women's movement.

Women representatives have thus benefited from this success of the women's movement. However, there has been limited interaction between women representatives and the women's movement - one of the important areas of weakness behind both the effectiveness of women MPs as well as that of the women's movement. This is, perhaps, the issue that the women's movement needs to address as part of its expanding agenda for the 1990s.

12

Panchayati Raj System and Rural Development in India

"India is poor because the villages of India are poor. India will be rich if the villages of India are rich. Panchayats should be given greater power; for we want the villagers to have a greater measure of real swaraj [self-government] in their own villages." [Jawaharlal Nehru, first Prime Minister of India]

After the independence, Community Development Programme was started in 1952 AD. But because it was not attached with the people, therefore it couldn't prove to be a success story. People took it as a burden put on them by the government. A team, under the leadership of Balwantrai Mehta tried to find out the cause for the failure of this programme and came up with the inference that there should be an organisation at village level, which would select the true beneficiaries and implement various government programmes and schemes.

This organisation would act as the representative of all the villagers and should ensure the development of the village as well as participation of villagers. In this way Balwantrai Mehta tried to achieve local self-government though Panchayats (the organisation). This concept of local self-government was the right step towards decentralized democracy. In this process, the State of Rajasthan for the first time adopted the three leveled structure of Panchayati Raj-Village Level, Intermediate Level and District Level. In 1977 AD. Ashok Mehta Committee was set up to review the working of Panchayats. The committee found out that Panchayati Raj is the soul of democracy and therefore it should be empowered with more authority. Those Panchayats which formed after 1977 AD. are known as Second Generation Panchayats. In West Bengal, the Panchayats became more effective after accepting the suggestions made in this report.

During the decade of 1990, it was realized that without constitutional power, the self-government can't be fruitful, therefore the Central Government passed the 73rd Constitutional Amendment Act in 1992, which became effective from 20th April 1993 (from the date of publication in the Gazette of India).

BASIC CONCEPTS OF PANCHAYATI RAJ

The basic concept of Panchayati Raj is that the villagers should think, decide and act for their own socio-economic interests. Thus Panchayati Raj Act is related to village self-governance, where the people in the form of an organisation will think, decide and act for their collective interest. Self-government allows us to decide about ourselves without hampering others interest. Whenever we talk about collective benefit one point is clear that there is no conflict between the villagers' collective interest on one side and societal and national interest on the other, rather they are complementary. Where the Panchayats end their activities the state govt. takes them up. The state govt. plays their major roles.

- To support the village Panchayats
- To co-ordinate the village Panchayats
- To ensure the implementation of this system.

Besides these, once the democratic institution in the villages and towns becomes strong, the people's representatives can express the problems of their constituency in a better way. This will help in policy determination for national interest. This plan for 'Swaraj' (Self-government) can't be fulfilled only by making a new law. For the success of self-government self reliance is must. The self-reliance means: every village must produce according to its capacity and try to increase its capacity, which can be achieved in following ways:

- By identifying economic and human resources of the Panchayat area,
- By estimating the capacity of these resource,
- By making decision for utilizing these resources,
- By formulating plans,
- By implementing plans,
- By evaluating plans.

Thus we find that self-governance is a concept which is the base for success of democracy. And for self-governance Panchayati Raj System is a must.

SOME IMPORTANT FEATURES OF THE ACT

Constitutional Status : The 73rd Constitutional Amendment Act was passed in 1992 but became effective from 20th April, 1993 after being published in the Gazette of India. This was included as Part IX of the Constitution of India. The rights and duties of the Panchayats have been included in schedule XI of the Constitution.

Three Leveled System : The Legislature of a state may, by law, make provisions for three leveled system-village level, intermediate level and district level.

Election : The representatives are elected for 5 years by the electorate of a Panchayat area.

Reservation of Seats : Some seats in the Panchayat shall be reserved for the Scheduled Castes, Scheduled Tribes and Women.

The number of reserved seats for Schedules Castes and Scheduled Tribes will be proportionate to the ration of population of SCs and STs to Total Population of the Panchayat area.

One third of the total seat will be reserved for women. It will include the reserved seats for SCs and STs.

Responsibility : Panchayats have two main responsibilities:

a. To plan for economic development and social justice.

b. To implement these plans.

Powers and Authorities : The Legislature of the State

may authorize a Panchayat to levy, collect and appropriate taxes, tolls and fees. It may also provide the Panchayat for making grants-in-aid to form the Consolidated Fund of the State. These funds can be used for implementing the plans.

Constitution of Finance Commission : Finance Commission has to be constituted in every state to review the financial position of the Panchayats and to make recommendation to the Governor regarding the allocation of fund to be Panchayats.

Panchayat and Environment : Although the 73rd Amendment Act has not mentioned the term "Environment" in the Schedule IX but out of the 29 duties some are related to environment in one way or the other, these are-

1. Agriculture, including agricultural extension.
2. Land improvement, implementation of land reforms, lands consolidation and soil conservation.
3. Minor irrigation, water management and watershed development.
4. Social forestry and farm forestry.
5. Minor forest produce.
6. Small scale industries including food-processing industries.
7. Khadi, village and cottage industries.
8. Rural housing.
9. Drinking water.
10. Fuel and fodder.
11. Non-conventional energy sources.
12. Education including primary and secondary schools.
13. Health and sanitation, including hospitals, primary health centres and dispensaries.
14. Maintenance of community assets.

CENTRE ON PANCHAYATI RAJ AND ENVIRONMENT

During the decade of 1990, it was realized that without constitutional power, the self-government or Panchayati Raj couldn't be fruitful; therefore the Central Government passed the 73rd constitutional Amendment Acts of 1992, which became effective from 20th April 1993. The basic concept of Panchyati Raj is that the villagers should think, decide and act for their own socio-economic interests. Thus, it is related to village self-governance, where the people in the form of an organisation will think, decide and act for their collective interests.

For integrated rural development decentralization of power and resources to Panchayati Raj Institutions (PRIs) is an essential element. It has been also realized that Panchayat can play effective role through drawing local people's participation in sustainable harvesting and management of local resources. If financial and technical assistance is provided to them, they will certainly take positive initiatives in solving local environmental problems. Agriculture, land improvement, forestry, tree planting, animal husbandry, village and cottage industries, drinking water, poverty alleviation programmes, health, sanitation, family welfare etc. are necessarily the concern of the village Panchayats. To fulfil the expectations of rural development consideration of environment in its totality (economic, political, technological, cultural, historical, moral and aesthetics) is very essential. Documenting environmental issues form local, national and international points of view for providing insight into environmental problems and to promote environmental consciousness among rural masses are equally important. Therefore, Ministry of Environment and Forests, Government of India, has set up ENVIS Centre on Panchayati Raj and Environment at Indian Environmental Society (IES), Delhi under the ENVIS scheme, with the following main objectives.

OBJECTIVES:

- To develop facilities for collection, compilation and dissemination of information related to environment and rural development to the Panchayats.
- To develop networking of Panchayati Raj Institutions and work as connecting link between Ministry and Panchayats.
- To provide regular input to Panchayat about latest happenings in the field of environment through Newsletter, other resource material and training programmes.

- To conduct training programmes on various crucial issues of environment and related areas prevailing in Panchayats.

IES publish a quarterly newsletter named "Panchayat" to disseminate various environmental news, government schemes and other information useful for empowerment of Panchayats and grass root people. Besides, the Centre has published resource materials for environmental awareness among common people and organizes training camps and workshops. The newsletter and booklets are widely distributed among user groups. The Centre also provides useful information about various publications and resource materials on Panchayati Raj and Environment as well as about organizations involved with Panchayats. The Centre is also compiling Success Stories in this context from various parts of the country.

Structure of Panchayat Raj

1. District Level = Zilla Parisad

People's Government

- o President
- o Vice-President
- o Elected members &
- o Ex-officio Members

Development Administration

- o Chief Secretary
- o Deputy Secretaries
- o Chief Accounts Officer
- o Chief Planning Officer

2. Block Level = Panchayat Samiti/Block Panchayat/Taluk Panchayat

People's Government

- o Chairman
- o Ex-officio-members

Development Administration

- o Block Development Officer
- o Standing Committee

3. Village Level = Mandal Panchayat/Gram Panchayat

People's Government

- o President
- o Vice-president
- o Elected members*

Development Administration

- o Secretary
- o Village Level Workers

*Elected members of Mandal/Gram Panchayat are elected by college of eligible voters of the Gramsabha

RURAL DEVELOPMENT-ROLE OF PANCHAYATI RAJ INSTITUTIONS IN THE RURAL

Sampoorna Grameen Rozgar Yojana (SGRY)

The objectives of the Sampoorna Grameen Rozgar Yojana is to provide additional employment in the rural areas as also food security, alongside the creation of durable community, social and economic infrastructure in the rural areas. The programme is self-targeting in nature with special emphasis to provide Wage Employment to women, SCs, STs and parents of children withdrawn from hazardous occupations. This Programme is being implemented into two streams :-

- The First Stream of the Programme will be implemented at the District and Intermediate level Panchayats. 50% of the funds are earmarked out of the total funds available under the SGRY and distributed between the District Panchayat and the Intermediate Panchayats in the ratio of 40:60.
- The Second Stream of the Programme will be implemented at the Village Panchayat level. 50% of the SGRY funds are earmarked for this Stream. The entire funds are released to the Village Panchayats through the DRDAs/District Pachayats.

Swarnjayanit Gram Swarozgar Yojana (SGSY)

The objective of SGSY is to bring the assisted poor families above the poverty line by providing them income generating assets through a mix of bank credit and government subsidy. The families of below poverty line (BPL) including artisans, identified through the BPL Census are eligible for assistance under the Scheme. While selecting the new activities priority may be given to those having inherent skill which is primarily constituted by the rural artisans. The role of PRIs in the implementation of this Scheme are as under:-

- The Gram Sabha will approve the list of BPL families.
- The list of key activities and the list of villages identified under the scheme in the Block should be approved by the Intermediate Panchayat.
- The list of swarozgaris finally selected should be made available to the Gram Panchayat for placing it before the next Gram Sabha.
- The Gram Panchayat would actively monitor the performance of the Swarozgaris particularly repayment of loan.
- The District Panchayat will review the performance under this scheme in its General Body Meetings.

Pradhan Mantri Gram Sadak Yojana (PMGSY)

This is a 100% Centrally Sponsored Scheme. This Scheme seeks to provide connectivity to all unconnected habitations in the rural areas with a population of more than 500 persons through good All-weather roads by the end of the Tenth Plan. In Hill States and Desert Areas, the objective would be to connect habitations with a population of 250 persons and above.

The role of PRIs in implementation of this scheme are as under:-

- The District Panchayats (or DRDAs where the District Panchayats do not exist) shall be the competent authority to select the variable best suited for the District, categories them and accord relative weightage to them and shall communicate it to all concerned.
- The Plan should be finalized by the Intermediate Panchayat. Any changes made by the Intermediate Panchayat should be separately mentioned and reasons, thereof, should be indicated.

- The Draft District Rural Roads Plan would be presented to the District Panchayat by the Chief Executive of the District Planning Committee. It should be discussed and adopted by the District Panchayat, with such changes, as may be considered appropriate, but strictly within the framework of the Manual.
- The Rural Roads constructed/upgraded under this Programme will be maintained by the concerned District/ Intermediate Panchayat. Efforts will be made to involve local peoples' participation in the maintenance of Rural Roads.
- All the Road Works will be subjected to Social Audit by way of discussion in the Gram Sabha and the relevant information in this regard will be made available to the Gram Sabha.

Indira Awaas Yojana (IAY)

This scheme provides assistance primarily to the BPL rural households belonging primarily to SCs/STs and freed bonded labour categories.

Benefits of the scheme have also been extended to families of servicemen of the armed and paramilitary forces killed in action.

3% of the houses are also reserved for BPL physically and mentally challenged persons living in rural areas.

The role of PRIs in implementation of this scheme are :-

- The Zilla Parishads or DRDAs on the basis of allocations made and targets fixed shall decide the number of houses to be constructed/upgraded Panchayat wise under IAY, during a particular financial year.
- The Zilla Parishads/DRDAs shall intimate the same to the Gram Panchayat. Thereafter, the Gram Sabha will select the beneficiaries from the list of eligible households, according to IAY Guidelines as per priorities fixed, restricting this number to the target allotted.
- Panchayat Samiti's approval is not required. The Panchayat Samiti should however, be sent a list of selected beneficiaries for their information.

Pradhan Mantri Gramodaya Yojana (PMGY)

This scheme envisages allocation of Additional Central Assistance to the States/UTs for providing/improving the outlay of Basic Minimum Services including "Rural Shelter" in the rural areas. The funds under this Scheme are released by the Ministry of Finance/Ministry of Home Affairs on the basis of recommendations made by the Ministry of Rural Development, being the nodal Ministry for implementation and monitoring of the scheme. The role of PRIs in implementation of this scheme are :-

- The Zilla Parishads/DRDAs will decide the number of houses to be constructed, Panchayat-wise, and the same will immediately be intimated to the Gram Panchayat.
- The Gram Sabha will select the beneficiaries from the list of eligible households, restricting this number to the target allotted.
- The Intermediate-level Panchayat (Panchayat Samiti) will invariably be sent a list of selected beneficiaries.

Credit Cum Subsidy Scheme

This Scheme targets rural families having annual income upto Rs.32,000/-. While subsidy is restricted to Rs.10,000/-, the maximum loan amount can be availed upto Rs.40,000/-under this scheme. The role of PRIs in implementation of this scheme are :- One of the Agencies for implementing the scheme is Zilla Panchayat. The identification of the most appropriate implementing agency under the Credit-cum Subsidy Scheme shall be left to the State Government.

Samagra Awaas Yojana

This is a comprehensive Housing Scheme with a view to ensuring integrated provision of shelter, sanitation and drinking water. This is being implemented in one block each off 25 districts of 24 States and one UT.

The role of PRIs in implementation of this scheme are :-

- The Zilla Parishad, the Block Samiti and the Gram Panchayat will be fully involved in the implementation of this Scheme.

- The special IEC funds of Rs. 5 lakh per district and habitat development funds of Rs. 20 lakh will be routed through DRDAs. DRDAs/ZPs and Public Health Department will be the main implementing agencies.

Innovative Scheme for Housing and Habitat Development and Rural Building Centres

The innovative scheme for housing and habitat development has been designed for standardizing and popularizing/ replicating/propagating cost-effective, environment-friendly housing construction technologies, designs and materials and evolving ideal types of sustainable rural human settlements consistent with agro-climatic variations and natural disaster proneness. The Rural Building Centres Scheme is inter alia designed with the purpose of technology transfer and information dissemination, skill up gradation through training and production of cost effective and environment friendly material components.

Panchayati Raj Institutions are one of the Implementing Agencies under these schemes.

Annapurna

The Annapurna Scheme aims at providing food security to meet the requirement of those senior citizens who though eligible have remained uncovered under the National Old Age Pension Scheme.

The role of PRIs in implementation of this scheme are :-

- The Panchayats identifies the Beneficiaries and communicate the same to Collector/CEO.
- The Gram Sabhas are required to select the Beneficiaries for the Scheme and the lists of beneficiaries so selected by Gram Sabha will be displayed by the Gram Panchayats.
- The Gram Panchayats distribute the Entitlement Cards to the Beneficiaries in Gram Sabha Meetings.
- The Gram Panchayats will give wide publicity to the Scheme and will also be responsible for dissemination of information in regard to the procedure for securing benefits under the Scheme.

Watershed Development Programmes Under DPAP and DD

The Drought Prone Areas Programme (DPAP), Desert Development Programme (DDP) and Integrated Wasteland Development Programme (IWDP) are being implemented on watershed basis and aim at drought proofing and controlling desertification by regeneration of depleted natural resource base. All these three programmes were brought under the Guidelines for Watershed Development with effect from 1.4.1995.

The role of PRIs in implementation of this scheme are :-

- The District Panchayats and other Panchayati Raj Institutions shall have very important role to play in Watershed Development Programmes.
- The PRIs shall have the right to monitor and review the implementation of the programme and provide guidance for improvements in the administrative arrangements and procedures with a view to ensure convergence of other programmes of Ministry of Rural Development such as SGRY, SGSY, IAY, CRSP, Rural Drinking Water Supply, etc.
- At the Village level, the Gram Panchayat shall be fully involved in the implementation of the programme, specially community organization, formation of SHGs and training programmes.
- Gram Panchayat will be responsible for operation and maintenance of assets created during the project.
- The Watershed Action Plan should have the approval of Gram Sabha and it should be a part of annual action plan of Gram Sabha.
- The District Panchayat/DRDA in whose favour the project has been sanctioned will be entitled to affect recovery of funds from any institutions/organization/ individuals and take appropriate action under law if the project is not properly implemented for funds are misutilised or not spent as per Guidelines.
- The Panchayats at any level are also entitled to take on the responsibility of implementing a cluster of

watershed projects in the capacity of Project Implementation Agencies(PIAs), if they so desire.

- PIAs will motivate the Gram Panchayats to pass necessary resolutions to make public contribution, conduct Participatory Rural Appraisal (PRA) exercises, prepare the development plans for the watershed, undertake community organization and training for the village communities, provide technical guidance and supervision of watershed Development activities, inspect and authenticate project accounts, undertake action research to adapt low-cost technologies and/or validate and build upon indigenous technical knowledge, monitor and review the overall project maintenance and further development of the assets created during the project period.
- Under the new initiate 'Haryali', the watershed programmes are to be executed by the Gram Panchayats by facilitating project funds to them. The District and Intermediate Panchayars are to act as PIAs

Computerisation of Land Records (CLR) and Strengthening of Revenue Administration & Updating of Land Records

Under these Schemes funds are released to Revenue Department of the States/UTs for implementation in various districts of the State and not to Panchayati Raj Institutions of State Governments.

The Panchayati Raj Institutions are not being involved in the implementation of these two Schemes.

Accelerated Rural Water Supply Programme (ARWSP)

Under ARWSP, the Central Government is to supplement the efforts of the State Governments in providing access to safe drinking water to all rural habitations of the country.

The role of PRIs in implementation of this scheme are :

- Panchayati Raj Institutions should be involved in the implementation of schemes particularly in selecting the location of standpost, spot sources, operation and maintenance, fixing of cess/water tariff, etc.

- The implementation of the Sector Reform Projects in the identified pilot districts, are also to be carried out either by the District Panchayats or through the District Water and Sanitation Missions (DWSM), which are to be registered societies under the supervision, control and guidance of District Panchayat.
- Wherever PRIs are themselves firmly in place and willing to take up the responsibility and are strong enough to do so, they implement the projects themselves instead of DWSM.
- At the village level, the individual Rural Water Supply Schemes are to be implemented through Village Water and Sanitation Committees which should be committees of Gram Panchayats.
- Drinking water supply assets are transferred to the appropriate level of Panchayats and such Panchayats are to be empowered to undertake operation and maintenance of drinking water systems.

Central Rural Sanitation Programme (CRSP)

This programme aims at improving the general quality of life in rural areas; accelerating coverage in rural areas; generating demand through awareness creation and health education; and controlling incidence of water sanitation related diseases.

The role of PRIs in implementation if this scheme are :-

- Total Sanitation Campaign (TSC) is a community based programme where Panchayati Raj Institutions are in the forefront.
- As per TSC Guidelines, the implementation at the district level is to be done by the District Panchayats. Panchayats at block and village level are to be fully involved for implementation of the programme.
- Where District Panchayat is not in a position to implement the programme, it is being implemented by District Water & Sanitation Mission which is chaired

by Chairperson of District Panchayat and the Village Committees are chaired by the Chairpersons of Gram Panchayats. In the later case, the Village Water & Sanitation Mission are part of the Gram Panchayat.

Swajaldhara

This programme aims at providing Community-based Rural Drinking Water Supply. The key elements of this programmes are namely, (i) demand-driven and community participation approach, (ii) panchayats/communities to plan, implement, operate, maintain and manage all drinking water schemes, (iii) partial capital cost sharing by the communities upfront in cash, (iv) full ownership of drinking water assets with Gram Panchayats and (v) full Operation and Maintenance by the users/Panchayats.

The role of PRIs in implementation of this scheme are :-

- Gram Panchayat shall convene a Gram Sabha Meeting where the Drinking Water Supply Scheme of People's choice including design and cost etc. must be finalized. Gram Panchayats are to undertake procurement of materials/services for execution of schemes and supervise the scheme execution.
- A resolution must be passed in the Gram Panchayat meeting calling for users/beneficiaries to contribute 10% of the capital expenditure. However, GP can remit towards community contribution from its tax revenue (Not from Government Grants) with the approval of Gram Sabha.
- Gram Panchayat will decide whether the Panchayat wants to execute Scheme on its own or wants the State Government Agency to undertake the execution.
- After completion of such schemes, the Gram Panchayat will take over the Schemes for Operation & Maintenance(O&M).
- Panchayat must decide on the user charges from the community so that adequate funds available with Panchayat to undertake O&M.

Information, Education And Communication (IEC)

Information, Education and Communication plays a pivotal role in creating awareness, mobilizing people and making development participatory through advocacy and by transferring knowledge, skills and techniques to the people. The IEC efforts aim at creating awareness and disseminating information on the Rural Development Programmes of this Ministry primarily to the target groups in rural, to the opinion makers and also to the public at large.

The Panchayati Raj Institutions are not being involved in the implementation of the Schemes under IEC Division.

Training Division

The Ministry of Rural Development provides funds to National Institute of Rural Development, State Institutes of Rural Development and Extension Training Centres for providing training to the elected representatives of Panchayats as well as Rural Development functionaries. Funds are also being released under this scheme for holding training courses, seminars, workshops etc on subjects relevant to rural development.

The Panchayati Raj Institutions are not being involved in the implementation of the Schemes under Training Division.

Panchayati Raj

PR Division has been releasing funds to NGOs/Institutions for Action Research Studies and Workshops/Seminar on Panchayati Raj.

The Panchayati Raj Institutions are not being involved in the implementation of the Schemes under Training Division.

Organisational Structure of DRDAs

Each district will have its own District Rural Development Agency. Ordinarily it would be a society registered under a Societies Registration Act. In respect of such states where DRDA does not have a separate identity a separate cell should be created in Zill Parishad which maintains a separate identity and separate accounts, so that the accounts are capable of being audited separately. This Cell should be directly under the charge of CEO or alternatively an officer who has the qualifications to be a Project Director. The accounts of DRDAs should under no circumstances be merged or amalgamated with those of the Zilla Parishads.

Each DRDA should be headed by Project Director, who should be the rank of a Additional District Magistrate. The Project Director should preferably be a senior scale officer of All India Services or a senior officer of the State Service, eligible of appointment to the All India Services. He would be in overall charge of the activities of the DRDA and responsible for interaction with the District/State administration as well as with the Government of India. The PD should be exclusively for DRDA work.

The District Rural Development Agency (DRDA) has traditionally been the principal organ at the District level to oversee the implementation of different anti-poverty programmes. The district Rural Development Agency is visualised as specialized and a professional agency capable of managing the anti-poverty programmes of the Ministry of Rural Development on the one hand and to effectively relate these to the overall effort of poverty eradication in the District. In other words, while the DRDA will continue to watch over and ensure effective utilization of the funds intended for anti-poverty programmes

DRDAs must themselves be more professional and should be able to interact effectively with various other agencies. They are expected to coordinate with the line department, the Panchayati Raj Institutions, the banks and other financial institutions, resources required for poverty reduction effort in the district. It shall be their endeavour and objective to secure inter-sectoral and inter-departmental coordination and cooperation for reducing poverty in the district. It is their ability to coordinate and bring about a convergence of approach among different agencies for poverty alleviation and would set them apart.

The DRDAs are expected to coordinate effectively with the Panchayati Raj Institutions. Under no circumstances will they perform functions of PRIs.

The DRDAs will maintain their separate identity but will function under the chairmanship of the Chairman of Zilla Parishad. They are expected to be a facilitating and supporting organization to Zilla Parishad, providing necessary executive and technical support in respect of poverty reduction efforts. Wherever the Zilla Parishads are not in existence of are not functional, the DRDAs would function under the Collector/ District Magistrate/Deputy Commissioner, as the case may be.

The DRDAs are expected to oversee the implementation of different anti-poverty programmes of the Ministry of Rural Development in the district. This is not be confused with actual implementation, which will be by the Panchayati Raj and other Institutions. The DRDAs will monitor closely the implementation through obtaining of periodic reports as well as frequent field visits. The purpose of the visit should be to facilitate the implementing agencies in improving implementation process, besides ensuring that the quality of implementation of programmes is high. This would include overseeing whether the intended beneficiaries are receiving the benefits under the different programmes.

The DRDAs shall keep the Zilla Parishad, the State and Central Government duly informed of the progress of the implementation of the programmes through periodic reports in the prescribed formats. Special report, as and when called for, shall be provided.

It shall be the duty of the DRDAs to oversee and ensure that the benefits specifically earmarked for certain target groups (SC/ST, women and disabled) reach them. They shall all necessary steps to achieve the prescribed norms.

The DRDAs shall take necessary step to improve the awareness regarding rural development and poverty alleviation particularly among the rural poor. This would involve issues of poverty, the opportunities available to the rural poor and generally infusing a sense of confidence in their ability to overcome poverty. It would also involve sensitizing the different functionaries in the district to the different aspects of poverty and poverty alleviation programmes. The DRDAs will strive to promote transparency in the implementation of different anti-poverty programmes. Towards this end, they shall publish periodically, the details of the different programmes and their implementation.

Keeping in view, the substantial investment that are being made in poverty alleviation programmes, the DRDAs shall ensure financial discipline in respect of the funds received by them, whether from Central of State Governments. They shall also ensure that the accounts are properly maintained including in respect of the funds allocated to banks or implementing agencies in accordance with the guidelines of different programmes.

Thus the role of the DRDA is in terms of planning for effective implementation of anti-poverty programmes; coordinating with other agencies-Governmental, non-Governmental, technical and financial for successful programme implementation; enabling the community and the rural poor to participate in the decision marking process, overseeing the implementation to ensure adherence to guidelines, quality, equity and efficiency; reporting to the prescribed authorities on the implementation; and promoting transparency in decision making and implementation.

In addition the DRDAs shall coordinate and oversee the conduct of the BPL Census and such other surveys that are required from time to time.

The DRDAs shall also carry out/aid in carrying out action research/or evaluation studies that are initiated by the Central/ State Governments.

The DRDAs should deal only with the anti-poverty programmes of the Ministry of Rural Development. If DRDAs are to be entrusted with programmes of other ministries or those of the State Governments, it should be ensured that these have a definite antipoverty focus. Entrusting of any programme to the DRDAs, other than anti-poverty programmes of the Ministry, be it of any other Ministry of Government of India or the respective State Government will have to be done with the approval of the Secretary, Rural Development of the respective State (s), who should examine such request in consultation with the Ministry of Rural Development,

Government of India. In such cases, it must be ensured that adequate provision is made for requisite staffing needed for proper implementation of the programme.

The administration of the DRDA shall be carried out by a governing body. The Governing Body of the DRDA will provide policy directions, approve the annual plan and also review and monitor the implementation of the plan, including the different programmes. They shall give such directions to the DRDA as may be necessary from time to time. The Governing Body of the DRDA will meet once in a quarter.

The composition of the governing body shall be as follows.

i. Chairman of Zilla Parishad Chairman

ii. All MPs and MLAs and MLCs of the District

iii. 1/3rd of Panchayat Samiti Chairpersons to be nominated by rotation in alphabetical order for a tenure of one year, one of whom must belong to SC/ST and another a woman.

iv. CEO of Zilla Parishad/District Collector-Chief Executive Officer/Executive Director

ROLE AND FUNCTIONS OF THE DISTRICT RURAL DEVELOPMENT AGENCY

If effective programme design is critical to successful implementation of rural development programmes, so is an effective delivery agency. None of the anti-poverty programmes can have impact unless they are implemented with clarity of purpose and a commitment to the task. It is here that the DRDAs play a critical role. The DRDAs are not the implementation through overseeing the implementation of different programmes and ensuring that necessary linkages are provided. To this extent the DRDA is a supporting and facilitation organization and needs to play a very effective role as a catalyst in development process.

The district Rural Development Agency is visualised as specialized and a professional agency capable of managing the anti-poverty programmes of the Ministry of Rural Development on the one hand and to effectively relate these to the overall effort of poverty eradication in the District. In other words, while the DRDA will continue to watch over and ensure effective utilization of the funds intended for anti-poverty programmes, it will need to develop a far greater understanding of the processes necessary for poverty alleviation/eradication. It will also need to develop the capacity to build synergies among different agencies involved for the most effective results. It will therefore need to develop distinctive capabilities rather than perform tasks that are legitimately in the domain of the PRIs or the line departments. The role of the DRDA will therefore be distinct from all the other agencies, including the Zilla Parishad.

DRDAs must themselves be more professional and should be able to interact effectively with various other agencies. They are expected to coordinate with the line department, the Panchayati Raj Institutions, the banks and other financial institutions, resources required for poverty reduction effort in the district. It shall be their endeavour and objective to secure inter-sectoral and inter-departmental coordination and cooperation for reducing poverty in the district. It is their ability to coordinate and bring about a convergence of approach among different agencies for poverty alleviation and would set them apart.

The DRDAs are expected to coordinate effectively with the Panchayati Raj Institutions. Under no circumstances will they perform functions of PRIs.

The DRDAs will maintain their separate identity but will function under the chairmanship of the Chairman of Zilla Parishad. They are expected to be a facilitating and supporting organization to Zilla Parishad, providing necessary executive and technical support in respect of poverty reduction efforts. Wherever the Zilla Parishads are not in existence of are not functional, the DRDAs would function under the Collector/ District Magistrate/Deputy Commissioner, as the case may be.

The DRDAs are expected to oversee the implementation of different anti-poverty programmes of the Ministry of Rural Development in the district. This is not be confused with actual implementation, which will be by the Panchayati Raj and other Institutions. The DRDAs will monitor closely the implementation through obtaining of periodic reports as well as frequent field visits. The purpose of the visit should be to facilitate the implementing agencies in improving implementation process, besides ensuring that the quality of implementation of programmes is high. This would include overseeing whether the intended beneficiaries are receiving the benefits under the different programmes.

The DRDAs shall keep the Zilla Parishad, the State and Central Government duly informed of the progress of the implementation of the programmes through periodic reports in the prescribed formats. Special report, as and when called for, shall be provided.

It shall be the duty of the DRDAs to oversee and ensure that the benefits specifically earmarked for certain target groups (SC/ST, women and disabled) reach them. They shall all necessary steps to achieve the prescribed norms.

The DRDAs shall take necessary step to improve the awareness regarding rural development and poverty alleviation particularly among the rural poor. This would involve issues of poverty, the opportunities available to the rural poor and generally infusing a sense of confidence in their ability to overcome poverty. It would also involve sensitizing the different functionaries in the district to the different aspects of poverty and poverty alleviation programmes.

The DRDAs will strive to promote transparency in the implementation of different anti-poverty programmes. Towards this end, they shall publish periodically, the details of the different programmes and their implementation.

Keeping in view, the substantial investment that are being made in poverty alleviation programmes, the DRDAs shall ensure financial discipline in respect of the funds received by them, whether from Central of State Governments. They shall also ensure that the accounts are properly maintained including in respect of the funds allocated to banks or implementing agencies in accordance with the guidelines of different programmes.

Thus the role of the DRDA is in terms of planning for effective implementation of anti-poverty programmes; coordinating with other agencies-Governmental, non-

Governmental, technical and financial for successful programme implementation; enabling the community and the rural poor to participate in the decision marking process, overseeing the implementation to ensure adherence to guidelines, quality, equity and efficiency; reporting to the prescribed authorities on the implementation; and promoting transparency in decision making and implementation.

In addition the DRDAs shall coordinate and oversee the conduct of the BPL Census and such other surveys that are required from time to time.

The DRDAs shall also carry out/aid in carring out action research/or evaluation studies that are initiated by the Central/ State Governments.

The DRDAs should deal only with the anti-poverty programmes of the Ministry of Rural Development. If DRDAs are to be entrusted with programmes of other ministries or those of the State Governments, it should be ensured that these have a definite antipoverty focus. Entrusting of any programme to the DRDAs, other than anti-poverty programmes of the Ministry, be it of any other Ministry of Government of India or the respective State Government will have to be done with the approval of the Secretary, Rural Development of the respective State (s), who should examine such request in consultation with the Ministry of Rural Development, Government of India. In such cases, it must be ensured that adequate provision is made for requisite staffing needed for proper implementation of the programme.

Rural Infrastructure Development Fund (RIDF)

In the Union Budget Speech 1995-96, Hon'ble Finance Minister announced that-

"Inadequacy of public investment in agriculture is today a matter of general concern. This is an area which is the responsibility of States. But many States have neglected investment in infrastructure for agriculture. There are many rural infrastructure projects which have been started but are lying incomplete for want of resources. They represent a major loss of potential income and employment to rural population." RIDF-I was launched in 1995-96 with an initial corpus of

Rs.2000 crore through contributions by way of deposits from domestic commercial banks both from public and private sector having shortfall in the agricultural lending subject to a maximum of 1.5% of the shortfall of the net bank credit to agriculture. Since 1996-97 i.e. RIDF-II, sources of deposits from commercial banks has been broad-based by including shortfall either in direct finance to agriculture and/or shortfall in priority sector lending.

RDIF-II(Yer 1996-97) contribution amounted to Rs.2500/-. Contributions have since increased progresively. RDIF IX (2003-04) contribution amounted to Rs.5500/-bringing the cumulate corpus fund of RDIF to Rs.34000/-.

Disbursements & Outstandings

Total sanctions as on 31 March 2003 aggregated Rs.29475 crore as on 30 March 2003. The total disbursements as on 31 March 2003 were Rs.17,145 crore and RIDF outstandings as on 31 March 2003 were Rs.13,062 crore. The tranch-wise sanctions have been higher than the corpus.

Sanction of Projects: Appraisal reports submitted by the ROs are scrutinised by State Projects Department at HO before placing the same to Projects Sanctioning Committee (PSC) for consideration of sanction. Projects are sanctioned by PSC-which is a committee of the Board of Directors with following Members:

1. Chairman of NABARD;
2. Managing Director of NABARD;
3. Secretary (Banking), MoF, GoI, on the Board of NABARD;
4. Secretary, Ministry of Rural Development, GoI, on the Board of NABARD;
5. Deputy Governor, RBI, on the Board of NABARD;
6. Nominee of RBI.

Normally seven or eight meetings of PSC are held in a year to sanction loans from the RIDF corpus. Sanctioning process under RIDF IX (2003-04) has been operationalised.

Borrowing Institutions: State Governments are eligible to borrow out of RIDF on project basis. It has been decided to extend loans to Panchayat Raj Institutions (PRIs), Non-

Governmental Organisations, Self-Help Groups, etc. w.e.f. 1 April 1999.

Activities/Sectors financed under RIDF: Only ongoing Irrigation, Flood Protection, Watershed Management projects were financed under RIDF-I as a 'last mile approach' to facilitate completion of the projects delayed on account of financial constraints.

The financing of rural Road & Bridge projects was started during RIDF-II. Subsequently, coverage of RIDF was broad-based in each tranche and at present, a wide range of activities such as Primary Schools, Primary Health Centres, Village Haats, Joint Forest Management, Terminal and Rural Market, Rain Water Harvesting, Fish Jetties, Mini Hydel and System Improvement Projects in Power Sector, Rural Drinking Water Supply Scheme, Citizen Information Centres, Anganwadi Centres and Shishu Shiksha Kendras are also being financed.

All new "project concepts" received from various State Governments are placed before the PSC for approval before accepting detailed projects from State Governments for financing.

Rate of Interest on RIDF Loan: The loan under RIDF-I were advanced to State Governments with interest rate at 13%. The rate of interest on loans under RIDF-II to RIDF-V was 12%. The rate of interest was further reduced to 11.5% under RIDF-VI and to 10.5% under RIDF-VII and is at 8.5% per annum under RIDF-VIII. The rate of interest has been linked to Bank Rate i.e. 2% above the bank rate with effect from 01 April 2002. The rate of interest under each tranche remains constant during entire disbursement period of the tranche. NABARD retain

Differential Rate of Interest to Banks: The rates of interest on deposits received from the banks under tranches I to VI were less by 0.5% than the rates of interest charged by NABARD on RIDF loans to the State Govts. With a view to encouraging commercial banks to enhance flow of direct credit to agriculture, it was decided by RBI to link interest on bank contribution to RIDF, from Tranche-VII, to the extent of the shortfall of their agriculture lending vis-a-vis the targets.

Period of Loan: The repayment period of 5 years including a 2 year grace period was provided under RIDF-I to RIDF-V. The repayment period has, however, been extended to 7 years including a grace period of 2 years since RIDF-VI and the same policy is continuing.

Normative Allocation: Normative allocations are made to all States on the basis of norms prescribed by the PSC. Currently, the allocation norms provide weightage to rural population (50%), geographical area (25%) and infrastructural development index (25%).

Some of the State Governments are not able to fully utilise the allocation and the State-wise allocations are reviewed by PSC from time to time and accordingly reallocated.

Nodal Department for RIDF: The Finance Department has been nominated by the State Governments to act as the Nodal Department for operationalising RIDF. The project proposals are routed through the Finance Department only and no proposals are accepted directly from any other Department of the State Government. Release of loan, repayment thereof, documentation, etc. are executed by Finance Department of the State Governments.

Appraisal of Projects: Regional Offices receive the detailed project reports from State Governments based on the their priorities and within the priorities decided under RIDF. The detailed project reports are subject to field and desk appraisal by a team comprising of NABARD officers as well as consultants, who are normally senior retired officers of the concerned departments of State/Central Government.

Documentation: Besides normal documents such as acceptance of Terms & Conditions of sanction, Time Promissory Note(TPN), the State Government has to execute mandate in favour of RBI.

The State Governments are required to furnish a certificate to the effect that the advances drawn are within the limits prescribed by the State Legislative Assembly under Article 293(1) as also a certificate indicating consent of the Government of India under Article 293(3) of the Constitution of India.

Phasing of the Projects: The normal phasing under RIDF-I was 2 years whereas under subsequent tranches of RIDF, it is 3 years. However, due to operational constraints, phasing has to be normally extended for the Trancne as a whole or for specific projects to enable the State Governments to complete the projects.

Release of Funds: The State Governments can avail advance against the loan sanctioned @ 20% on acceptance of the terms & conditions of sanction and 10% on commencement of work either for the annual phasing or the total sanction as per local conditions and needs of the project.

The State Governments, thereafter, are provided loans on reimbursement basis against the actual expenditure incurred in execution of sanctioned projects. The RIDF loans are released by Regional Offices of NABARD.

Cost Escalation: Normally it is expected that RIDF projects could be completed on time within the approved cost. However, cost escalation is considered on account of change in design during execution and revision in Schedule of Rates (SOR).

Monitoring of RIDF Projects: Although monitoring is basically the responsibility of the State Governments, yet an effective monitoring mechanism developed by NABARD is one of the strong features of RIDF. Currently, 10,000 projects which constitute about 12% of the ongoing projects are annually field monitored by our Districts Development Managers, staff of ROs and Consultants. Selective sector-wise monitoring is undertaken by the HO and through external agencies also.

Monitoring Committees: In addition to the field monitoring, institutional mechanism has been developed for sectoral and project-wise review at the level of Superintending Engineers, Chief Engineers, Head of the Departments, Administrative Secretaries & Chief Secretaries to facilitate timely completion of RIDF projects. The mechanism has stabilised and is working satisfactorily. Recently, NABARD has started organizing capacity building workshops for the govt. staff working in various line departments connected with RIDF projects.

Bibliography

Alam, Bilquis: *Women Members of Union Parishad, A Few Statistics*, NILG, Dhaka, 1981.

Arvind, Sharma : *Women in World Religion,* New York Press, New York, 1990.

Benjamin, J.: *Socio-religious Status of Panchayati Raj in India*, New Delhi, Ashish Publishing, 1991.

Bhai, N.: *Harijan Women in Independent India*, Delhi, BR Publishing 1986

Burton, Antoinette: *British Feminists, Indian Women, and Imperial Culture, 1865-1915*, Chapel Hill, University of North Carolina, 1994.

Calman, J.: *Toward Empowerment: Women and Politics in India*, Colorado, Westview Press, 1992.

Chandra, S.K.: *Development of Women Entrepreneurship in India. A Study of Public Policies and Programmes*, New Delhi, Mittal 1991

Dak, T.M.: *Women and Work in Indian Society*, Delhi, Discovery, 1988.

Dikshit, D.P.: *Political History of Panchayati Raj*, New Delhi, Abhinav, 1980.

Erikson, E. H.: *Panchayati Raj and Society,* New York, W. W. Norton, 1993.

Fine, M.: *Women with Disabilities: Essays in Psychology, Culture, and Politics*, Philadelphia, Temple University Press, 1988.

Gilligan, C.: *Psychological Theory and Women's Development in Panchayati Raj,* Cambridge, Harvard University Press, 1993.

Hasan, Mushirul: *India's Partition: Process, Strategy and Mobilization*, New Delhi, Oxford UP, 1993.

Jain, D.: *Women's Quest for Power in Panchayati Raj*, Sahibabad, Vikas, 1980.

Janaki, N: *Women and Law in Panchayati Raj*, New Delhi, Kali, 1996.

Jordan, J. V.: *Women's Growth in Diversity*, New York, Guilford Press, 1997.

Judith, E.: *The Sexual Exploitation of Panchayati Raj*, Cambridge, Polity Press, 1986.

Jumani, U.: *Poverty: Self-employment for Poor, Rural Women in India*, London, Sage 1991.

Karl Marilee: *Women and Empowerment in Panchayati Raj System in India*, Zed Books Limited, London, 1995.

Lalitha N. and B.S. Nagarajan: *Self Help Groups in Rural Development*, New Delhi: dominant Publishers and Distributors, 2002.

Mathur, B.B.: *Women and Depressed Class Population in Panchayati Raj System*, Allahabad, Chugh, 1994.

Minakshi, C.: *Administration and Social Life under Panchayati Raj*, Madras, University of Madras, 1977.

Mohiuddin Khan: 1988, *Development Strategies for Panchayati Raj*, Dhaka, Bangladesh.

Mueller, R.: *Women's Work in Third World Agriculture*, Geneva, ILO, 1985.

Nair, Janaki: *Women and Law in Colonial India*, New Delhi, Kali, 1996.

Palriwala, R.: *Structures and Strategies of Panchayati Raj*, New Delhi, Sage 1990.

Panini, M.N.: *Accounts of Women Fieldworkers Studying their Own Communities*, Delhi, Hindustan, 1991.

Rose K.: *Where Women are Leaders : The SEWA Movement in India*, New Delhi: Vistar Publications, 1992.

Sharma, A : *Women in Panchayati Raj*, New York Press, New York, 1990.

Singh, S.: *Role of Women's in Panchati Raj System in India*, New Delhi, Sage, 1995.

Vyas, A. & Singh, S.: *Women's Studies in India. Information Sources, Services and Programmes*, New Delhi, Sage, 1993.

Index

M

O

P

R

S

T

U

V

W

Z

□□□